TEAM WORK AND GROUP DYNAMICS

TEAM WORK AND GROUP DYNAMICS

Greg L. Stewart
Vanderbilt University

Charles C. Manz
University of Massachusetts, Amherst

Henry P. Sims, Jr.
University of Maryland

JOHN WILEY & SONS, INC.

New York   Chichester   Weinheim   Brisbane   Singapore   Toronto

Acquisitions Editor	Ellen Ford
Marketing Manager	Tracy Guyton
Senior Production Editor	Kelly Tavares
Senior Designer	Laura Boucher

Cover photo by Bill Binzen/The Stock Market

This book is printed on acid-free paper. ∞

The paper in this book was manufactured by a mill whose forest management programs include sustained yield harvesting of its timberlands. Sustained yield harvesting principles ensure that the numbers of trees cut each year does not exceed the amount of new growth.

Library of Congress Cataloging-in-Publication Data
Stewart, Greg L.
   Team Work and group dynamics / Greg L. Stewart, Charles C. Manz,
Henry P. Sims, Jr.
      p.   cm.
   Includes index.
   ISBN 0-471-19769-6 (pbk. : alk. paper)
   1. Teams in the workplace.   2. Teams in the workplace—Case
Studies.   I. Manz, Charles C.   II. Sims, Henry P., 1939-   .
III. Title.
HD66.S747   1999
658.4'036—dc21
                                                                98-28153
                                                                    CIP

10 9 8 7 6 5 4

To our families:
Lisa, Brandon, Ryan, Jason, and Analisa;
Karen, Chris, and Katy;
Laurie, Jonathan, Amy, and Andrew;
our favorite teams.

Preface

The idea of organizing work around teams challenges a number of traditional management approaches and structures that form the bedrock of our understanding about organizations. Your first reaction may to be to view teams either as a significant threat or as a wonderful opportunity for your own worklife and career. Regardless of your reaction, teams appear to be here to stay and may represent the most powerful organizational change since the Industrial Revolution.

Contemporary business organizations are increasingly structuring work around teams because teams can lead to substantial improvement in both the quality and quantity of a firm's services and products. A majority of employees also report that they prefer working in team environments, suggesting that teams can indeed provide organizations with a method of simultaneously increasing both productivity and quality of worklife for employees. Teams therefore hold a great deal of promise for changing the way business is conducted.

Not all teams are successful, however. The faulty design of many teams assures their failure before they are even created. Other teams experience initial success but quickly falter when their internal processes collapse as they face adversity and challenge. Perhaps an even greater number of teams continue their existence in organizations but fail to reach their full potential. Fortunately, research and practice teach us quite a bit about how teams can be made more effective. Thus, our purpose in writing this textbook is to share knowledge about teams. We strive to share it in a way that students are able not only to understand the complex issues associated with teams but also to develop the tools they need to increase their effectiveness as team designers, leaders, and members.

The knowledge we share comes from two primary sources. One source is a long stream of theory and research related to group psychology. Researchers across the decades have examined group processes. Their observations and findings provide a structure for understanding teams, as well as a framework for determining possible methods of team improvement. Another source of knowledge is the practical lessons being learned by the numerous business organizations adopting teams. These organizations face complex problems that arise from the specific application of teams in business contexts. Combining the "real-world" experiences of these teams with small-group theory and research brings team issues to life and provides a holistic picture of teams in the workplace.

In order to link team research and practice, we combine research summaries with extended case descriptions of actual teams in business organizations. The research summaries are compiled from the extensive literature written by scholars concerned with understanding groups and teams. We do not, however, attempt to discuss every aspect of teams that researchers have explored. Instead, we focus only on the key issues that we feel are most critical for team success. This focus allows us to summarize the literature in a way that does not require us to spend a great deal of time explaining psychological concepts that are only tangentially related to teams in business organizations. The case studies we use are adapted from *Business Without Bosses: How Self-managing Teams Are Building High-performing Companies*, a book previously written by Charles Manz and Henry Sims, and published by John Wiley and Sons. These cases have been well received by both students and business leaders. They provide a rich picture of teams in action.

By combining case studies and research summaries into a single text, we hope to eliminate a great deal of the inefficiency and confusion that we and our colleagues have faced while teaching about teams without a relatively complete and well-integrated textbook. In the past our approach has been to assemble a variety of readings from a number of sources including group psychology textbooks, academic articles, business trade books, and popular press case studies. Business students have frequently found the psychology textbooks and academic articles to be too technical and theoretical for their purposes. The trade books and popular press articles have provided good practical advice but often lack a theoretical research foundation that is critical for developing a deeper understanding of team concepts. Moreover, students often find it difficult to tie all the concepts from the numerous sources together in a meaningful way. Our fundamental goal has thus been to provide a solution to these problems by developing an integrated textbook that combines knowledge from both research and practice into a model that provides students with an opportunity to learn about teams in an efficient, yet comprehensive, manner.

Unit 1 of the book explores some of the forces that have led to the widespread adoption of teams in business organizations. We introduce a model of teams that includes inputs, processes, and outputs. Each of the following three units then focuses on an element of the model. Unit 2 describes inputs and focuses on how teams can be designed to increase effectiveness. Unit 3 discusses processes within teams and illustrates how positive relationships within a team can contribute to effectiveness. Unit 4 focuses on outputs and explains a training process whereby team effectiveness can be increased. Units 2, 3, and 4 also include cases. A case opens each unit and provides a background setting and an illustration of many of the unit's concepts. In each unit a research summary then provides an analysis of important concepts, followed by two additional cases that illustrate specific aspects of the topic. The cases and research summaries are not, however, designed to align perfectly. Issues covered in the cases are not always discussed in the research sections, and all topics described in the research summaries are not illustrated in the cases. This reduces redundancy and resembles conditions in actual organizations where students will be required to synthesize complex issues. Nevertheless, each case summary does conclude with a "Key Lessons" section that points out ties between the case and the research summaries, as well as additional lessons that the case teaches.

This book would not have been possible without several teams that we wish to thank. First, we thank our team of professional colleagues. In particular, we thank our colleagues who helped with the preparation of the various cases throughout the book: David Keating, Anne Donnellon, John Newstrom, Barry Bateman, Harold Angle, Frank Shipper, Alan Cheney, and Kenneth Smith. Among the many other colleagues we thank Tom Mahoney, Bruce Barry, Murray Barrick, Chris Neck, Vikas Anand, Chris Argyris, Michael Byerlein, Tom Cummings, Dennis Gioia, Richard Hackman, Robert House, Ed Lawler, Ted Levitt, Ed Locke, Fred Luthans, Gerry Hunt, Skip Szilagyi, Bob Marx, Karen Manz, Jim Mancuso, Barry Macy, Richard Cherry, and Phil Podsakoff. All of these people have significantly shaped our views and helped us to see team issues more clearly. Each of our respective universities—the Owen Graduate School of Management at Vanderbilt University, the Isenberg School of Management at the University of Massachusetts-Amherst, and the Robert H. Smith College of Business at the University of Maryland-College Park—has provided us with the support necessary to conduct our research and writing. Charles Manz would also like to thank the Isenberg School of Management for his recent appointment as the Nirenberg Professor of Business Leadership, and especially Charles and Janet Nirenberg whose generous gift made the position possible. Our thanks extend to the supportive leaders and administrators who have helped create an environment of excellence: Marty Geisel, Nancy Hyer, Tom O'Brien, Tony Butterfield, Rudy Lamone, Ed Locke, Howard Frank, and Susan Taylor.

Second, we thank the team of reviewers who took the time to read and comment on earlier drafts of this book. Their ideas and feedback have definitely improved the product. We also thank the editorial and production team at John Wiley and Sons, particularly Ellen Ford, our editor. Their guidance and support has been a valuable aid.

Third, we thank our family teams. Their love and support make all that we do possible and meaningful.

Finally, we thank all who read and study this textbook. We hope that you will find it both rewarding and informative. We also look forward to hearing your comments and feedback, as we know that they will undoubtedly help us to understand teams better.

Greg L. Stewart
Charles C. Manz
Henry P. Sims, Jr.

Contents

UNIT 1 INTRODUCTION   1

What Is a Team?   3
Why Do People Form Teams?   4
How Have Teams Evolved in Work Organizations?   6
Do Teams Make Sense Today?   9
Are Teams Effective?   10
How Is This Book Organized?   13
What We Hope You Learn in This Unit   14

UNIT 2 INPUTS TO TEAMS: DESIGNING
EFFECTIVE WORK TEAMS   17

Case 2.1   The Evolution Toward Teams at TIM   17

Inputs to Teams   29
Task Applications   30
Technology and Interdependence   32
Team Self-leadership   34
Team Goals   36
Team Composition   38
    Task and Socioemotional Roles   38
    Individual Characteristics That Facilitate Team Success   39
    Fit Between Team Members   42
    Diversity in Teams   43
What We Hope You Learn in This Unit   44

Case 2.2 Designing Teams at the Fitzgerald Battery Plant   47

Case 2.3 The Early Implementation Phase of Teams at IDS   52

**UNIT 3   TEAM PROCESSES: DEVELOPING
              SYNERGISTIC TEAM RELATIONSHIPS   70**

Case 3.1   Team Processes at the Fitzgerald Battery Plant   70

Team Processes   81

Team Development   82
       Forming   82
       Storming   83
       Norming   84
       Performing   86
       Adjourning   88
Socialization   88
Power and Influence   90
       Power Bases   90
       Influence Strategies   92
Conflict   94
       Sources of Conflict   94
       Types of Conflict   95
       Conflict Resolution   96
Leadership   97
       Leadership Structures   98
       Leadership Behaviors   100
       How Leadership Affects Teams   101
       Supervisor Resistance to Teams   105
What We Hope You Learn in this Unit   106

Case 3.2   Overcoming Supervisor Resistance at Charrette   108

Case 3.3   Teams Processes to Decrease Individual Autonomy   118

UNIT 4 TEAM OUTPUTS: ASSESSING AND IMPROVING TEAM PERFORMANCE

UNIT 4 TEAM OUTPUTS: ASSESSING AND IMPROVING TEAM PERFORMANCE   126

Case 4.1 Team Performance at Lake Superior Paper Company   126

Team Outputs   138

Determining Team Effectiveness   139
     Goods and Services Produced   140
     Team Viability   140
     Member Satisfaction   141

Team Effectiveness Potential   142
     A Taxonomy of Team Potential   142
     Social Facilitation   143

Interteam Cooperation   145
     Social Identification   146
     Conditions that Foster Competition Between Teams   147
     Encouraging Team Cooperation   148

Improving Team Effectiveness   150
     Overview of the Training Cycle for Teams   151
     Analyzing Training Needs   152
     Developing the Training   153
     Conducting the Training   154
     Evaluating the Training   154

Common Challenges to Team Effectiveness   155

Fundamental Requirements for Team Effectiveness   158

What We Hope You Learn in this Unit   160

Case 4.2 Coordinating Teams at AES   163

Case 4.3 The Team at W.L. Gore & Associates   177

Index   189

Introduction

Unit I introduces the concept of teams. It examines both the historical development of team-based work organizations and current trends supporting the adoption of teams. This information shows that, in many organizations, teams have the potential to improve both productivity and employee satisfaction. However, some work teams are ineffective; thus, transitions to work teams must be carefully planned and implemented. Moreover, work teams may not be appropriate for all organizations. An input–process–output model of teams is introduced as a useful framework for understanding issues related to teams.

"What new management program will they introduce today?" Jane wondered as she rushed to the supervisor meeting at the hospital where she had worked for over 35 years. Having worked as a head nurse for the past 20 years, Jane was certain that she had heard about every possible proposal for helping the hospital become more effective. Yet, she knew the hospital was in trouble. Changes in the healthcare industry were creating a stressful environment that demanded radical decreases in operating costs. Specialization of tasks among doctors, nurses, and other healthcare providers was also increasingly resulting in the fragmented delivery of patient services. Taken together, these trends seemed to be contributing to a disgruntled staff, and a record number of the nurses on her floor had quit their jobs during the past year. "Someone around here had better come up with a long-term solution soon," she thought as she entered the training room.

As Jane slid into a seat near the back of the room she heard Bill—the hospital's lead administrator—begin a presentation about using teams to improve both employee satisfaction and patient care. Bill became rather dramatic as he picked up a stick and snapped it in half. Next, he picked up a bunch of sticks together and attempted to break them. They bent but did not break. "A stick by itself," he said, "can be broken easily. But if all the sticks stay together, they will not break." Slowly he smiled. "The same is true of us," he emphasized, "We either learn to succeed as a team or we fail."[1]

As the meeting ended, Jane's mind kept returning to Bill's example. She agreed that hospital employees needed to work together more, but she just wasn't sure about the idea of teams. Were teams really appropriate for the nurses on her floor? If the hospital adopts teams will she be required to give up her individuality? How might the introduction of teams affect her supervisor job? Could teams really succeed?

The above case illustrates some major changes that are taking place in work organizations. Competitive pressures are forcing business firms to cut costs, increase efficiency, and improve quality. At the same time, workers are demanding more satisfaction from their jobs. These trends suggest that organizations with work structures that are both highly productive and intrinsically satisfying for workers will succeed, while those that fail in either area will likely join the ranks of the extinct.

Among the more noteworthy and promising approaches for achieving the dual goals of higher productivity and increased worker satisfaction is the design of organizations around teams. Team-based organizational designs hold a great deal of promise for improving the way work is accomplished, but extensive evidence suggests that effective teams are not easy to design and implement in the workplace. The purpose of this textbook is to guide you along a path of discovery that helps you not only to ask the right questions about designing, implementing, and supporting teams, but also to provide appropriate and intelligent answers.

Much of our discussion throughout this textbook will describe the potential benefits of teams. However, not all teams are successful. Our experience and research have taught us that many business organizations fall short in their attempts to implement teams. We therefore attempt not only to extol the virtues of teams, but also to reveal the troubles, problems, issues, and challenges that frequently accompany team design and implementation. By understanding both the benefits and the difficulties of teams we can apply theory and research that provide guidance for implementing and facilitating teams. We can also more fully understand the types of organizations and work units where teams are most likely to succeed.

Throughout the text we combine theory and practice. Although teams are a relatively new development in work organizations, researchers have studied the dynamics of small groups for almost 100 years. These studies have led to a number of general group-level theories that can be applied to the specific context of teams in work organizations. We do not pretend to extensively cover all theories related to groups and teams. Instead we focus on the points that we feel are most critical. We also include a number of cases that illustrate applications of the theoretical concepts and provide a "real-world" context for seeing how teams actually function. The combination of theoretical discussions and case descriptions provides a foundation for logical thought that draws from both academic research and current organizational practice to develop a holistic view of teams. The concepts illustrated in these cases do not always fit neatly into the theoretical frameworks, and many of the specific theoretical points are not found explicitly in the case descriptions. However, examining both cases and theories does provide complementary perspectives of teams that blend theory and practice.

Before we get too deep into theories and cases, it is helpful to review the answers to a few fundamental questions concerning teams. Such a review provides a background for understanding what teams are, as well as how they have developed historically in work organizations. Unit 1 will thus focus on the following questions:

1. What is a team?
2. Why do people form teams?
3. How have teams evolved in work organizations?
4. Do teams make sense today?
5. What evidence is there that teams can be beneficial for organizations?

WHAT IS A TEAM?

The question of what a team is represents a good starting point for beginning our journey toward a greater understanding of teams. There are many types of teams, and numerous different labels for teams are being used in business organizations. Perhaps the most basic distinction in labels surrounds the difference between teams and groups. A group is normally defined as two or more people who interact in some way. Teams are usually thought of as groups with shared commitments and goals, suggesting that a team is more than a group.[2] While this distinction between teams and groups makes some sense, it is impossible to clearly determine the point where a group becomes a team. Throughout this book we will thus use the terms "group" and "team" somewhat interchangeably.

A *team* is a collection of individuals who exist within a larger social system such as an organization, who can be identified by themselves and others as a team, who are interdependent, and who perform tasks that affect other individuals and groups.[3] To be a team, members and observers must therefore be able to distinguish clearly those people who are included in the team from those who are part of the larger social system but not included in the team. For instance, a large number of unacquainted and dispersed business executives observing a football game would not be seen as a team because neither they nor the other game observers would identify them as a unique group. Moreover, the business executives would not be working together and relying on one another's contributions (interdependence) in order to accomplish something that would affect other people. In contrast, employees working in an automobile plant form a team when they perceive themselves as a unique group within the plant, when they and others can clearly identify who is a team member, when their work tasks require them to work closely with one another, and when they produce a good or service that is used by others.

A critical notion implicit in our definition is that employees organized into teams typically work together to complete a whole or a distinct part of a product or service. This allows them to see their accomplishments and thereby gain a sense of meaningfulness from their work. Many teams also make decisions on a wide range of issues, including such traditional management prerogatives as determining who will perform which task, solving quality problems, settling conflicts between members on the team, and selecting team leaders. Because we feel that relatively autonomous teams hold the most promise for simultaneously improving organizational productivity and employee satisfaction, many of the cases in this book place particular emphasis on issues associated with teams that are frequently referred to as empowered or self-managing. The basic characterstics of these teams were summarized by Richard Hackman of Harvard University. He said they have a distinct, recognizable task that workers can identify with (e.g., be able to service all of a mutual fund's customer's needs); members with a variety of skills related to the group task; discretion over issues such as how the work is done, scheduling the work, and assigning tasks; and compensation and performance feedback for the group as a whole.[4]

WHY DO PEOPLE FORM TEAMS?

Why do people choose to live close to one another? Why do they spend so much of their time working in groups? Small-group researchers have long pondered the answers to questions similar to these. In general, their theories can be summarized as falling into one of two categories.[5] The first category of answers takes a functional perspective and suggests that we join groups because groups are able to accomplish things that individuals cannot accomplish when they work alone. The second category of answers is more interpersonal in nature and focuses less on the accomplishment of tasks and proposes that we join groups because they help us to fulfill our social needs.

Functional Perspectives

One functional theory of formation posits that groups first formed because working together was the only way that individuals could survive the demands of their environment and thereby continue living. Compared to individuals, groups more effectively produced food and provided defense against invasion by enemies. Groups were also necessary for survival because they allowed people to care for one another when they became ill, as well as to provide social support to individuals in times of stress. Moreover, groups facilitated reproduction by assuring association with individuals of the opposite sex. The theory of formation for survival is thus based on the notion that we join groups because we would die if we didn't. This may sound a bit harsh, but some theorists actually believe that evolutionary forces have created a process of natural selection whereby people with no desire to associate with others have become mostly extinct. The desire to form groups is thus seen as an adaptive mechanism that helps us to survive.

Another functional perspective focuses less on survival and suggests that groups not only help us to survive but also help us to improve the quality of our lives. From this perspective we join groups because they make our efforts more efficient. Groups help us to complete common tasks more quickly and thereby provide extra time for either leisure or further accomplishment. This notion is somewhat supported by historical evidence that suggests the standard of living of a society is higher when people work cooperatively in teams. Groups also allow us to accomplish collective tasks that make our lives more comfortable but that we would be unable to accomplish alone. For instance, modern roads and automobiles provide us with the opportunity for extensive travel, but neither of these would be possible if people had not chosen to work together and pool their efforts. The desire to form groups is thus seen as an economic choice because it allows us to improve our well-being.

Functional perspectives on group formation are carried over into business applications of teams. Organizations are often structured around teams because teams have the potential to help workers become more productive. Efforts can be pooled, and employees with unique strengths can work together more effectively. For instance, hotel employees such as desk clerks, bellhops, and food servers can provide better guest service when they form a team and work cooperatively than when they work individually. This service improvement occurs because the particular unique strengths of each employee can be matched to the unique and changing needs of each guest.

Interpersonal Perspectives

A somewhat different and interpersonal theory of group formation suggests that we join groups because we have innate social desires that can only be fulfilled in the presence of others. From this perspective people are seen as having a need for *affiliation* with others. The basis for this need is often traced to childhood experiences involving family relationships. Children receive acceptance and protection from their parents, and then later in life affiliate with groups to duplicate those desirable states. People also join groups to provide them with the opportunity to fulfill their needs to exercise *power* over others. Similar to the control of parents over the behavior of children, leaders in groups are able to influence the actions of others. Another basic psychological need is the desire to give and receive *affection*. Again, similar to families, groups provide people with the opportunity to develop emotional relationships that allow them to feel accepted. People have different needs for affiliation, power, and affection, which means that individuals may join groups for different reasons. Nevertheless, the desire to form groups is seen as resulting from psychological drives that influence us to associate with other people.

Another twist to the interpersonal perspective posits that we join groups because we want information from other people. A desire to compare ourselves with others is at the heart of this theory. Because we want to understand ourselves, we seek information about the behavior and attitudes of others. We then compare this information about others with information about our own attitudes and behaviors. The comparison process allows us to validate our actions and beliefs. A common example of the social comparison process occurs when professors return exams and papers to students. Scores are of little meaning to students until they obtain information from their peers. However, once students learn how others performed, they begin a comparison process that helps them understand their own performance. Their personal perception of the quality of their performance is based largely on how well they did relative to others. This desire for social comparison is so strong that it drives people to form groups in order to understand and evaluate themselves.

Similar to the functional perspective, the interpersonal perspective of team formation can be linked to the explosion of teams in modern businesses. Workers frequently report higher job satisfaction when they work in teams rather than independently as individuals. The dignity and freedom workers receive are especially publicized in many organizations that adopt teams. One example of this dignity and freedom is provided in the transition to teams that took place at the Charette Corporation (see Case 3.2), where the team system helped relatively uneducated and troubled workers gain the respect they needed to improve their performance. In particular, teams permit stronger social relationships and tend to provide a work environment that is interpersonally satisfying. Adding this benefit to the functional benefits associated with increased productivity suggests that in some settings teams may indeed be able to accomplish something that most other work design innovations fail to achieve: simultaneous improvement in both organizational productivity and quality of worklife for employees.

HOW HAVE TEAMS EVOLVED IN WORK ORGANIZATIONS?

The early days of the team system were heavily influenced by a concept known as sociotechnical systems (STS) theory, which emphasizes the need to optimize both the social and technical aspects of work.[6] The technical aspects of work include the equipment and processes for producing goods and services, and have historically been maximized through mass production and bureaucratic structures. In contrast, the social aspects of work concern relationships among workers and have historically received very little attention. The result has been organizations that can efficiently produce a standardized product or service but that can neither adapt to changes in their environments nor satisfy many of the social needs of workers. While details of a specific application of STS in an actual organization are provided in the IDS case that is included in Unit 2, it is important here to point out that the underlying goal of STS is to jointly create excellence in both the technical and the social systems of organizations.

The application of STS principles typically results in a shift to performing work in groups; technology and people are matched together in clusters, or teams. The main rationale is that teams can more effectively apply resources to deal with the total variance (changes and unpredictable events) in work conditions than can individuals acting on their own. Today, the formal analysis techniques of STS are found less frequently, but the philosophy of matching the technical system and the social system remains and is an important part of successful team design.

The teams that have evolved from STS are a distinctly Western phenomenon (teams have been used in the United States, Canada, Europe, and Mexico), although they are frequently confused with Japanese management practices. Both are often associated with the idea of participatory management, but each approach is targeted at a quite different population, with distinct cultural values. In particular, Japanese organizations use teams in a culture that supports collectivism, where the interests of an organization are seen as more important than the interests of individuals. In such work systems, teams lower in the organizational hierarchy are expected to willingly follow the directions given by top-level leaders. Although effective in Japan, similarly designed team systems have been less effective in Western countries that focus more on individualism than collectivism. Following the principles of STS, Western organizations have therefore moved toward empowered teams that provide line workers greater discretion over work processes.

In 1990, Edward Lawler, director of the Center for Organizational Effectiveness at the University of Southern California, estimated that about 7 percent of U.S. companies were using some form of self-managing teams.[7] Only a decade earlier, he had estimated in personal conversations to us that about 150 to 250 work sites were using teams. Clearly, the number of companies using teams has grown considerably, and a recent report found 47 percent of the Fortune 1000 companies using self-managing teams with at least some employees.[8] We believe that nearly every major U.S. company is currently trying or considering some form of empowered work teams somewhere in their organization, and our own informal estimate is that within the next few years 40 to 50 percent of the U.S. workforce may work in some kind of empowered team. Hundreds of applications have already taken place across industries in multiple settings. A list of several settings that we are aware of is provided as Table 1.1.

The Procter & Gamble Company is generally considered an important U.S. pioneer in applying teams to their operations. Their work began in the early 1960s, although it was not publicized and virtually escaped media attention. P&G saw the team approach as a significant competitive advantage and through the 1980s attempted to deflect attention away from its efforts. The company thought of its knowledge about the team organization as a type of trade secret and required consultants and employees to sign nondisclosure statements. Nevertheless, Procter & Gamble's successes with teams received considerable off-the-record attention from a small group of consultants across the country who were inspired by the P&G success and learned techniques through an informal network. Many of them originally worked at P&G and were attracted away to other companies by lucrative job offers because of their unique knowledge and expertise.

Through the 1970s and 1980s, General Motors Corporation was also a locus

TABLE 1.1   Settings Where Work Teams Have Been Applied

Pet food plant
Parts manufacturing
Paint manufacturing
Coal mines
Auto manufacturing
Supply warehouse
Paper mill
Hospitals
Financial offices
Insurance offices
Government organizations

of active experimentation with teams and was significantly less secretive than Procter & Gamble. Many of the GM team implementations have been very successful and have served as models for other changes around the country. The focus on teams ultimately led to the Saturn experiment, currently GM's most successful division in terms of customer satisfaction. GM remains an interesting enigma, however; it is a textbook case of how success with teams at one location does not necessarily transfer to another location within a large corporation. Furthermore, the GM experience highlights the fact that teams are not the sole answer to the competitiveness challenge. Diffusing the team concept throughout diversified companies has proven to be a considerable challenge.

Other prominent companies have been active with teams, among them Gaines, Cummins Engine, Digital Equipment, Ford, Chrysler, Motorola, Tektronix, General Electric, Honeywell, LTV, Caterpillar, Boeing, Monsanto, AT&T, and Xerox.

Teams have also had a different impact on the various sectors of our work society. The most extensive experience derives from the manufacturing sector, where the team concept was first introduced in the 1960s. In many areas of the manufacturing sector, it's no longer a question of whether or why to use teams but of fine-tuning to specific sites. The service sector has significantly lagged the manufacturing sector in adoption of teams. Perhaps the slow progress of service teams stems from the increased difficulty in designing effective teams. The high variability associated with service settings requires a different type of team. Nevertheless, competitiveness has started to become a hot issue in service, and we expect service providers to increasingly use teams, albeit somewhat different teams than are common in manufacturing settings. The IDS case we report later in this book is an example of the potential of these service teams. While we still have much to learn, teams in the service sector are likely to be the most exciting applications in the near future.

DO TEAMS MAKE SENSE TODAY?

One way of looking at reasons why businesses are moving toward teams is to examine psychological theories that explain why people join some groups but not others. The fundamental core of these theories is *social exchange*.[9] Social exchange posits that every team provides both rewards and costs. Rewards come from positive interactions that provide economic and social benefits. For instance, employees may support joining a team because it gives them the opportunity to produce more goods and services than when they work alone, which in turn may lead to higher wages. Teams may also provide employees with social rewards like friendship, self-esteem, and a feeling of control. However, teams also have costs. These costs may include reduced efficiency that occurs when teams spend a lot of time meeting together and negotiating decisions, as well as strained interpersonal relationships resulting from negative social interactions.

Employees will desire to work in teams as long as the rewards of the team are greater than the costs. One critical element of the cost-reward equation involves the desires of individual employees. Some employees report numerous individual benefits from working in teams, while others report a relative increase in costs. Indeed, some employees are uncomfortable in teams and tend to leave organizations that transition to teams. Nevertheless, societal trends appear to be making teams increasingly rewarding for a large number of workers, as modern workers more and more place a high value on the benefits of empowerment and interpersonal relationships that accompany teams. Because changes in the desires of workers offer a compelling explanation of why teams increasingly make sense for business organizations, we briefly review trends in worker preferences.

The generation receiving most attention now is the large group born between the mid-1940s and the 1960s, who grew to maturity during a time of unprecedented prosperity and social turmoil and are variously called the "baby boom," the "now generation," the "new breed," the "new values worker," and the "'60s kids."[10] Baby boomers have a set of life and work values in some areas that are very different from that of their parents and grandparents. Most of all, they are less tolerant of hierarchical control. Many have lower overall job satisfaction and less desire to lead or manage, move up the organizational hierarchy, and defer to authority. These workers often believe that they are entitled to a "good" job, have a desire to control their own destiny, and have a low absenteeism threshold.[11] In addition, they have a lower respect for authority and a greater desire for self-expression, personal growth, and self-fulfillment. In other words, these workers are not satisfied to report to work merely for the paycheck. They want something more.

To complicate matters, a newer set of workers, including the "baby busters" and "generation X," has recently been entering the workforce. These employees also carry values and expectations that are significantly different from those

of traditional organizations. They are slower to commit and less loyal to organizations. (It's also true that organizations are less loyal to employees.) They
were recently described in this way: "They don't bow to any authority. Younger
workers will not respect you because you're the boss. They want to know why
they're being asked to do things. They question authority, and they have a dis-
regard for hierarchies."[12] They are also described as competitive and as desir-
ing an opportunity to learn and have fun at work.

These characteristics of the new employee generations, when coupled with
rises in education and standards of living during this century, pose major challenges for organizations. The new workers' aspirations for self-fulfillment cannot be met by conventional approaches of the past. Teams have a special capacity
to answer the needs of the new generation of employees. This is not a new
idea. Over fifteen years ago *Business Week* concluded that "U.S. industry must
reorganize work and its incentives to appeal to new worker values, rather than
try to retrofit people to work designs and an industrial relations system of 80
years ago."[13] The newer employees have an especially acute need to be treated
as valuable and respected contributors and to be given the opportunity to learn,
develop, and influence their work and their organizations. The rewards of work
teams come closer to meeting these demands than most other tested work system alternatives. Teams often break down the traditional, hierarchical work systems and can provide employees with the freedom to grow and improve
themselves. With teams, employees frequently feel that they can control and
manage themselves to really make a difference. Team-based work systems can
thus fulfill many of the needs of modern workers, suggesting that teams may
indeed be a key to increasing the overall satisfaction of workers.

ARE TEAMS EFFECTIVE?

As pointed out earlier, the shifting interests and desires of workers are an important explanation for the shift toward teams in businesses. However, issues of
productivity and quality—the important elements of competitiveness—are probably the strongest drivers of the move toward teams. In the end, the team approach will be adopted only if teams really do work.

The team concept has been credited with improving productivity and quality in many organizations. Teams are a way to undertake continuous improvement designed to increase productivity. Today, teams are seen as a critical
element of many total quality management (TQM) programs (see, for example,
the Texas Instrument Malaysia case presented in Unit 2). Moreover, teams typically breed reduced conflict between management and labor. Frequently cited
reasons why teams make sense for modern business are listed in Table 1.2.

Specific evidence that evaluates the effectiveness of teams can be divided
into two categories: qualitative evidence, often reported in the popular press,
and more rigorous scientific data, derived from well-designed quantitative research studies.[14] *Business Week* claims that teams can increase productivity by
30 percent or more and can also substantially improve quality.[15] Other exam-

TABLE 1.2 Organizational Benefits Frequently Credited to Teams

Increased productivity
Improved quality
Enhanced employee quality of work life
Reduced costs
Reduced turnover and absenteeism
Reduced conflict
Increased innovation
Better organizational adaptability and flexibility

ples reported in the popular press include an Alcoa plant in Cleveland, where a production team came up with a method for making forged wheels for vans that increased output 5 percent and cut scrap in half. At Weyerhaeuser, the forest-products company, a team of legal employees significantly reduced the retrieval time for documents. At Federal Express, a thousand clerical workers, divided into teams of five to ten people, helped the company reduce service problems by 13 percent. At Rubbermaid, a multidisciplinary team from marketing, engineering, and design developed a new product line; subsequently, sales in the first year exceeded projections by 50 percent.[16]

While these qualitative data generally support the effectiveness of teams, not all evidence, especially from more rigorous academic research, is completely supportive. Perhaps the difficulty of evaluating the team concept in terms of any hard scientific data was best expressed by John Miner:

> The results are often positive. It is hard to predict whether the outcomes will be greater output, better quality, less absenteeism, reduced turnover, fewer accidents, greater job satisfaction, or what, but the introduction of autonomous work groups is often associated with improvements. It is difficult to understand why a particular outcome such as increased productivity occurs in one study and not in another, and why, on some occasions, nothing improves. Furthermore, what actually causes the changes when they do occur is not known. The approach calls for making so many changes at once that it is almost impossible to judge the value of the individual variables. Increased pay, self-selection of work situations, multiskilling, with its resultant job enrichment and decreased contact with authority almost invariably occurs in autonomous work groups.[17]

In another report, researchers attempted a rigorously scientific review of the effectiveness of the team approach. Despite 1,100 studies conducted in actual organizations, they concluded that "there are not many well-designed studies that evaluate the impact of self-managed groups."[18]

One revealing scientific report of the bottom-line effect of teams is contained in a study conducted by researchers at the Texas Center for Productivity and Quality of Work Life.[19] Their analysis contrasted the success of various changes involving human resources, work structure, and technology—for example, training, reward systems, and work teams. Very strong effects, especially in terms of financial outcomes, were observed with team applications. Another study by researchers at the University of Minnesota quantitatively examined the introduction of teams at an assembly plant. This study concluded that over time the introduction of teams improved both labor productivity and the quality of the product being manufactured.[20] These and other emerging studies are beginning to provide rigorous scientific evidence that teams can positively influence the bottom-line financial performance of work organizations.

A vast body of experience related to the effectiveness of teams also seems to lie unreported in the scientific literature. Those close to the self-management movement informally report substantial productivity gains and cost savings that typically range from 30 to 70 percent when compared with traditional systems. Many who have experienced the power of teams believe that they have the potential to exert substantial effects on the bottom line. Perhaps the notion was captured best by Charles Eberle, a former vice president at Procter & Gamble, who speaks with the advantage of years of practical experience:

> At P&G there are well over two decades of comparisons of results side by side—between enlightened work systems and those I call traditional. It is absolutely clear that the new work systems work better—a lot better—for example, with 30 to 50 percent lower manufacturing costs. Not only are the tangible, measurable, bottom line indicators such as cost, quality, customer service and reliability better, but also the harder-to-measure attributes such as quickness, decisiveness, toughness, and just plain resourcefulness of these organizations.[21]

Why then do companies and employees often resist the change to teams? There are several philosophical and practical barriers to the ready acceptance of the team concept. Teams often take a long time to yield substantial benefits, and many organizations abort their transitions to teams before barriers can be overcome and improvements realized. Perhaps the biggest dilemma frequently encountered in changing to teams arises because of the transition needed in managerial thinking and philosophy. Empowering teams throughout the organization can be a very unnerving process for managers, who may perceive it as a threat to their own status and power. In addition, leading teams for new management and leadership perspectives and strategies often do not seem to come naturally to managers whose only experience is in a traditional hierarchical system.

Indeed, the transition to teams can be a troubling process. Teams often represent a whole new management paradigm. Nevertheless, research evidence is beginning to show that this new paradigm, though not appropriate for all organizations, can indeed be beneficial for many modern organizations. Throughout this text we describe several issues that should be taken into account when determining both whether teams are appropriate for a given organization and how the transition to a team-based system can be facilitated.

HOW IS THIS BOOK ORGANIZED?

Having reviewed some basic issues concerning teams and their historical development in the business world, we are now ready to dive into theories and cases. In order to theoretically understand teams, researchers have adopted a model that suggests teams can be understood in terms of their inputs, processes, and outputs.[22] An illustration of this model is shown in Figure 1.1. The underlying idea is that a team is made up of several inputs, including the tasks the team undertakes, the technological process the team uses to accomplish those tasks, the level of autonomy given to the team, the goals provided to the team, and the composition of individuals who make up the team. These characteristics combine through processes such as communication, cooperation, influence, and leadership to produce outputs such as productivity and employee satisfaction. Because of the usefulness of this model for understanding teams, we divide the remainder of this book into three sections, each section being based on one part of the model.

The following unit (Unit 2) focuses on *inputs*, which are extremely important to consider when teams are designed and first introduced into organizations. A case about teams working at a Texas Instruments manufacturing plant located in Malaysia is presented first. The case provides a background for introducing concepts related to team design. Theory concerning several primary design inputs is then described. Two other cases, one about the Fitzgerald Battery Plant of General Motors and the other about IDS Financial Services, are then used to illustrate key points. Taken together, the cases and theory provide a rich view of team design processes and highlight the effect of many critical inputs for teams.

The next unit (Unit 3) focuses on the *processes* that occur as the various inputs combine. A case that revisits the Fitzgerald Battery Plant uses conversations in teams, as well as discussions about leadership, to illustrate intrateam interactions. The unit then builds on this case to look at group development over time, socialization, influence, conflict, and leadership. The theoretical discussion is followed by two additional cases. One case examines the leadership process at Charette Corporation—a wholesale distributor. Another case describes how a

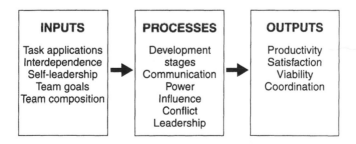

Figure 1.1 Input, process, output model of teams

CEO used his power and influence to exert control in his organization in a way that was dysfunctional for team empowerment.

The final unit (Unit 4) addresses outputs in terms of performance. This section begins with a case describing Lake Superior Paper Company and provides explicit examples of effective teams in the paper mill industry. A discussion then focuses on different facets of performance and illustrates that performance is multidimensional and cannot be summarized by simple measures of output. Methods of improving performance are also described. Once again two additional cases follow. A case about AES Corporation provides an excellent example of an organizational structure that is effective in fostering cooperation among teams. Lastly, a case description of W. L. Gore and Associates is included as a preview of the future where organizations may very well be constructed of small, self-forming teams that come and go as conditions change.

WHAT WE HOPE YOU LEARN IN THIS UNIT

After studying this opening unit of the text, you should be able to describe some critical characteristics of teams. More importantly, you should be able to better classify when workers are actually organized into teams. Although an understanding of when workers are actually operating in teams may not seem that important in and of itself, we have found that many organizations think they are using teams when they really are not. For instance, one of us went to a manufacturing plant to study teams but was disappointed to find that the smallest team consisted of over 150 individuals. Closer examination revealed that this plant really didn't have any teams that would meet the definition we have presented. In the end, many leaders in the organization assumed that they were using teams when in reality their workers lacked the interdependence and group identity necessary for them to operate as teams.

We hope that you have also gained an understanding of the dual benefits that teams have the potential of providing for organizations: increased employee satisfaction and increased productivity. Both aspects of work are critical if organizations hope to remain successful over the long term, and both psychological theory and mounting research evidence suggest that team-based organizations can often succeed in each area.

Finally, you should be able to describe both the historical development of teams and current trends that suggest teams should continue to be used in organizations. The historical perspective is important for understanding how the current movement toward teams differs from past management approaches that focused solely on technical production rather than the workers' social needs. People have grown weary of working in these organizations, and both productivity and quality of outputs have begun to decrease. The movement toward using teams in the workplace has in some ways been relatively slow to develop. However, current trends associated with both the needs of modern workers and improving productivity indicate that the number of organizations using teams will continue to grow and that teams may eventually become the dominant organizational form for accomplishing work.

NOTES FOR UNIT I

1. The story about the sticks is inspired by one told by Kelvin Throop III in *Analog,* May 1994, p. 81.

2. A discussion on the potential differences can be found in J. R. Katzenbach and D. K. Smith "The Discipline of Teams," *Harvard Business Review* 71 (1993): 111–120.

3. This definition is taken from Richard A. Guzzo and Marcus W. Dickson, "Teams in Organizations: Research on Performance and Effectiveness," *Annual Review of Psychology* 47 (1996): 307–338.

4. See J. Richard Hackman, "The Design of Work Teams," in Jay W. Lorsch (ed.), *Handbook of Organizational Behavior,* (Englewood Cliffs, NJ: Prentice-Hall, 1987), pp. 315–342.

5. A more thorough explanation of these different theories can be found in Donelson R. Forsyth, *Group Dynamics,* 2nd ed. (Pacific Grove, CA: Brooks/Cole, 1990).

6. For an academic development of Sociotechnical Systems Theory, see T. Cummings, "Self-regulated Work Groups: A Socio-technical Synthesis," *Academy of Management Review* 3 (1978): 625–634.

7. From a speech given at the International Conference on Self-managed Work Teams, University of North Texas, Denton, Texas, 1990.

8. This estimate is taken from Susan G. Cohen, Gerald E. Ledford, Jr., and Gretchen M. Spreitzer, "A Predictive Model of Self-managing Work Team Effectiveness," *Human Relations* 49 (1996): 643–676.

9. These ideas were introduced by J. W. Thibaut and H. H. Kelley, *The Social Psychology of Groups* (New York: John Wiley, 1959).

10. This section is based in part on Charles C. Manz and Roger Grothe, "Is the Workforce Vanguard to the 21st Century a Quality of Work Life Deficient-Prone Generation?" *Journal of Business Research* 23 (1991): 67–82.

11. See, for example, Joseph A. Raelin, "60's Kids" in the Corporation: More Than Just 'Daydream Believers,'" *Academy of Management Executives* 1 (1987): 21–30.

12. See "Baby Busters Enter the Work Force," in *Futurist* (May–June 1992): 53. The article is based on Lawrence J. Bradford and Claire Raines, with JoLeda Martin, *Twenty Something: Managing and Motivating Today's New Work Force* (New York: Master Media Limited, 1992).

13. "The New Industrial Relations," *Business Week,* May 1981, pp. 84–88.

14. This section borrows heavily from Henry P. Sims, Jr., and Peter Lorenzi, *The New Leadership Paradigm* (Newbury Park, CA: Sage, 1992).

15. John Horr, "The Payoff from Teamwork," *Business Week,* July 10, 1989, pp. 56–62.

16. John Dumaine, "Who Needs a Boss?" *Fortune,* May 7, 1990, pp. 52–60.

17. John B. Miner, *Theories of Organizational Structure and Process* (Hinsdale, IL: Dryden, 1982), pp. 110–111.

18. Paul S. Goodman, Rukmini Devadas, and Terri L. Griffith Hughson, "Groups and Productivity: Analyzing the Effectiveness of Self-Managing Teams," in *Productivity in Organizations* (San Francisco: Jossey-Bass, 1988).

19. B. A. Macy and H. Izumi, "Organizational Change, Design, and Work Innovation: A Meta-Analysis of 131 North American Field Studies—1961–1991," *Research in Organizational Change and Development* 7 (1993): 235–313.

20. Rajiv D. Banker, Joy M. Field, Roger G. Schroeder, and Kingshuk K. Sinha, "Impact of Work Teams on Manufacturing Performance: A Longitudinal Field Study," *Academy of Management Journal* 39 (1996): 867–890.

21. Quoted by Kim Fisher, "Are You Serious About Self-Management?" (paper delivered at the International Conference on Self-Managed Work Teams, Dallas, October 1991).

22. This model has been presented by J. Richard Hackman, "The Design of Work Teams," in Lorsch (ed.), *Handbook of Organizational Behavior*, pp. 315–342. See also Deborah L. Gladstein, "Groups in Context: A Model of Task Group Effectiveness," *Administrative Science Quarterly* 29 (1984): 499–517.

UNIT

2

Inputs to Teams: Designing
Effective Work Teams

Unit 2 focuses on team inputs and design issues and begins with a case description of a team implementation at Texas Instruments Malaysia. A theory and research section then examines inputs into teams such as task applications, team technologies, team autonomy, team goals, and team composition. Two additional case descriptions follow. One describes what teams do at the Fitzgerald Battery Plant. The other describes how a financial services company—IDS—implemented teams. Taken together, these cases and research summary provide insights about designing effective teams.

CASE

2.1

The Evolution Toward Teams at TIM

This case was written by Alan B. Cheney, Henry P. Sims, Jr., and Charles C. Manz.[1]

This case provides a long-term perspective of an organization implementing teams. Several different types of teams are discussed. Over time the teams have become more sophisticated and have evolved to the point where they increasingly lead themselves. The importance of providing team members with necessary technical and social skills is also clearly demonstrated as numerous training programs are described.

At a place most North Americans can't locate on a world map, on the other side of the world from us, just north of the equator, lies a bustling city of 1.2 million people. In the streets of Kuala Lumpur one can hear a variety of languages, the most common being Chinese, Tamil, Bahasa Malaysia, and English. (Many people in Kuala Lumpur speak very good English.) This city is the setting for the story of this case, a story about a company that has evolved over the years from a traditional management structure to TQM (total quality management) to self-managing work teams. (TQM, of course, is a philosophy and set of practices intended to improve the quality of an organization's products and/or services.) What has happened at this plant is one of the best examples in the world of a planned evolution toward work teams.

The Company: Texas Instruments Malaysia

Texas Instruments established a wholly owned subsidiary, Texas Instruments Malaysia (TIM), in November 1972 on a 15-acre site near Kuala Lumpur. The 250,000-square-foot facility was built to produce integrated circuits for use in computers and related products. Twenty years later, it produces about 3 million high-volume integrated circuits each day, many of which are shipped to companies in Japan. TIM employs 2,600 people, all but a handful Malaysian nationals.

Malaysia is a good place for multinational companies to do business (see the box). In addition to a favorable business climate, the Malaysian workforce tends to be well educated, hard working, loyal, and dedicated to quality. Apparently, the attraction is mutual. The results of TIM's annual employee attitude survey represent the highest favorable percentage of all Texas Instruments plants in East Asia and one of the highest percentages worldwide.

The positive atmosphere and mutual respect are evident at the plant. The employees smile and greet visitors, even on the plant floor. The cafeteria, which features indoor stalls selling foods from Malaysia's three major ethnic cultures (Malays, Chinese, and Tamil), is often adorned with banners celebrating holidays. There are frequent afterhours celebrations, such as family dinners recognizing company service anniversaries, the annual recreation committee ball, and the annual sports day. Employee quality awards are frequently given, and an excellent company magazine, *Gema TIM,* appears bimonthly. The company is also active as a corporate citizen, from sponsorship of the Malaysian Young Enterprise Program to blood drives.

Much of TIM's atmosphere and success can be linked to Jerry W. Lee, the managing director. One of his contributions has been a dedicated focus on total quality and employee involvement.

The Malaysian Economy

Malaysia is one of the world's fastest-growing economies. Like other newly industrialized countries in East Asia, Malaysia is friendly to business and leaves little of its economic growth to chance. It attracts multinational corporations with its political stability and 10-year government plan for improving its physical and human resources. In 1990 Prime Minister Mahathir Moharnad's government announced 2020 Vision, which details Malaysia's plan for becoming a fully developed nation by 2020. Among other things, the plan proposes that manufacturing continue to be the primary means of economic growth by being the major vehicle for export earnings. It also proposes a broadening of Malaysia's industrial base beyond electronics and textiles, which now dominate it. For example, Malaysia is now the world's third largest producer of computer chips, behind only the United States and Japan. Texas Instruments was a relatively early foreign player in contemporary Malaysia; now foreign investment capital is pouring into the economy, much of it from North Asian companies. The Malaysian-American Electronics Industry Association represents 15 American manufacturers located in Malaysia.

The Evolution of TIM's Organizational Structure

The TIM workforce is relatively mature, with 60 percent having more than 10 years of service. With cost improvement and "delayering," the organization will continue to change in the direction of a flatter structure. Thus, the future holds diminished opportunity for traditional organizational advancement up the ladder. In addition, Malaysia's booming economy and industrialization are projected to yield a shortage of experienced professionals in the labor market.

The aggregate meaning of all of these factors is that TIM has been seeking a way to provide internal achievement opportunities for employees, while improving their skills and qualifications. The TIM response has been to push responsibility to the lowest level. The story of how they have done this through teams is the theme of this chapter. Jerry Lee calls this "building the flexible organization."

The evolution of the form of organizational structure at TIM started in 1972. The baseline, or originating structure of the plant, was the traditional functional/vertical hierarchy, characterized by separate and specialized departments and attitudes that can be described as protectionist and "cover your rear". The plant remained organized in this way until 1980 and the beginning of what is now referred to as the Eleven Year Search." (Figure C2.1-1 outlines the evolution of TIM's organizational structures.)

In 1980 Mohd Azmi Abdullah read about Peter Drucker's concepts of worker self-management and began to discuss them with others.[2] Particularly interesting to the TIM managers were Drucker's three prerequisites for self-management: productive work, continuous feedback enabling self-direction, and a continuous learning environment. Mohd Azmi Abdullah remembers, "We thought, 'This looks very good, but how do you apply it?' We couldn't find any methodology to do it, so we weren't able to try it then." But a seed was planted.

By 1982, TIM's structure had evolved to a matrix form, characterized by an intertwining of the traditional vertical organization with project management. This structure created project teams which consisted of functional specialists who came together to work on specific projects. These teams were externally managed and had little autonomy to work creatively. As is common with matrix structures, conflict occurred between project management needs and the vertical hierarchy.

This was the beginning of teams at TIM. However, three years later TIM was swept up in what was becoming a worldwide phenomenon: the discovery of and emphasis on total quality. At that time, the perspectives of Deming and Juran were most influential. The story of these two pioneers, of their initial rejection in the United States and embrace in Japan, is well known and we won't rehash it here. It is important to note, how-

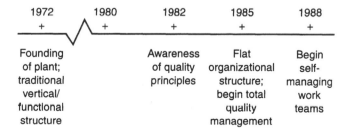

Figure C2.1-1 Organizational changes at Texas Instruments Malaysia

ever, that at TI Malaysia, perspectives and contributions from both U.S. and Japanese management have always been considered and evaluated with some interest, perhaps because of Japan's geographical and cultural proximity.

Since 1980, total quality has been a focus of Texas Instruments worldwide. In a company brochure called Management Perspective: Customer Satisfaction Through Total Quality, chairman, president, and CEO Jerry R. Jenkins writes, "Over the past few years, we have changed our culture within TI to focus on Total Quality. Today, this concept is well-established and the essentials of guaranteeing customer satisfaction are in place, but we must realize Total Quality is a continuous process and our journey along this path is never-ending." At Texas Instruments, the three components of customer satisfaction through total quality are: customer focus, continuous improvement, and people involvement. Jenkins writes, "More than any other factor, dedicated TIers contributing ideas through teamwork is vital to our continued success." This commitment to total quality by the parent corporation was an important backdrop to the change at TIM.

Quality Improvement Teams and Effectiveness Teams

Among Juran's ideas, those addressing operator self-control especially captured the attention of Mohd Azmi Abdullah. Like Drucker, Juran stressed prerequisites to increased employee participation: knowledge of what one is supposed to do, ability to monitor one's own performance, and ability to regulate one's own activities through a decision-making process. Juran also proposed a model for building self-control into operations. At TIM, his ideas found form in advice teams like quality circles and quality improvement teams designed to involve employees in finding ways to improve quality and cut costs.

Quality improvement teams, which were formed to resolve specific problems or issues, started in the management and engineering offices. The reason, Mohd Azmi explains, is that "according to Dr. Juran, 80 percent or more of problems are management-controllable problems. For example, many systems, design, and other problems are not operator controllable." The first quality improvement teams consisted of managers and professionals from different departments; they were cross-functional. A QIT team might be formed to look at reducing cycle time. The manufacturing manager, appointed to form the team, would recruit members from other departments—accounting, planning, production, facilities, and so forth. By forming quality improvement teams in this way, departmental barriers began to break down. Breaking down interdepartmental barriers eventually led to the actual removal of physical barriers. Today at TIM, individuals representing all functions—assemblers, process engineers, manufacturing engineers, planners, and equipment engineers—sit together in a common area.

Following the success of quality improvement teams at the management and professional support levels, effectiveness teams (quality circles) were created among line workers. Made up of employees from the same work area, they met regularly to solve specific quality, productivity, and customer service problems. Sometimes viewed as a precursor to self-managing work teams, quality circles have contributed to several important paradigm shifts for companies that have used them successfully.[3] Among these contributions are a realization of the value of worker input into solving work-related problems, the value of cross-functional (interdepartmental or across-jobs) problem solving, and a clear demonstration of how involved and committed most workers will become when invited into the decision-making process.

As in other companies that sponsor quality circles, TIM employees are encouraged to form effectiveness teams among themselves. A team leader is selected and trained. Then each team selects a work-related problem as a project and meets regularly to discuss it. The teams follow a reciprocal technology and engage in problem solving. Each team eventually devises recommendations to solve problems. They also make formal presentations to plant management. However, because these teams are advice teams, they do not implement their solutions.

One effectiveness team from TIM's solder dip function (one of the steps in making semiconductors) has nine members—technicians and expediters. They work on different shifts but still manage to meet weekly to work on their project. Their first project, which solved a difficult production problem, won an incentive award. For their second project, they chose to look for ways to improve a process called the solder pot crank system. Again their recommended changes were implemented, solving another production problem and saving the company more time and money. Again, team members were given an incentive award (an all-expenses-paid weekend trip), were written up in *Gema TIM*, and made a presentation. The team leader Lien S. S. had this to say: "ET [the effectiveness team] has given us the opportunity to solve our work problem and made our work much easier. We also learned to solve problems systematically, which we were never taught in school. It brings us together as one family working for a common objective. Our communication has improved. We understand each other, and there is better cooperation and, best of all, we are recognized!"

One of the major vehicles for learning to solve problems systematically is the "QC [quality circle] Story," a problem-solving procedure used extensively in Japan. Following are the steps usually employed in a typical QC:

1. Selecting a theme (problem). This includes reasons why the quality circle chose the problem, a Pareto diagram (which shows key factors contributing to the problem), and specific goals for the team's activities.

2. Understanding the situation. Team members use SPC (statistical process controls) tools such as histograms and cause-and-effect diagrams to analyze the problem and identify variances in quality.

3. Setting the target. Specific improvement targets (goals) and target dates are set based on available data.

4. Analyzing factors contributing to the problem and applying countermeasures to enable the quality circle members to attain their target.

5. Measuring results. Tangible results, such as decreased or eliminated variances in quality, are reported, as are intangible results, such as workers' increased realization of the importance of daily quality controls or improved quality procedures.

6. Developing measures to prevent backsliding. Team members develop countermeasures aimed at preventing any recurrence of the problem. Procedure manuals are often created or updated in order to standardize the improvements.

7. Developing insights and looking to future directions, a concept summed up as *kaizen*.

Because of the positive response to effectiveness teams, in December 1989, a council was formed to coordinate team activities and promote expansion of the program. The council is responsible for providing support and encouragement to individual teams, coordinating training for team leaders and members, and providing guidance as necessary to ensure completion of team projects. The council plans to create a resource center with audiovisual equipment and reading material, foster awards for teams completing their projects, and organize rallies for team members including an annual convention. Effectiveness teams that complete their projects are recognized in the TIM magazine and can present their projects at the annual TI Malaysia/TI Singapore ET Presentation.

Quality at the Source

The QC Story is just one of the tools TIM employees use. Beginning in 1985, TIM managers began to put operator self-control into practice. First, they taught operators how to recognize problems and arrive at solutions; then they gave them the responsibility, discretion, and authority to implement the solutions.

Extensive training was begun to give operators the knowledge and skills needed to monitor their own work, to look for and recognize variances in quality, and to know what to do when they saw problems. In many cases, this training simply polished or standardized existing worker skills. TIM, like most other companies, had been set up in a line manufacturing format, with each operator on the line performing a specific job. At the end of the production line, quality control inspectors, in a separate function, were responsible for catching quality problems. Workers on the line were not encouraged, or even allowed, to point out problems they saw. That was the job of highly trained QC inspectors. Stories abound all over the world of line workers "not paid to think," quietly watching defective materials go down the line. Sometimes it even became a game: "Will the QC inspectors catch that piece of Ha! They missed it!" As a result, quality, and the customer, often suffered.

Juran had declared that three requirements had to be met if operator self-control was to work. The first, knowledge of what one is supposed to do, was accomplished at TIM by expanding the job of each operator to include monitoring the quality of his or her own work. Quality awareness training was given, and job descriptions were changed to promote quality at the source.

Juran's second prerequisite, the ability to monitor one's own performance, was accomplished through training that provided knowledge and skills in quality inspection and control. Statistical process control techniques, developed in the 1950s in Japan, were taught to line operators, and tools such as Pareto analyses, control charts, fishbone or cause-and-effect diagrams, and run charts were introduced.

The third requirement, the ability to regulate one's own activities through a decision-making process, was taught through the use of Deming's PDCA (Plan-Do-Check-Act) cycle, the QC Story, and other frameworks for problem solving and decision making. The QC inspectors did all this training. As a result, after much of the training was accomplished, a sizable number of QC jobs were eliminated. The people who had formerly performed those jobs were given new responsibilities at the plant, since the QC function had become an integral part of each operator's job.

After operators were taught the principles and tools of quality at the source, they were empowered to practice them. A major aspect of empowerment is the authority to act on decisions. At TIM, operators are allowed to shut down the line when a defect is found. Previously, only QC inspectors had this authority by formally writing out a machine shutdown tag.

Self-managing Work Teams as a Total Quality Tool

TIM is now using self-managing work teams as an integral component of their workplace transformation. These teams are production teams that actually make the semiconductors. The teams operate as an assembly line, which is appropriate for producing a relatively standardized product that must meet stringent requirements for quality. Mohd

Azmi says, "All quality activities here are aimed at trying to satisfy customers. Customers look at quality, cost, service, and so forth. But at TIM, people development shares equal priority with customer satisfaction. Why? If our people are not developed and trained to deliver, you cannot have customer satisfaction. Personal development is the cause and customer satisfaction is the effect or result." Employees are quite proud of their ability to satisfy the rigorous quality requirements of their Japanese customers. Mohd Azmi says, "It is not easy to penetrate the Japanese market. They'll come and audit you for months. They'll go out and inspect the road to your factory and if they find a cigarette butt, they'll chew you out, saying, 'You think your people can produce quality products, and they have no discipline!' We listen to them, though, and make a lot of improvements." All over the TIM facility are brass plates with the word KAIZEN. Here, however, they try to make continuous improvement more than a slogan. Another striking symbol of the commitment to total quality can be found near one of the main entrances to the plant. It is the Quality Garden, a lush and attractive garden surrounding a marble monument on which is inscribed TIM's commitment to TQM. We were told that Japanese visitors are especially impressed by this beautiful and constant reminder.

The Quality Garden (Shrine)

The Texas Instruments Malaysian plant is located in an exotic setting compared to the other locations we describe in this book. Kuala Lumpur, with its lush tropical plants and rich cultural diversity, creates a fascinating backdrop for teams. The large industrial complex itself, however, at first seems similar to a thousand other production facilities. There are several buildings with a factory-setting appearance interwoven with paved parking lots filled with rows of employee cars. Inside, a honeycomb of work rooms are bustling with production activity. Off the long hallways are meeting rooms, restrooms, drinking fountains, and many company displays, all contributing to the familiar feel of a factory, albeit a very clean, orderly one.

A visitor who entered through a particular main factory entrance into this production environment could easily overlook a small garden area immediately to the right of the door. This well-kept garden features a beautiful display of carefully arranged native tropical plants, creating a natural picture that is visually pleasing to the eye.

At the center of the garden is a small stone-looking structure that appears to be a compact monument of some kind. It is the plant's quality shrine—a continual reminder and symbol of TIM's commitment to quality. The garden is a particularly appropriate symbol of the total quality emphasis at TIM. The garden and the stone form a natural blending of numerous living organisms to create a total quality product. It represents in a creative and powerful way the dedication to total quality.

After redesigning the work to integrate quality at the source, TIM managers went on in 1989 to begin implementing what they call the flexible organization. The design of the flexible organization has three components: a quality steering team (the plant manager and his reports), a process management team (middle managers and engineers, chartered with providing guidance and expertise), and self-managing work teams. These three groups have two basic functions in common: to maintain and to improve, the two pillars of continuous improvement. Following Juran's model, the maintain function guarantees the maintenance of processes, actively looks for problem situations, monitors quality, and promotes total participation. The improve function embodies KAIZEN, the continuous improvement of work standards and quality. "Hold the gain—improve—hold the gain—improve."

To begin moving toward self-managing work teams, TIM first instituted total productive maintenance, another concept developed in Japan, that attempts to maximize equipment effectiveness with a total system of preventive maintenance covering the entire life of the equipment. People are motivated to achieve this result through voluntary group activities. Like quality at the source, it is designed to include workers as more than mere operators of equipment; they are charged with maintaining the working order of their own equipment. And as with quality at the source, where the work of quality control inspectors is largely replaced by the workers themselves, total productive maintenance takes routine maintenance responsibility from a maintenance department and places it on the machine operators.

Several steps are required to set up this concept. First, teams of machine operators learn to clean their machines using standard cleaning procedures. Next, they learn to adjust the machine when something goes wrong. Previously, they were instructed to stop a machine with even small maladjustments and tell their supervisor. The supervisor then filled out a maintenance request order, which was sent to Maintenance and answered perhaps the next day (or after!). Although many seasoned operators knew how to perform these minor adjustments, they were not permitted to do so.

In the next step, workers learn to clean and oil their machines. Then they become responsible for total inspection of the machine operation using the manual, which is followed by preventive maintenance. They learn in detail how each machine operation affects the quality of their product. Finally, each operator becomes responsible for total preventive maintenance. Generally, the full process takes three years.

TIM's V. P. Murugan explains, "In the early days, a machine was repaired only after it broke down. Then time-based preventive maintenance was introduced. That was further improved by the addition of condition monitoring and reliability engineering. Total productive maintenance is productive maintenance involving total participation. Its success depends on everyone's cooperation and participation." According to Murugan, the advantages of total productive maintenance are increased productivity through the elimination of equipment losses, better quality, a minimum inventory of spare parts, zero pollution, a safe working environment through elimination of accidents, and a pleasant working environment. At TIM, a particular method, the Five S's, is used. Each S represents a Japanese word and component of involvement: *Seiri* ("cleaning"), *Seiton* ("tidiness"), *Seiso* ("sweeping and washing"), *Seiketsu* ("good housekeeping"), and *Shitsuke* ("discipline"). Murugan calls the Five S's "simple rules to keep any place clean and orderly, be it your house or workplace."

Self-managing Teams at TIM

The goal is to have all manufacturing people at TIM involved in self-managing work teams. More than 85 percent are now members of self-managing teams. Following quality circles, quality at the source, and total productive maintenance/autonomous maintenance, the next important building blocks toward the flexible organization were team daily administration and daily management. Daily administration, explains A. Subramaniam, involves teams taking on routine activities formerly performed by supervisors: marking attendance, setup, control of material usage, quality control, monitoring cycle time, safety, and line audits. TIM used several American companies as benchmarks for setting up daily administration for teams. For example, Milliken & Company, which produces textiles, has very good flow and maintains that if a team does good flowcharting, it can reduce problems by 50 percent. Florida Power & Light says that everything they do keeps customer satisfaction in mind, "so each person is challenged to keep the impact on the customer in focus." Japanese companies were also used as benchmarks. Toyota Motor, for example, maintains that employees have to know why certain operations are done the way they are, and so inspired TIM to write down why certain things are done in a certain way. There are written explanations even for marking attendance and housekeeping.

Daily management allows teams a great deal of autonomy, as TIM defines it: "A team working together and managing their process without any need for supervision." Mohd Azmi notes that daily management involves "a control activity that incorporates quality, cost, delivery, and service as the customer satisfaction drivers that link all critical sources of problems, from management to the lowest organization level. It involves a standardized procedure for identifying and solving problems and is applicable to every level in the organization." Low Say Sun, training and development administrator, adds, "They are expected in daily management to detect abnormality and take corrective action as well as make improvements in their work area using problem solving techniques and quality control tools. It will be just like running a business company. Of course there will be facilitators or managers whom they can turn to for help. In other words, there will be somebody to take care of the team. Training will be provided to enable them to manage their operation and process well." To begin, team members receive about 50 hours per person of training in the QC Story, quality control tools for problem solving, team building, daily management, analysis, capacity, communication, and other areas. The training function was increased by eight people, whose sole job is to teach, coach, and support members toward maturity as fully functioning self-managing teams. Many of the trainers are former production supervisors who have been displaced by the changeover to self-managing teams.

Difficulties Along the Path

Was everyone equally on board when it became clear that TIM was headed in the direction of self-managing teams? Subra remembered:

> There was concern that some of the senior technicians would not like self-management and want to leave. What we found is that they actually enjoy the teaching aspects and find more fulfillment in doing that than in doing their old jobs. "The most important thing in this or any program is good communication right from the start. Never hide anything from the workers. Tell them up front what is involved, how long it is going to take, what is their role, how they will be affected. Everything has to be told up front. Our plant manager meets every month, without fail, with all the employees. He has explained during these meetings the basics, and then I follow up with the workers in meetings of thirty people more of the details, answering their questions." [Note that the issue of senior technicians is a problem that will emerge in other cases in this book.]

Not all managers and supervisors have made the transition. Subra recounts how one manager "completely dominated his team with his self-centeredness. He never was able to adapt to the give-and-take of the team system and the sharing of authority. He wanted to make all the decisions himself." Eventually he left TIM for an electronics company that has a traditional management style. "From a technical viewpoint, we regretted his loss," said Subra. "He was excellent at the technical side, but he was never able to accept the team system. I've talked to him recently, and he's much happier in a traditional management setting."

Another issue is the question of what to do with former supervisors. This group is quite vulnerable to anxieties, not entirely unfounded, about job security. Many former supervisors have become trainers, facilitators, and technical specialists. Some have chosen to leave TIM. But no one has been laid off.

Did workers ask for more money when they realized self-management meant increased responsibility in their jobs? Subra said they were told up front that there will be no monetary incentive in going into self-management and teams. "Even if we were to divide the pay for the supervisory positions that are eliminated among the 1,600 manufacturing employees, it would come to only U.S.$10 per employee. We talk more about the freedom and skill development that they will get." However, TIM is considering a gain-sharing approach. When aggressive improvement goals are exceeded, employees may share the monetary gain.

Performance Outcomes

One outcome of TIM's quality improvement activities is enthusiastic employees. A technician told Mohd Azmi:

> You know, Azmi, before these self-managed teams started, when I set up the equipment and I had problems, I just put a hold tag saying "hold for engineer" on that lot. The next day, the engineer would come and fix the problem. But you know, now that we have gone through all this training for self-managing teams, and I know why my job is so important in relationship to my customer, I feel very bad. Now I understand. Now I know that if I put the lot on hold for the engineer, I will create one more day of cycle time, which is not good for our customer. Now I know that customer satisfaction is our number one priority.

Low S. S. explains, "Self-managed teams are the way most companies in the future will go. Today's workers are more educated, motivated, responsible, and more capable of doing their job without being closely supervised. We can be proud that TI Malaysia is among the first in TI worldwide to have adopted teams. It is a creative way for you to use your talents and it provides an opportunity to learn and develop yourself to be a better person, while at the same time makes life more interesting and rewarding." Mohd Azim adds:

> Technicians, in the past, some of them, as they stepped into the plant, parked their brains outside the fence. They came in with a body and hands, and they went to work and they went home. But today, we have got technicians who come to work with a brain and work and also take home work. Can you believe it? And feel happy! I believe it is something the people want, something they really want.

> Now, by getting into the self-managing teams concept, we are creating an environment where there is a certain amount of freedom to choose what they want to do. I believe some of them who never in the past enjoyed their jobs now have the opportunity to express themselves. And sometimes there are surprises. In the past, we had operators that we assumed were not very smart and couldn't contribute much. Today many of those same people come in and show fishbone diagrams and Pareto diagrams and ask why a certain lot has increased cycle time or why there are other problems. Now they come forward and show us analyses! We

are very excited because there is a lot of potential that we can tap if we provide the necessary training, coaching, and support. I think we can get a lot.

As for the numbers,

- TIM attributes a savings of $50 million in 10 years to quality improvements alone.
- There is a significant positive change in attitude, demonstrated by the fact that annual attitude survey results increase each year, and for the last two years, have been among the highest within TI worldwide.
- Thirty-five percent of TIM's production goes to Japanese customers, as opposed to none prior to 1985. Every major Japanese electronics company buys products from TIM, and several have exclaimed that quality at TIM rivals Deming Prize winners in Japan.
- As a result of putting operator self-control into practice, sustainable increases in yield and quality have been recorded. The average outgoing quality part-per-million defect has been reduced tenfold.
- In 1989, TIM received Malaysia's Award for Manufacturing Excellence.
- In December 1991, TIM was the winner of the 1991 Ministry of International Trade and Industry Excellence Award for Quality Management.
- From 1980 to 1991, units shipped increased from 400 million to almost 1 billion per year, while the number of semiconductor employees decreased from 2,500 to 2,000, showing a dramatic increase in output per person.
- The operators-to-supervisors ratio increased from 60:1 to 200:1, while the number of supervisor positions decreased from 79 to 18. The plan is to reduce supervisory positions even further.
- There have been demonstrable increases in cleanliness and machine "up time"; the equipment mean time between failures has increased four times, and downtime is only 25 percent of what it was in the past.
- Worker absenteeism is very low.
- Product cycle time has been cut in half.

KEY LESSONS TO BE LEARNED FROM THIS CASE

1. The design and implementation of teams at TIM has been guided by an overall philosophy that stems first from the parent company, and second, from the unique overlay that TIM uses to interpret this philosophy. This suggests that effective teams are designed with input characteristics that are congruent with organizational culture, at both the corporate and plant levels.

2. The transformation to teams has been inspired from the top down by an executive, the managing director, who expresses a clear vision that views employee development and self-management as the centerpiece of the drive toward excellence. This suggests that team-based designs often need a champion within the organization to continually help others see the potential benefits.

3. The transformation toward increasing team self-leadership has been accompanied by a move from a vertical hierarchy to a flat, delayered organization. This illustrates how effective team designs must be congruent with the broader organizational structure.

4. The quest for excellence through total quality has been an organizational goal that has served as a driver of change. This highlights the importance of having a pervasive goal that helps motivate teams toward change.

5. Self-managing production teams could only be implemented after team members had gained social and technical skills necessary to lead themselves. This illustrates the critical role of employee training and selection to ensure that teams are composed of individuals who possess characteristics that allow them to contribute necessary task and social inputs.

6. The design and implementation of teams has been marked by a patient but steady progress over a relatively lengthy period of 12 years. At no time was an overnight transformation expected. This highlights the need to design teams that are congruent with organizational and environmental factors. It also highlights the potential for guiding teams toward increased interdependence and self-leadership as conditions change.

NOTES FOR THE TIM CASE

1. We thank the staff at Texas Instruments Malaysia, especially Jerry Lee, Mohd Azmi Abdullah, A. Subramaniam, and Gene Carlone. Quotations in case are taken from interviews.

2. Peter F. Drucker, "The Responsible Worker," in *Management: Task, Responsibilities, Practices* (India: Allied Publishers Private Limited, 1975).

3. For more on this topic, see Henry P. Sims, Jr., and James W. Dean, "Beyond Quality Circles: Evolution into Self-managing Teams," *Personnel* (January 1985): 25–32.

INPUTS TO TEAMS

"Do we really need teams?" Steve asked himself as he hung up the telephone. George, the new CEO, was encouraging all plants and departments of the small-parts manufacturer to structure themselves around self-managing teams. Although Steve believed that teams might be helpful in the plant he supervised, he had thus far resisted teams because he was unsure how to design teams that would be truly effective.

"What type of teams do we need?" Steve wondered aloud as he stared out his office window. "Do we really need to organize the line workers into teams, or should we just develop quality circles?" he questioned. This stream of thought continued as Steve asked himself additional questions such as whether a move to teams would really require workers to work together more closely, whether hierarchical relationships within his plant would need to be changed to accommodate teams, and whether he could use goals and objectives to facilitate teams. "All of these issues seem so important, but where do I find direction to help me make the right decisions?" he queried himself.

Just then Becky, the plant's human resource director, interrupted Steve and asked him to approve a plan to hire 20 additional workers. Steve had previously discussed the team concept with Becky, so he decided to pursue some additional questions.

"If we decide to design the work at this plant around teams, will we need to hire people with different skills?" Steve asked.

"Well, probably, but I'm not entirely sure what those skills are or how team employees should differ," responded Becky.

"Will it matter who we put together to form each team?" questioned Steve.

"I'm not sure, but I will do some research and find out what I can about putting together effective work teams," Becky said.

Becky returned to her office, and Steve continued to ponder issues related to team design. "If we're going to do this, I want it done right," he thought. He then committed himself to learn more about teams before he began to adopt them at his plant.

This short case description illustrates some of the complex decisions that must be made when work teams are designed. Many of these decisions concern inputs into teams. Work teams that are designed with effective inputs have a much greater chance of being successful than do teams that lack critical inputs. In this unit we will discuss theory and research related to the task applications teams perform, the work technology (levels of interdependence) teams use to complete their work, team autonomy (self-leadership), and team goals. These inputs are associated with the tasks a team undertakes, as well as the structure of the organization within which the teams work. We will also discuss theory and research related to the combinations of individuals who comprise teams, as well as the inputs these members provide. Combining a knowledge of these individual-level inputs with knowledge about task and organizational inputs provides answers to many important questions about how work teams should be designed.

TASK APPLICATIONS

Differences in the tasks they perform necessitate that an automobile manufacturing team be designed very differently than a medical surgery team. Based on the tasks that they perform, work teams can be classified into four different categories: advice teams, production teams, project teams, and action teams.[1]

Advice teams are given the tasks of developing suggestions, making decisions, and providing recommendations. A common example is quality circles. At Texas Instruments Malaysia (TIM) (Case 2.1), advice teams were referred to as "quality improvement teams." These teams were organized at TIM with the purpose of giving advice about ways to reduce manufacturing cycle time. The manufacturing manager recruited team members from other departments including accounting, production planning, and facilities. The team met to develop specific suggestions related to cycle time reduction.

Several important characteristics of advice teams are represented in the TIM example. Team members were representatives from several different parts of the organization. The organizational structure for the teams was parallel to the main organizational structure. Thus, the advice team did not have authority or responsibility to carry out specific work tasks. Team members had other primary duties, and their contributions to the advice team were in parallel to the primary functional contributions they provided to the organization. In general, this TIM quality improvement team and other advice teams have nonspecialized duties and spend little time coordinating their efforts with other teams or business units.

Production teams are given the task of producing goods or services. They are structured around primary work tasks, and their purpose is to continuously provide goods or services. Assembly teams, maintenance teams, and flight attendant teams are examples of this type of team. The self-managing teams at TIM provide a good example. These teams spend the majority of their time producing circuits. They repeat their work cycle over and over in order to produce a relatively homogeneous output. Their work is not highly specialized, but they must closely coordinate their tasks with other teams and departments.

Project teams are given tasks related to specialized ventures. They often form to complete a specific set of duties, and they disband once those actions are completed. Task forces, planning teams, and research groups are common examples. The design team described in the IDS case (Case 2.3) provides a concrete example of a project team. This team consisted of 11 workers who for a period of time were relieved of their usual job duties in order to work on a team with a specific mission. The team gathered data, conducted analysis, and made important decisions. In the end, the design team created an effective plan for introducing teams throughout IDS.

As with most project teams, the design team at IDS spent a lot of time planning, investigating, and making reports. Team members were experts who provided specific inputs that were required to complete the team's core mission. The team coordinated its efforts with people outside the team as appropriate but worked primarily on its own without extensive ongoing coordination with other parts of the organization.

Action teams come together for a brief performance of highly specialized tasks. Examples are negotiation teams, surgery teams, and cockpit crews. Action teams differ from project teams in that, because they only come together for a short period of time, they must coordinate their efforts with other units inside the organization. One example is a Life Flight team at a large metropolitan hospital. This team is given the task of transporting accident victims via helicopter. In essence, a different new team consisting of a pilot and two trained medical technicians is formed for each flight. Other units of the organization (i.e., nursing, pilots association) provide support and training for the individual team members. The team members are experts who have clearly defined roles that are determined before each particular team is formed. This predetermination of roles allows members of Life Flight and other action teams to quickly perform their work. Once the team's task is performed, the team disbands and other units within the organization take over to complete the service or good.

The tasks that a team undertakes provide them with a purpose. Table 2.1 highlights key differences in features that are associated with different task applications. Highly specialized tasks usually result in project teams or action teams, while ongoing tasks usually call for advice or production teams. The task application also influences the amount of interaction a team has with other parts of the organization. Production teams and action teams interact a lot with other units, whereas advice teams and project teams tend to work somewhat independently. The optimal type of team thus depends largely on what is trying to be achieved. If recommendations are all that are desired, then advice teams may be sufficient. However, if the desire is to have teams produce goods or services, then a production team is best for ongoing, nonspecialized work. When the desired end is a short-term, specialized contribution, then an action team is best when close external coordination is required, while a project team is best when only limited ongoing coordination is needed.

TABLE 2.1 Team Types

Task Application	Purpose	Coordination with Other Teams	Time Frame
Advice	General	Low	Long
Production	General	High	Long
Project	Specialized	Low	Short
Action	Specialized	High	Short

Source: Adapted from Sundstrom, De Meuse, & Futrell (1990).

TECHNOLOGY AND INTERDEPENDENCE

Another input into teams is the technology, or process, through which individual contributions are combined into a group outcome. At one extreme is a team of insurance sales representatives who work in different geographic areas and seldom interact. This process of combining individual efforts is relatively simple and requires little interaction between team members. At the other extreme is a strategic planning team that spends endless hours meeting together and working on a cooperative solution. In this case the process of combining individual contributions is relatively complex and requires extensive team member interactions. This difference in interaction within teams is known as interdependence. *Interdependence* is defined as the amount of interaction that is required for team members to complete their work tasks.[2]

A relatively low form of interdependence occurs when teams simply pool their individual inputs. Each person works in relative isolation on specific tasks. The individual outputs are then combined into a team output. This is known as *pooled interdependence,* which occurs when the contributions of any individual team member are not generally affected by the unique contributions of other team members. Pooled interdependence can be an efficient way of accomplishing work when there is little or no need to coordinate the inputs of team members. Pooling of inputs can, however, help reduce the risks associated with variations in individual performance, such as when a particular sales representative has a bad month because of changes in the local economy of her sales territory.

In many college courses, teams of students use pooled interdependence to write group papers. Often each person on the team is assigned a specific section of the paper to write. The students go off and work individually on their sections and then use a word processor to combine the various inputs into a group paper. If no additional steps are taken (which having read many group papers, we know does sometimes occur), then the group has written a paper using pooled interdependence. While this pooling process is very efficient, the end product is usually not a very good paper. The sections don't link together well, and there is seldom adequate coverage of all important points. Certain steps in the process of writing an effective group paper thus require teams to adopt higher levels of interdependence, illustrating that teams are most effective when the level of interdependence they adopt matches the tasks that they perform.

Sequential interdependence requires a higher level of coordination between team members. Tasks move from one team member to another, and the output of each worker becomes the input for other workers. However, work generally moves in only one direction, with rational planning being used to develop a master schedule that coordinates team member efforts. The assembly line is a classic example of this type of interdependence. Even though the inputs of individual team members are closely linked, the need for ongoing interaction is minimized by the rational plan that sequentially coordinates inputs.

Teams of students writing group papers could use sequential interdependence. This occurs when one team member writes a part of the paper and then passes the paper on to another team member who writes some and then passes it on to someone else. Each team member takes what was written before and adds to it. Team members who work on the paper later in the process can see what others have written. Not only can they adapt the portion that they write to fit with the previous sections, but they can also alter the parts of the paper that were written earlier. This sequential process normally yields a paper that is better than a paper written with a pooled process. Coordination is somewhat higher, but there is still only limited interaction among team members.

Reciprocal interdependence requires team members to work together very closely. They continuously react to one another's inputs. Tasks move back and forth between team members, and each team member must be willing to rapidly adapt his or her inputs to coordinate with the rest of the team. In the most extreme cases of reciprocal interdependence, teams work together physically and continually collaborate to combine their individual outputs into a unique group output.

Reciprocal interdependence can once again be illustrated in the approaches students adopt to write group papers. When team members get together and brainstorm ideas, they interact closely and continuously build on the inputs of one another. What one team member says will likely influence what another team member says. This reciprocal process for writing a paper can be carried to the extreme when all the members sit around a computer and attempt to write a paper as a team. Team members discuss each sentence, and the suggestions and ideas of each team member are strongly influenced by the suggestions and ideas of others. The end result of this extreme reciprocal interaction is likely to be a high-quality paper, if the paper ever gets finished. One of the critical trade-offs for such high coordination is decreased efficiency, and many student teams who attempt to write a paper with reciprocal technology end up moving to lower levels of interdependence to complete some portions of the overall task.

The examples we have shared regarding how student teams write papers begin to illustrate that appropriate team interdependence is somewhat contingent on the tasks a team performs.[3] Some tasks such as selling insurance are perhaps best accomplished by people working individually. Other tasks such as strategic planning and medical surgery are most appropriate for reciprocal interdependence.[4] Nevertheless, teams performing a common task can be organized with different degrees of interdependence, and thus interdependence is largely a design characteristic that can be strategically determined. One example is automobile manufacturing.[5]

Toyota has developed methods of automobile manufacturing that adopt teams with sequential interdependence. These teams consist of members who have very specific duties. The work cycle of each team member is repeated approximately every minute. The output of one member serves as the input of another member, but the work is so standardized that there is little need for interaction between the workers. In contrast, Volvo has experimented with production methods that are more consistent with reciprocal interdependence.

Teams have been given an entire part of the car to assemble. The work cycle can take several hours to complete, and team members can do different things each time a cycle occurs. Individual roles within the teams are not prescribed, and workers must interact with one another to determine how they will approach the tasks.

So which form of interdependence is best? The answer is that it depends.[6] Pooled interdependence is effective when the work can be accomplished by individuals and there is little information or help to be gained from interacting with others. However, employees working under pooled interdependence are not organized into teams that must work cooperatively. Sequential interdependence does require teamwork and is appropriate when a team's work demands are stable. Rational planning can be used to coordinate individual inputs, and a very consistent product or service can be produced efficiently. In contrast, higher levels of reciprocal interdependence are most appropriate when a team's work requirements are dynamic. Rapid variations in the work environment, or instability of inputs and outputs, create a setting where the contributions of team members cannot be planned in advance. Information dispersed among team members can also be most effectively integrated through reciprocal interdependence. In addition, higher forms of interdependence usually generate greater worker satisfaction.

Teams can also adopt different forms of interdependence for the different subtasks that they perform. In the case of students writing a paper, a team might first adopt pooled interdependence as everyone goes to the library and researches the assigned topic. The team may then move to reciprocal technology to brainstorm ideas and write an outline for the paper. Sequential or pooled technology can then be used to write each specific section. In the end another round of reciprocal technology might help in the process of editing the paper. Through this process, the team is able to balance efficiency and coordination in order to produce a quality paper.

This adoption of different approaches to interdependence is also illustrated in the Fitzgerald case (see Case 2.2). Battery production teams are designed to use primarily sequential and pooled technology to produce the batteries. However, they use reciprocal technology when they meet together to discuss personnel issues and production process improvement.

TEAM SELF-LEADERSHIP

Another way teams vary in their design is related to their ability and freedom to lead themselves. This capacity for team self-leadership often depends on inputs that stem from hierarchical relationships within organizations. The control structure of some organizations allows teams a great deal of freedom to govern themselves. Other control structures place teams under tight external control with very little autonomy. One way of viewing these differences is shown in Figure 2.1, which provides a continuum ranging from externally managed teams to self-leading teams.[7]

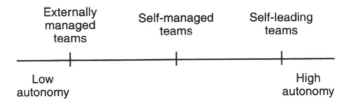

Figure 2.1 A continuum of team self-leadership

Externally managed teams have strong leaders who make decisions for them. Team members are given little latitude to determine how to do their work. They carry out prescribed tasks and make sure that assigned work is completed. Externally managed teams are not allowed to make decisions and are often discouraged from making creative suggestions. Their role is to stay within established boundaries.

One interesting example of an externally managed team was a group of government service employees who had the task of writing a series of reports.[8] The leader of the team required that all information flow through her office. Team members did not meet together and were discouraged from trying to do more than their small part of the report. The team leader made all assignments and had control over the end product. The team itself had no power to decide what the end product should look like or for that matter how it should approach its work. In the end this process led to a relatively dysfunctional team with members who were unable to find satisfaction and enjoyment in their work.

Self-managing teams exercise more freedom than externally managed teams. They are expected to manage themselves and focus on improving the work process. These teams are empowered to alter the way things are done and to govern themselves by performing traditional leadership duties such as time keeping, member discipline, materials management, repairs, and quality testing. (See the accompanying Fitzgerald case for an extensive list of self-managing team activities.) Taking on managerial duties provides the team with greater responsibility and authority than externally managed teams. However, self-managed teams do not possess the high degree of empowerment that characterizes self-leading teams. They do not set strategic objectives and are ultimately subject to external control.

The teams described in the final stages of the TIM case are a good example of self-managing teams. Team members are trained in quality improvement processes so that the teams themselves rather than external managers can manage the production process. Each team member receives about 50 hours of training in areas such as quality control, team building, daily management, and communication. After they receive the training, team members take on more and more managerial responsibility. The team is expected to detect any abnormalities in the production process and take any necessary corrective actions. In many ways, each team operates its own business. However, ultimate strategic direction at TIM is still set by upper-level managers, suggesting that an even higher level of empowerment (team self-leadership) is possible.

Self-leading teams are at the high end of the continuum for autonomy. In addition to determining *how* to do work, they decide *what* to do and *why*. Self-leading teams not only elect their own leaders, but they also decide whether the team will even have a leader. They build on team member commitment and allow their work to be guided by intrinsic motivation. These teams are given strategic information and often interact with customers and suppliers outside the organization. The team itself, rather than some external authority, is seen as the ultimate source of control.

Some interesting aspects of team self-leadership are described in the IDS case (Case 2.3). In many ways, the Design Team was able to lead itself. The team was given the broad mandate of determining how teams should be implemented in the organization; yet, they were given a great deal of autonomy and latitude in carrying out the mandate. Much of this is summed up by their leader who reported, "[I] gave them as much freedom as possible, because I didn't want anything to impact their decision. I even told the design team that I'd not be seen." The team went on not only to conduct analysis and arrive at solutions to problems but also to determine the very issues that they should address. This was a highly empowered team that in many areas had the ability to set overall strategic direction.

Self-leading teams are not appropriate for all situations.[9] One key contingency is the nature of the team members. Self-leading teams are most appropriate when workers have a high need for autonomy and a high level of technical ability and individual self-leadership ability. This means that high levels of team self-leadership require a great deal of training. Another contingency is the nature of the work.[10] Externally managed teams can sometimes be effective when work is routine, while self-leading teams are most appropriate when work is creative or customized. Self-leading teams are also best for dynamic environments that require a high degree of flexibility.

TEAM GOALS

A pervasive recommendation for designing teams is to make sure that they have a clear, engaging sense of direction. This sense of direction is normally communicated through goals. A *goal* is defined as something that is trying to be accomplished, or the object of actions."[11] Over 400 studies have investigated the effect of goals on performance, and most of them have concluded that performance can be increased through the establishment of specific, moderately difficult goals.[12] The majority of these studies have, nevertheless, examined the influence of individual-level goals and performance, with only a handful of studies actually looking at team-level goals and performance. Issues surrounding goals become more complex at the team level, as both individual members and the team as a collective can have goals.

One type of goal is an *overall goal that is shared by team members*. These goals concern what the group as a whole is trying to accomplish. Examples include a manufacturing team's goal to produce 300 radio assemblies per day or a flight attendant team's goal to complete its beverage service for every flight. A critical aspect of these team goals is that they are expressed in terms of work for a collective unit and not for each individual team member. The majority of research suggests that this type of goal is effective for improving performance.[13] One reason these team-level goals are beneficial is because they increase effort.[14] When group members have a shared goal, they seem to work harder and longer on the tasks that are required for high performance. This effect is particularly strong when the group's tasks are relatively routine and clearly understood. However, some evidence suggests that strong group goals may in some instances be counterproductive when a team's tasks are ambiguous, for focusing too much on a certain goal precludes a team from exploring options and preferences that may not have even been known when the goal was established.[15] Teams that have multiple goals, some of which may be competing goals, also experience difficulty.

A second type of goal that can exist for teams is the *individual goals of team members*. An example is an individual sales representative's goal to sell a million dollars worth of goods. This goal is helpful because it can motivate the sales representative to increase effort. However, the drive to achieve the sales goal can sometimes harm the overall performance of a customer service team if the individual sales representative's behavior is counterproductive to other team members. For instance, the sales representative may cut corners and make promises that result in long-term decreases in customer satisfaction, which may be the primary collective goal of the team. Individual goals have thus been found to improve overall team performance in some instances and to harm team performance in other instances.

Some of the discrepancy about the value of individual member goals appears to be resolved by taking into account differences in interdependence. When interdependence is low, individual goals are beneficial because they motivate team members to work hard.[16] In contrast, when interdependence is high, individual goals can be harmful because team members will often focus on their own performance at the expense of the team's overall performance.[17]

One way of overcoming the potentially negative effect of individual goals is to always supplement them with team goals. For instance, the sales representative's individual goal of one million dollars in sales could be combined with a team level goal such as 90 percent of clients will report that they receive a very high level of service from the team as a whole. Another method is to develop individual goals related to maximization of team performance. In this case, the sales representative's goal would be to have a 90 percent satisfaction rating for the clients with which he serves as the primary contact person. A combination of this type of individual goal and the overall group goal has been linked to significantly improved levels of team performance.[18]

TEAM COMPOSITION

Another critical design feature of teams concerns the individuals who comprise the team. Team staffing is a critical input into the design of effective teams. Most of us became aware of this as children. Teams are composed every day as children meet together to play competitive games. Two children are usually chosen as "captains." The other children then line up and the two "captains" alternate choosing other players. Many of us probably remember hoping that we were not the last one chosen. But what determines the order in which the players are chosen? Is it friendship? Is it skill? In reality it is probably some combination of both friendship and skill. No one wants to play on a team with people they do not like. At the same time, nobody likes to lose, and choosing teammates with needed skill improves the chance of success.

Choosing members for a work team is quite similar. Some team members provide beneficial social and emotional inputs; other members provide valuable task inputs. The inputs for any team depend on the composition of its members. A small-parts manufacturing team such as those described in the TIM case can only complete its work if team members are capable of operating the machines required to manufacture the product. The task skills of team members are thus critical for success. However, the manufacturing team will not reach maximum productivity over an extended time period unless team members also provide social support that helps develop effective communication channels and synergistic interpersonal relationships. Similar to children on a playground, team members like to spend time with others whom they like.

In order to provide task and social inputs, team members need certain knowledge, skills, and abilities so that they can provide particular inputs. If a team does not include someone with the ability to provide a critical input, its success suffers. *Team composition,* which is defined as the mixture of individual inputs and skills included in the team, is thus a critical element of work teams. In order to understand the effects of team composition, we first explore the task and socioemotional inputs required of team members. We then explore how these inputs are related to characteristics of individuals, which provides guidance for team member selection.

Task and Socioemotional Roles

One way of better understanding team member inputs is to examine the roles team members enact. A *role* is a set of behaviors that is characteristic of a person in a specific situation. For instance, students usually listen to lectures, participate in discussions, ask questions, take notes, and complete exams. The role of student is defined by these behaviors because they are common to most people who are students. However, most students are also engaged in other roles such as boyfriend, girlfriend, spouse, club member, and roommate. Each of these roles has a different set of behaviors associated with it, and behavior is usually dependent on the role that an individual is enacting at a given time. When they are acting as a student, their behavior is different than when they are acting as a club member. Several different people can simultaneously enact the role of student. Roles can thus be shared by a number of people and are dependent on the particular situations in which people find themselves.

Roles within work teams are similar. A number of different team members may enact the same role, and any one person may fill a number of roles. The roles create a pattern of relationships that influence not only how each team member acts but also how others treat him or her. Of course, each person can enact a unique role, but research suggests two basic categories of roles within teams: task and socioemotional.[19]

Task roles encompass behaviors that focus on accomplishing work goals. Team members enacting task roles spend a lot of time doing work tasks. In the Fitzgerald case (Case 2.2) team members enact task roles when they initiate equipment repair, prepare material and labor budgets, and conduct quality control inspections. *Socioemotional roles* encompass behaviors that structure relationships and fulfill the social and emotional needs of members. Team members who enact socioemotional roles spend their time in social interchanges that have objectives such as encouraging other team members and mediating conflicts. Members of the Fitzgerald teams enact these roles when they conduct weekly group meetings, discipline team members for absenteeism and tardiness, and negotiate job assignments.

Individual Characteristics That Facilitate Team Success

Team members cannot provide task and social inputs unless they have the necessary knowledge, skill, and ability. Members' capability to provide desirable inputs can be obtained either through effective team member selection or through training and development. With either process, the goal is to ensure that a team is composed of employees with characteristics that allow them to enact roles that provide critical inputs. Many times it is easier to select members who already possess critical capabilities rather than to try training them once they are included in the team. Team composition is thus one area of team design that can be used to facilitate early team success.

Research suggests that, consistent with roles, some employee characteristics provide task inputs, while others facilitate socioemotional inputs. Because understanding these characteristics helps guide team staffing decisions, we first focus on some characteristics associated with task inputs and then on some characteristics associated with socioemotional inputs..

Characteristics That Provide Task Inputs

Team members' mental and physical abilities are individual characteristics necessary for enacting most task roles. Numerous tasks can be completed only by people with *specific abilities*. For instance, the task of tracking a team's financial expenditures requires accounting ability. The task of operating an X-ray machine requires knowledge and skill associated with X-ray procedures. The nature of the group's work thus plays a large part in determining individual abilities that are needed to enact specific task roles. Teams will be successful only if they include members with the required task skills and abilities.

In contrast to abilities required to perform a specific task, *self-management skills* are related to performance for almost all tasks.[20] Many self-management skills are detailed in the accompanying Fitzgerald case (Case 2.2). Examples of specific behaviors associated with these skills include self-observation, self-goal setting, and antecedent/consequent modification. Self-observation encompasses efforts to monitor behavior and gather information about performance. Self-goal setting occurs as employees establish targets for desirable behavior. Antecedent modification is carried out through the alteration of environmental cues. Consequent modification occurs after behavior when employees reward themselves for performance. For example, a self-leading team member might monitor her performance and realize that she often fails to replace the filter on a machine. She would then establish a goal to replace the filter at regular intervals. To help her remember, she might place a sign on the machine that cues her to change the filter. After she changes the filter, she can experience self-reward by celebrating the fact that she has accomplished an important task.

Characteristics Congruent with Socioemotional Inputs

The individual characteristics needed to successfully enact socioemotional roles are less easy to describe. Socioemotional roles are inherently interpersonal, meaning that the desirability of characteristics for any member depends in large part on the characteristics of other members. However, a few common social inputs can be identified.[21]

One critical socioemotional input is *conflict resolution*. Because a moderate amount of conflict is beneficial for a team, the highest contributing members do not avoid conflict, nor do they try to totally eliminate it. They encourage conflict that is constructive and discourage conflict that is destructive. We will explore this difference between positive and negative conflict more fully in Unit 3; however, the point here is that team members enact a valuable socioemotional role when they help the team implement constructive conflict resolution strategies. This is usually accomplished by team members who use "win-win" negotiation strategies rather than "win-lose" strategies.

Collaborative problem solving is also beneficial. Team members are helpful when they involve other team members and generate optimal solutions to problems. This requires them to encourage participation from each team member, as well as to ensure that all sides of important issues are examined. Team members with the ability to guide the team through collaborative problem solving can thus provide a valuable social input.

Effective *communication skills* are required for enacting almost all socioemotional roles. Team members communicate effectively by engaging in informal conversation, listening actively and nonevaluatively, and maximizing congruence between verbal and nonverbal messages. Team members enacting effective socioemotional roles also focus on developing appropriate communication networks.

Communication networks represent patterns of who communicates with whom.[22] One important way that communication within teams differs is in its amount of centralization. For instance, highly centralized networks require all communication related to the team to flow through a central individual, such as a leader or facilitator. In contrast, highly decentralized networks allow each team member to communicate directly with any other member of the team. Centralized communication networks are most effective for completing relatively simple tasks, while decentralized networks are best for performing complex tasks. Team members are thus most helpful when they have the ability to develop a communication network that matches the level of task difficulty. More often than not, this means the development of decentralized networks in contemporary organizations that face complex tasks.

An example of the need for a decentralized communication network can be seen in the government service team that was described earlier. The team faced a complex task of producing a series of reports. They experienced strong external leadership, and the leader required all communication to flow through her. This highly centralized network was ineffective for bringing together the various viewpoints that were required to produce high-quality reports. Team members felt little identity with the team and reported very low levels of job satisfaction. The team and its product would have benefited greatly by including a leader, or perhaps even another team member, who helped them develop a decentralized communication network.

Personality traits also represent individual characteristics that are associated with numerous socioemotional inputs. Teams benefit from socioemotional inputs such as active participation in group discussions and exhibitions of leadership. These facilitating roles are naturally carried out by extroverted team members, which suggests that *extroversion* is a desirable trait for team members. However, research suggests that too many extroverts can harm team performance.[23] One particular study found this in student teams, as four and five member teams performed best when they included two or three extroverts. Too few extroverts seemed to result in teams with many important socioemotional roles that were not enacted. Yet, too many extroverts resulted in teams that did not cooperate well. Perhaps this is because the socioemotional roles of leader and information giver require complementary roles of follower and listener. Effective teams thus have a balance of extroverts and introverts, meaning that the desirability of extroversion for any one team member is dependent on the extroversion of other team members.

Other personality traits have also been found to facilitate important socioemotional inputs.[24] Teams composed of members who score high on measures of *agreeableness* (descriptors of this trait include cooperation, caring, and tolerance) have been found to become cohesive and able to maintain positive working relationships. Teams without members who are anxious and stressed (a trait that personality researchers label *emotional stability,* which includes descriptors such as stable, relaxed, and tolerant of stress) also seem to function better over the long-run. This makes sense when you think about team relationships.

An interesting example of the effect of personality might be a small music band. Including a single disagreeable member can destroy interpersonal relationships and create an environment where band members are uncomfortable. A member who is always stressed out and worrying also tends to continually bring up negative issues related to the performance and future of the band. This negative communication increases the stress levels of other band members and thus has a compounding effect. One way to increase the likelihood of team success is to make sure that all team members have group-facilitating personality traits such as agreeableness and emotional stability.

Fit Between Team Members

As described in relation to the personality trait of extroversion, research has begun to focus on the overall mix of individual personality traits. Team member compatibility is an important factor for understanding team composition, and a common prescription for teams is to choose members who are compatible with each other. This compatibility is often referred to as "fit."[25] Fit is difficult to define, and most people respond that "they will know it when they see it." However, *team fit* exists when there are positive social relationships among team members. With the exception of a few traits such as extroversion, positive relationships usually result from some level of team member similarity. People are attracted to others with similar interests and beliefs; attraction leads to decreased conflict and increased social interaction. The positive social interactions result in synergistic relationships that facilitate cooperation. However, if there is too much similarity, it can sometimes be difficult to obtain synergy, meaning that effective teams balance similarity with diversity.

Areas of similarity include personal values, political orientations, personality traits, hobbies, and leisure preferences.[26] Many of these characteristics are not directly related to job tasks. However, teams can become rather homogeneous in these areas. One explanation is the *attraction–selection–attrition hypothesis*.[27] This hypothesis posits that homogeneity results from three processes. The first process is attraction, which occurs when people desire to join a team whose values and beliefs are similar to theirs. This process is illustrated each year as people choose the university they will attend. Many base their choice on similarity with current students.

The second process—selection—occurs when teams make their choices about who they will allow to join the team. Because we all have a tendency to like people who are similar to us, existing team members frequently support the inclusion of others who have characteristics similar to their own. This bias is often unintended but creates a self-perpetuating cycle whereby the team progressively takes on the characteristics of those who make hiring decisions. The effect of selection can again be seen in the admission of students to universities, as people with characteristics similar to current students and alumnae often have a greater chance of acceptance to the university of their choice.

The third and final process is attrition. This occurs when individuals leave a team. Just as students leave universities when they don't feel accepted by other students and teachers, team members who do not share common likes and dislikes often feel left out and become dissatisfied with being a team member. When these people leave, attraction and selection processes result in their being replaced with someone who has a better fit with the team. Attraction, selection, and attrition thus operate to help teams to become homogeneous over time.

Support for the attraction–selection–attrition hypothesis was found in a study examining teams of retail sales clerks.[28] These teams had consistent emotional climates. Some teams were positive and upbeat, whereas others were negative and gloomy. Successful teams displayed positive emotions. Nevertheless, the personalities of the members (either positive or negative) were surprisingly similar within teams, supporting the notion that teams evolve toward homogeneity. Similar support for the operation of processes that increase team member similarity has been found in studies of top-management teams. These teams have found that individuals are likely to leave teams when they are not similar to the other members on such dimensions as age, education, career experience, and tenure with the organization.[29]

Diversity in Teams

Is an evolution toward fit and a composition of homogeneity beneficial? One argument suggests it is beneficial because similarity results in constructive social relationships that produce cooperation. The counterargument is that homogeneity is harmful because it results in cronyism that harms creativity, as well as limits the variety of viewpoints that can make synergy potent. Both arguments make sense and are somewhat supported by research, which leads to the conclusion that homogeneity is beneficial for teams that must cooperate and complete routine tasks, but is harmful for teams working on tasks that require creative solutions.[30] One study quantitatively demonstrated this by comparing culturally diverse teams with culturally homogeneous teams.[31] In the early stages of team performance, the culturally homogeneous teams were found to have more positive social interactions and performance. However, over time the processes of the culturally diverse teams improved and became as effective as those of the homogeneous teams. After about four months, the culturally diverse teams also scored higher than the homogeneous teams for some measures of creative performance. The TIM case also provides a good illustration of how culturally diverse work teams can be highly effective.

On another dimension, theoretical arguments have been made that employees will enjoy working in groups that are composed of members who are similar to themselves, particularly in terms of race. However, research suggests that this effect is not the same for all racial groups. In one study, white employees reported lower commitment and productivity when they were in groups of mostly African American and Hispanic workers. African American workers had consistent levels of commitment and productivity regardless of group racial composition. Hispanic workers had their lowest commitment and productivity in groups predominantly composed of minorities, and their highest commitment and productivity in groups consisting of about half white employees and half minorities. These findings suggest that the links between group diversity and worker perceptions are complex, and additional research needs to be done to understand how individuals react to groups with varying composition. In the meantime, organizational leaders are wise to remember that choosing teams based on homogeneity can violate equal employment opportunity laws. Moreover, demographic trends indicate that many new entrants into the workforce over the next several years will be minorities, perhaps making it impossible for organizations to maintain homogeneous teams.

WHAT WE HOPE YOU LEARN IN THIS UNIT

After studying this unit, you should be able to describe several different inputs into teams, as well as their potential effects. Understanding these differences and being able to apply them to actual work teams can help in the process of designing teams. As shown in the opening case vignette, numerous decisions must be made, and each of these decisions can have a lasting impact on team processes and performance.

The first input we discussed was the type of team that is desired. Team task applications should drive the type of team that is formed, and understanding how teams differ provides knowledge that can help guide decisions about choosing one form of team over another. Wise choices take into account the amount of time the team is expected to endure, the degree of specialization included in the team assignments, and the relationship of the team to other parts of the organization. The very act of classifying a team based on its task applications provides some insight into how the team is expected to interact and perform.

The second input was interdependence. Teams adopt different levels of interdependence to accomplish their work, and research has established that the optimal amount of interdependence depends largely on a team's tasks and environment. We hope that you can now examine a team's environment and task duties in order to better describe which type of interdependence is most appropriate. In the end, teams that work together closely are best for nonroutine work and dynamic work environments.

Team self-leadership is another critical input that can be influenced through the team design process. Although the next section (Unit 3) will discuss specific styles of leadership that are congruent with the various forms of team autonomy, this section has addressed the importance of hierarchical relationships with the rest of the organization. In particular, designing organizations so that teams have extensive self-leadership increases their capacity to change and remain flexible.

This unit has also provided information that should aid the process of setting motivational goals for teams. These goals provide an overall direction for team member effort, as well as define the outputs that the team is expected to contribute to the organization. By shifting the focus away from individual goals to team goals, team members are encouraged to work together and not to compete with one another to enhance individual accomplishments.

The final category of inputs comes from the contributions that individuals make to teams. Because both task and socioemotional inputs are needed, it is critical to staff teams in a manner that optimizes individual characteristics related to both technical skills and social relationships. By learning the kind of individual inputs that facilitate team success, you should be able to better determine the desirable characteristics of team members. You should also be able to see the bigger picture of interteam relationships and thereby make team staffing decisions that facilitate positive social interactions among team members.

NOTES FOR UNIT 2

1. These team types are taken from E. Sundstrom, K. P. De Meuse, and D. Futrell, "Work Teams: Applications and Effectiveness," *American Psychologist* 45 (1990): 120–133. Slightly different labels for these team types are provided by Susan G. Cohen and Diane E. Bailey, "What Makes Teams Work: Group Effectiveness Research from the Shop Floor to the Executive Suite," *Journal of Management* 23 (1997): 239–290.

2. The concept of task interdependence is based on the work of J. D. Thompson, *Organizations in Action* (New York: McGraw-Hill, 1967). See also A. H. Van de Ven and D. L. Ferry, *Measuring and Assessing Organizations* (New York: John Wiley & Sons, 1980) and G. P. Shea and R. A. Guzzo, "Groups as Human Resources," *Research in Personnel and Human Resources Management* 5 (1987): 323–356.

3. See G. P. Shea and R. A. Guzzo, "Groups as Human Resources," *Research in Personnel and Human Resources Management* 5 (1987): 323–356. See also K. Y. Williams and M. C. Thomas-Hunt, "It's Not All in the Task: A Closer Look at Interdependence in Groups," paper presented at the Academy of Management Conference held in Boston, August 1997.

4. See G. L. Stewart and M. R. Barrick, "Designing Effective Work Teams: Task Interdependence, Team Self-leadership, and Task Routineness," paper presented at the Annual Meeting of the Academy of Management, Boston, August 1997.

5. These points about the automobile industry are taken from P. S. Adler and R. E. Cole, "Designed for Learning: A Tale of Two Auto Plants," *Sloan Management Review* (1993): 85–94.

6. See Stewart and Barrick, "Designing Effective Work Teams."

7. For more on differences in team-level self-leadership, see C. C. Manz, "Self-leading Work Teams: Moving Beyond Self-management Myths," *Human Relations* 45 (1992): 1119–1140.

8. This description is based on the case entitled "Credit Analysis Team" written by M. L. Davis-Sacks and included in J. R. Hackman, *Groups That Work (and Those That Don't)* (San Francisco: Jossey-Bass, 1990).

9. C. C. Manz, "Self-leading Work Teams: Moving Beyond Self-management Myths," *Human Relations* 45 (1992): 1119–1140. See also Stewart and Barrick, "Designing Effective Work Teams."

10. Stewart and Barrick, "Designing Effective Work Teams."

11. E. A. Locke, K. N. Shaw, L. M. Saari, and G. P. Latham, "Goal Setting and Task Performance: 1969–1980," *Psychological Bulletin* (July 1981): 126.

12. E. A. Locke and G. P. Latham, "Work Motivation and Satisfaction: Light at the End of the Tunnel," *Psychological Science* 1 (1990): 240–246.

13. A meta-analysis supporting the benefits of group goals is reported by A. M. O'Leary-Kelly, J. J. Martocchio, and D. D. Frink, "A Review of the Influence of Group Goals on Group Performance," *Academy of Management Review* 37 (1994): 1285–1301.

14. L. R. Weingart, "Impact of Group Goals, Task Component Complexity, Effort, and Planning on Group Performance," *Journal of Applied Psychology* 77 (1992): 682–693.

15. O'Leary-Kelly et al., "A Review of the Influence of Group Goals."

16. T. Matsui, T. Kakuyama, and M. L. U. Onglatco, "Effects of Goals and Feedback on Performance in Groups," *Journal of Applied Psychology* 72 (1987): 407–415.

17. T. R. Mitchell and W. S. Silver, "Individual and Group Goals When Workers Are Interdependent: Effects on Task Strategies and Performance, *Journal of Applied Psychology* 75 (1990): 185–193.

18. See D. F. Crown and J. G. Rosse, "Yours, Mine, and Ours: Facilitating Group Productivity Through the Integration of Individual and Group Goals," *Organizational Behavior and Human Decision Processes* 64 (1995): 138–150.

19. This material, including the lists of generic task and socioemotional roles, is taken from R. F. Bales, "Task Roles and Social Roles in Problem-solving Groups," in E. E. Maccoby, T. M. Newcomb, and E. L. Hartley (eds.), *Readings in Social Psychology* (New York: Holt, Rinehart and Winston, 1958). Also, see K. D. Benne and P. Sheats, "Functional Roles of Group Members," *Journal of Social Issues* 4, no. 2 (1948): 41–49.

20. For information about self-management, see C. C. Manz and H. P. Sims, Jr., "Self-management as a Substitute for Leadership: A Social Learning Perspective," *Academy of Management Review* 5 (1980): 361–367. Also see C. C. Manz, *Mastering Self-leadership: Empowering Yourself for Personal Excellence* (Upper Saddle River, NJ: Prentice-Hall, 1992).

21. This information is taken from M. J. Stevens and M. A. Campion, "The Knowledge, Skill, and Ability Requirements for Teamwork: Implications for Human Resource Management," *Journal of Management* 20 (1994): 503–530.

22. See M. E. Shaw, "Communication Networks," in L. Berkowitz (ed.), *Advances in Social Psychology*, vol. 1, pp. 111–147 (New York: Academic Press, 1964).

23. This information is taken from B. Barry and G. L. Stewart, "Composition, Process, and Performance in Self-managed Groups: The Role of Personality," *Journal of Applied Psychology* pp. 62–78 (1997).

24. M. R. Barrick, G. L. Stewart, M. J. Neubert, and M. K. Mount, "Relating Member Ability and Personality to Work Team Processes and Team Effectiveness," *Journal of Applied Psychology* 83 (1998): 377–391.

25. For a review of the fit concept, see J. A. Chatman, "Matching People and Organizations: Selection and Socialization in Public Accounting Firms," *Administrative Science Quarterly* 36 (1991): 459–484.

26. These dimensions of fit come from R. D. Bretz, S. Rynes, and B. Gerhart, "Recruiter Perceptions of Applicant Fit: Mapping the Construct or Constructing the Map?" *Journal of Vocational Behavior* 43 (1993): 310–327.

27. The attraction–selection–attrition hypothesis is developed by B. Schneider, "The People Make the Place," *Personnel Psychology* 40 (1987): 437–452.

28. See J. M. George and K. Bettenhausen, "Understanding Prosocial Behavior, Sales Performance and Turnover: A Group-level Analysis in a Service Context," *Journal of Applied Psychology* 75 (1990): 698–709; J. M. George, "Personality, Affect, and Behavior in Groups," *Journal of Applied Psychology* 75 (1990): 107–116.

29. S. E. Jackson, J. F. Brett, V. I. Sessa, D. M. Cooper, J. A. Julin, and K. Peyronnin, "Some Differences Make a Difference: Individual Dissimilarity and Group Heterogeneity as Correlates of Recruitment, Promotions, and Turnover," *Journal of Applied Psychology* 76 (1991): 675–689; M. F. Wiersema and A. Bird, "Organizational Demography in Japanese Firms: Group Heterogeneity, Individual Dissimilarity, and Top Management Team Turnover," *Academy of Management Journal* 36 (1993): 996–1025.

30. For a review of the literature concerning group heterogeneity, see S. E. Jackson "Team Composition in Organizational Settings: Issues in Managing an Increasingly Diverse Work Force," in S. Worchell, W. Wood, and J. A. Simpson (eds.), *Group Process and Productivity,* (Newbury Park, CA: Sage, 1992) pp. 138–173. Also see D. C. Hambrick, T. S. Cho, and M. Jen, "The Influence of Top Management Team Heterogeneity on Firms' Competitive Moves," *Administrative Science Quarterly* 41 (1996): 659–684.

31. W. E. Watson, K. Kumar, and L. K. Michaelsen, "Cultural Diversity's Impact on Interaction Process and Performance: Comparing Homogeneous and Diverse Task Groups," *Academy of Management Journal* 36 (1993): 590–602.

CASE

2.2

Designing Teams at the Fitzgerald Battery Plant

This case was written by Henry P. Sims, Jr. and Charles C. Manz.[1]

During the design of a team system, decisions must be made about which managerial responsibilities will be carried out by the team rather than by an external supervisor. This case provides an illustration of a manufacturing facility that empowered teams to perform almost all duties that had previously been completed by external supervisors. When the team is designed so that team members, rather than external supervisors, perform these functions, critical task and socioemotional inputs to the team are contributed by a number of people rather than by a single leader.

The Fitzgerald Battery Plant of General Motors uses an innovative and highly effective system of employee self-managing teams. The plant, located in rural Fitzgerald, Georgia, was established in 1974 by General Motors Corporation to manufacture sealed maintenance-free automotive batteries. Generally, the technology can be described as sequentially interdependent; the output of one team member becomes the input of another team member. Moreover, the output of one team becomes the input of another team. There are small-parts production operations and some small-assembly operations.

The plant's personnel—about 320—have been organized into teams from the beginning. People at the plant simply use the term *teams;* we classify them as self-managing teams because they have freedom to determine how their work is carried out. There are three levels of teams. At the top are managers in the support team, so named because "we support the people who actually do the work." In the middle is a group of individuals who have technical and operational responsibilities—the coordinators. In traditional plants, these employees would be called foremen, general foremen, or technicians, but the role of these coordinators is quite different from the traditional one of foreman. Several of the coordinators have operational responsibility over the manufacturing teams, but this responsibility tends to be that of advice and facilitation rather than direction. At the operating level, the employees are organized into approximately 33 operating teams, ranging in size from 3 to about 19 members. People are grouped into teams composed of natural work units that have closely connected, interdependent tasks. Each team has recognizable boundaries, in both physical space and task responsibilities. The products of each team are measured according to input and output, and each team is considered to be a business unto itself. The output of one team becomes the input for other team(s), but the connections among teams are typically buffered by inventories of material between clusters of manufacturing processes. This makes the interdependence sequential rather than reciprocal.

Wages are based on a pay-for-knowledge concept rather than the traditional pay-for-position principle; that is, employees are paid for what they are capable of doing rather than the task they are doing at a particular moment. This system encourages the acquisition of knowledge and skill needed for many task inputs. It also facilitates task flexibility and variety. An employee must demonstrate competence at all jobs on two different teams in order to advance to the highest pay level. This typically takes about two years. One result is high flexibility of response, since most employees can enact numerous task roles and they are not financially penalized for short-term assignments to tasks that might command a lower rate in a more traditional pay system. This breadth of job experience, in turn, fosters an unusual appreciation for the "other guy's problems."

The plant's team system features an innovative method for influencing and motivating employee behavior. In addition to the traditional physical production tasks, each team is expected to perform a wide range of responsibilities, many of which are traditionally considered to be within the jurisdiction of supervisors or managers. Generally, the teams engage in various task and socioemotional roles that focus on production scheduling, process adjustments, product improvement, and, especially, quality problem solving. Teams also deal with internal personnel problems, such as the absenteeism of a team member.

Many of these activities take place during team meetings, which normally serve as problem-solving forums. Each team has at least one half-hour regularly scheduled team meeting per week, and special meetings are called to deal with specific problems. All meetings are held on company time, and employees are paid their regular wage while attending. Meetings are usually conducted by an elected team leader. Coordinators or support team members may attend parts of meetings but are not routinely present.

Team Member Inputs

When the plant was started up, an effort was made to involve the teams in at least a portion of the roles and responsibilities typically carried out by management at more traditional plants. Because many responsibilities were vested within the teams themselves, traditional foremen or bosses were not needed. Following is a description of how the teams handled responsibilities typically performed by traditional bosses. Each of these new roles required team members to provide certain task or socioemotional inputs.

Initiate equipment and machinery repair.

Overall, team members tended to make minor repairs themselves in order to keep production flowing. Although major repairs were carried out by the maintenance department, frequently they were initiated by team members. We recall the statement of a team member in a weekly team meeting: "They better get that bearing replaced this weekend, or that machine will break down next week, and we'll lose a day's production!" Most of all, team members seemed to have an unusual degree of ownership in their production equipment; they were very concerned about making the equipment work in the right way.

Ensure that needed production materials and spare parts are available.

In many traditional plants, workers allow a production material to become depleted in order to take a break that is unscheduled and unauthorized by management. At this plant, the ability to make sure production materials and spare parts were available was vested in the team itself. Internal team leaders spent a great deal of their time ensuring that the materials were available to meet production requirements.

Perform quality control inspections and compile data.

For the most part, team members did the quality inspections and compiled their own quality statistics, typically assigning this role to one member. The plant had no separate quality control inspectors, although occasionally a small central quality control department audited team quality data.

Prepare material and labor budgets.

Every year teams undertook a planning exercise in which they prepared a team budget. Accountants from the office did the budgeting, independently and in parallel, and the two proposed budgets were discussed and reconciled in order to arrive at a final budget. Team members required training and appropriate information to carry out this exercise.

Prepare daily log of quantity produced and amount of in process inventory.

For the most part, teams compiled their own in-process inventory records, subject to occasional auditing from production scheduling. Teams knew their own production schedule and kept their own records of how much they produced and the quantity of their in-process inventory.

Recommend engineering changes for equipment, process, and product.

As they worked with equipment, teams occasionally requested changes that would lead to significant process or product improvements. One engineer at the division level expressed a preference for placing new or experimental equipment at Fitzgerald. "They make it work!" he exclaimed.

Conduct safety meetings.

Scheduled safety meetings were conducted, normally by the team leader or a coordinator or other technical person. During the early stages of the start-up of the plant, safety performance was poor. Over the years, however, the safety record improved continuously, and by the time of our visits, Fitzgerald's safety performance was in the top quartile of all General Motors plants.

Shut down the process or assembly if quality is wrong.

The team could stop production to solve process or quality problems. Teams had the authority to stop production without asking management permission. Shutdown decisions were made with great discretion and almost always to solve a serious quality or process problem since such a decision might have ramifications for other teams.

Train new members of work group.

All teams carried out training, which is important in terms of developing the wide range of skills required for each new member to advance along the pay scale. Occasionally, the external coordinator would pitch in or conduct some special training, and there were more formal training programs for team members.

Review quarterly performance of company, plant, and group.

Each quarter, the plant manager met separately with each team to review company, plant, and team performance. These occasions provided an opportunity for an exchange of communication between the plant manager and team members.

Make specific job assignments within work group.

Each team made its own job assignments. The practices were quite different across teams; one team might rotate jobs every hour, while another would make assignments strictly on a seniority basis. Overall, teams seemed to find a way to satisfy individual member preferences without compromising productivity goals.

Select and dismiss the group leader.

Teams elected their own team leader from their membership. Elections were conducted whenever a current leader resigned or was challenged by another team member. (Teams also had the authority to dismiss a team leader, but this was virtually never done. Instead, an ineffective team leader might be encouraged to resign or might be challenged by another.) A few teams had had the same leader since the start-up of the plant; others had had several team leaders over the years.

At first, popular individuals tended to be elected leader; however, teams soon found that the best leaders were those who had organizing, planning, interpersonal, and conflict resolution skills. Eventually, so-called popularity diminished as a criterion for election to team leader.

Management appointed coordinators—leaders who were external to the team (although many had served as team leaders). Each coordinator had responsibility for one to three teams. Although coordinators filled the space in the organizational hierarchy typically occupied by a foreman or general foreman, their role was quite different. We will explain this role more fully in Unit 3 when we discuss leadership.

Establish relief and break schedules.

Teams had great discretion in establishing their own schedules. Since most of the teams were buffered by short-term in-process inventories, they could schedule breaks as they wished. They carried out this role responsibly, often timing breaks to facilitate mainte-nance or production setup. For example, a short tool or process change might be un-dertaken while the team was on break.

Keep record of hours worked for each group member.

The plant had no time clocks. Each team member kept a record of his or her number of hours worked and turned in weekly time records to the team leader and then to the coordinator. When asked, "Don't they cheat?" one team member replied, "Who do they cheat? Other team members! You may be able to get away with it once or twice, but that's all. You can't fool your teammates."

Select new members for the group and dismiss members.

Teams had considerable discretion over who would join or leave their group. Most in-tergroup mobility was facilitated by the coordinator, who used interpersonal skills to ex-plore new assignments to different groups. Great effort was made to match the preferences of individuals with teams. Employees would move from one team to another for any of several reasons—for example, to earn a higher pay rate, to perform a different type of work, or to seek more compatible teammates.

Evaluate group members for pay raise.

Under the pay-for-knowledge system, an employee had to pass performance tests for all tasks on two different teams to gain the highest pay rate. Performance tests were con-ducted by a coordinator, team leader, or senior team member.

Conduct weekly group meetings.

Teams usually met every week for a half-hour, on company time. In addition, shorter meetings were conducted almost every day, and occasionally a lengthier problem-solving meeting might be conducted to work on special production or quality issues.

Discipline group members for absenteeism or tardiness.

This authority was vested within each team, but not all teams utilized the authority. Coordinators identified this as the most difficult responsibility to get the teams to un-dertake.

Select new employees for the plant.

New employees were selected through an assessment center process. An evaluation team, consisting of one manager, one coordinator, one team leader, and two members of dif-ferent teams, observed candidates during interpersonal exercises and provided ratings and final judgments.

KEY LESSONS TO BE LEARNED FROM THIS CASE

1. Self-managing teams are given responsibility for a wide range of roles and functions, many of which are traditionally considered managers' work. This il-lustrates how teams can take over many of the roles traditionally performed by supervisors.

2. If teams are provided with the training, information, equipment, materials, and, especially, the opportunity, they can accomplish significant work. This provides a clear example of how properly equipped teams can enact the necessary roles to assure that the team receives the required task and social inputs.

3. An overriding goal of increasing team self-management can help the team to accept greater responsibility. This demonstrates how a team goal can facilitate processes within the team and help it to increase its capacity to lead itself.

4. Mature self-managing teams can be a significant source of organizational competitiveness, as well as satisfaction, for the workforce.

NOTES FOR THE FITZGERALD CASE

1. We acknowledge the support of Richard Cherry, who helped to provide access to collect the data for this case and has served as a colleague and adviser over several years. We also acknowledge the exceptional helpfulness and cooperation of management and employees at Fitzgerald.

   For readers interested in training, a training case based on the Fitzgerald story, "The Greenfield Case," is available from Organization Design and Development, 2002 Renaissance Blvd., Suite 100, King of Prussia, PA 19406, 213-279-2002.

   Parts of this chapter were previously published as Henry P. Sims, Jr., and Charles C. Manz, "Conversations Within Self-Managing Teams," *National Productivity Review* 1 (1982): 261–269.

CASE

2.3

The Early Implementation Phase of Teams at IDS

This case was written by Henry P. Sims, Jr., Charles C. Manz, and Barry Bateman.[1]

This case illustrates a process used to design effective teams in a service setting. Interestingly, the organization used a number of project and advice teams to design ongoing production teams. Each team was driven by a set of specific goals that helped them to stay focused on the task at hand. This case also illustrates the use of sociotechnical systems planning during the team design stage. Sociotechnical systems planning helped ensure that the production teams would be provided with the necessary task and social inputs. Nevertheless, even with extensive planning, the introduction of teams was met with some resistance and a variety of problems that had to be overcome. In the end, the introduction of teams increased the interdependence of workers and thereby improved service performance in this dynamic work setting.

This case describes how teams can be applied to an office setting of a company in a service industry. The employees who were the focus of a change to self-managing teams were "knowledge workers"—those whose work is mainly to transform information. Relatively little work has been done to apply self-managing teams in settings with predominantly knowledge workers; thus the effort we describe here is one of the pioneering changes in the service sector.

The story presented here reviews the early start-up stages of self-managing teams in an office situation. The company used the technique of sociotechnical systems (STS) analysis to execute this change. The company pioneering this effort was IDS Financial Services, Inc., of Minneapolis, Minnesota, a subsidiary of American Express Company. The story presents a picture of key structures and processes that are critical during the early stages of team development. Although the story can be described as quite successful, it also provides insight into the challenges, frustrations, and difficulties that inevitably accompany such a significant change.

The Organization

IDS, the current name for a company that started as Investors Diversified Services, has been described as the quiet financial giant from Minneapolis. Originally founded in 1894, today it offers a wide range of financial services and products, including personal financial planning, insurance and annuities, mutual funds, certificates, limited partnerships, consumer banking, lending, and brokerage services. The company's products and services are distributed by a nationwide network of more than 6,500 financial planners, whose efforts are supported by more than 3,600 employees in the company's home office.

In 1990, IDS owned or managed more than $58 billion in assets, including $22 billion under management in 36 mutual funds. Since it was acquired by American Express in 1984, its earnings have grown at a compound annual growth rate of 22 percent.

IDS planners work with individual clients to identify financial goals and objectives and to devise a complete financial strategy tailored to the individual's needs. A client who implements an IDS financial plan typically purchases one or more of the financial products offered by the company. On a day-to-day basis, the financial planners deal with home office service representatives employed by Mutual Fund Operations, now called the Transaction Services Department. Their contact is by mail and telephone and typically involves a transaction on behalf of a client. Thus, the financial planners—independent field agents who interact directly with the client—are highly dependent on the quality, accuracy, and speed of the behind-the-scenes or backroom services provided by employees of the Operations Division.

Nature of the Work at IDS

IDS's Mutual Fund Operations can be viewed as a service organization that processes information. The prototypical customer is an independent financial planner who is responsible for providing financial advice to clients. Most of the actual work revolves around an information or financial transaction, typically initiated by mail or telephone—for example, investing a certain amount of money in an IDS mutual fund for a client, withdrawing or redeeming from an account, or arranging a specific payout plan for retirement purposes. The more routine transactions are typically carried out by core workers.

Although most of the transactions are relatively straightforward, some require special technical or legal expertise to ensure compliance with laws and regulations. Transactions that involve interactions with legal trusts or estate settlements require special clerks—individuals with specialized and extensive knowledge who focus on special problems and who are available to support the core workers. Senior clerks serve as problem solvers and quasi-supervisors.

Overall, the work can be characterized as an input/output flow of information and financial resources across the organization's boundaries. Although much of the work is impersonal, requiring action only on information flow, a significant element in the process is the interpersonal relationship (by distance) with the financial planners. An important aim of the organization is to retain the planners as satisfied customers. Accuracy and absence of errors are critical for maintaining both efficiency and customer goodwill.

The Competitive Situation

As a part of the change under consideration, the management team in Mutual Fund Operations had assessed the opportunities for improvement that existed within the division and identified the following major business trends:

- Major growth in the financial planner and client base.
- More home office services being provided directly to clients.
- Increasing need for flexibility, especially for changing volumes.
- A continuing increase in the number of products sold.
- A volatile market.
- An increased use of technology by clients, planners, and home office staff.
- Increased competition.

Two key questions emerged from this analysis: (1) How can business processing errors be prevented (in essence, the quality issue)? (2) How can the organization be more adaptable to changing volumes, products, and the financial environment (the flexibility issue)? A partial answer to these questions lies in an expanded utilization of technology, but, most of all, an increased dependence on the quality of the organization's human resources. Issues of quality and flexibility inevitably mean a need for improving the ability and motivation of the organization's workforce. One of the alternatives proposed for consideration was an organizational change to teams.

Changing the Work Design

When we collected data for this story, a small portion of the organization had just converted to a self-managing team; the other employees continued to work in the traditional work unit operation. This organizational change was the result of a process of conscious analysis and design that had been sponsored by management and performed by employees who did the work.

Some of the motivation for the change came from a dissatisfaction with the status quo. One manager who recognized this fact said, "About 30 percent of our staff was assigned to error corrections." Another manager said, "We've done a lot of tweaking in the last few years. The organization is so massive and so complex that we were tweaked out. I think we all realized we needed something new."

The division was profitable, but none of the managers thought that operations were running smoothly. Over the years, the organization had evolved into what one manager described as a patchwork of responsibilities structured by a seemingly illogical combination of function, product, and processes. Job specialization was deeply embedded, and the total organization was described as fragmented. "A customer might call and get transferred four or five times before they could reach someone who could help." Accuracy was a problem. The division had encountered a temporary crisis in 1987 when, during the stock market crash, the system was overloaded and almost collapsed. The average response time to a customer during that day was about seven minutes. Furthermore, the division was generally not regarded as a desirable place to work and had a high turnover rate.

Vice-president Bill Scholz brought a special vision to this situation. He foresaw the possibility that the division might sink to a survivor mode in the future, and so he wanted to act now to preclude this possibility. Over months, he and his staff considered many alternatives, including functional reorganization and supervisory training. After this period of introspection and study, they decided to embark on an organizational redesign effort spearheaded by a sociotechnical systems analysis.

Structures for Change

In order to implement the change, several temporary organizational structures were formed. During the planning stages, the fundamental organizational structure remained intact, but several committees or implementation teams were formed to facilitate the process: the steering committee, the design team, and the pilot team. Each of these teams received process and technical assistance from a consultant team consisting of an inside consultant and an outside consultant experienced in the use of sociotechnical systems analysis.

The Steering Committee

The steering committee was established and convened by Bill Scholz. It consisted of Scholz and his staff of managers (including Jim Punch, then operations manager, now vice-president), the vice-president for management information systems, and the vice-president of human resources, and it was assisted by the small consulting team. One of its members expressed the objectives of the committee in this way: "I think our particular target was getting the program going, the people in place and establishing other guidelines." Another member added, "The objectives never focused on efficiency or on dollar savings. It focused on better accuracy, better service to clients . . . reductions of errors. We didn't say we were going to reduce expenses by a hundred million dollars. We have not deviated one iota; we're interested in accuracy; we're interested in quality."

One member commented on the process of the steering committee: "One thing I noticed is the way that we work together on the steering committee. It was very hard because it was very different from how we worked before. Before, it was, 'This is my world and I make the decisions of what happens here.' But it's not what is happening today. This is still a learning process for us."

The steering committee preceded the design team and provided initial parameters and periodic guidance to it. One steering committee member provided this viewpoint: "We kept them protected. We got periodic updates of where they were—cut the roadblocks, gained permission. We published parameters or boundaries for them. They also knew we had the right of veto, which was up front. But a real change in role from making the decision." Another described the charter to the design committee as "potent"—they were invested with decision-making discretion about anything that was happening in the division. The steering committee empowered the design team.

The steering committee also acted as liaison to top management and other parts of the organization. "We spent a lot of time developing plans to get senior management sold on this thing," and, "We published volumes of questions and answers. We asked ourselves the hardest questions. You're being a pioneer in this deal."

One major issue, job security, was addressed early. "We had a major off-site meeting for all of our employees when the thing kicked off. We took them to a hotel and gave them croissants and walked them through it. We guaranteed employment for everybody right off the bat. No loss of employment will occur because of the process. We didn't say your job won't change."

The steering committee had to be sensitive to the degree to which they provided guidance to the design team. Bill Scholz "gave them as much freedom as possible, because I didn't want anything to impact the decision. I even told the design team that I'd not be seen."

One senior manager talked about his mixed reactions to the process: "I found the process somewhat painful. Being senior in years and having enjoyed traditional organizations all my career, and now coming to the end of my career—But, it's really been refreshing. It put some new excitement into the last few years." Several managers wondered whether employees would be able to make decisions of the same quality as managers. Despite these reservations, the steering committee decided to proceed and announced the prospective change to the entire division. The next step was to form the design team.

The Design Team

The design team was selected from 57 volunteers. One member explained, "Everybody was invited to a meeting that explained the process. I listened to what they were proposing, and I did apply for a position on the team." Another said, "We were afraid it was an efficiency drive. In fact, it wasn't. It was right up front that there would be no jobs lost because of this project."

The design team was composed of 11 people—8 core workers, 2 supervisors, and 1 senior clerk—and was supported by the professional external consultant who was experienced with analysis. No formal leader was designated.

Each team member was relieved of his or her usual job and devoted full time to the design team efforts, meeting every day from 8:00 A.M. to 4:30 P.M., and meeting with the steering committee about once every two weeks to exchange information and seek guidance. The original plan called for the design team to accomplish its objectives in three to six months. In fact, the team's efforts took eight and a half months.

The team followed three major steps: developing a plan, conducting the technical (task) analysis, and doing the social analysis. Data gathering and analysis included interviewing and surveying the financial planners, clients, and employees; documenting work flows; and identifying errors and determining causes of key variance.

Team members described the communication climate with the steering committee as "mediocre to fair." One team member characterized it as "very, very difficult. It's probably the major problem in the process. We were supposed to do things by consensus decision. And it's a terrible, tedious, long process with all those people. And everybody had to have a role in making their viewpoint known. It takes a long time to learn how to do that without wasting time."

One or two members came close to leaving the team. "Burnout–communication problems," one said. "I felt like I was going to go crazy. The team had high expectations that we could sit in the meeting and, in half an hour, go right through issues and get the decisions made. The design team was highly motivated, and expectations of what they could achieve were very high. Perhaps we were too perfectionist."

The role of the supervisor received considerable attention from the design team. "The existing supervisors were given a lot of attention. They were quite nervous about the whole process. One of the rumors they'd heard about STS is that supervisors were to be eliminated." In fact, supervisors were not eliminated, although their role was changed considerably. Their title was changed to "facilitator," and "their goal would be to enable the team to become self-directing." One design team member anticipated problems with both supervisors and managers: "They will have difficulty adapting. The problem of this process is that the managerial staff have difficulty letting go of decision making. They will need to learn how to allow the team to make decisions."

The design team determined that teams would be organized according to geographical or regional lines and that each team would have 25 to 40 members. When questioned whether this number might be too large, one design team member replied, "We actually have teams within the teams." Each team was intended to be multifunctional; it would include all of the different functions and processes within the organization, and it would be empowered to make the decisions needed to process the work in a timely and accurate fashion.[2]

Most of all, the design team emphasized how the work could be designed to improve effectiveness. One member said: "Effectiveness really highlights what we wanted to get at, and that was quality. We wanted to do the work right the first time and to eliminate the errors out there. We wanted the work to be done effectively so that we don't have to go back and do it again." This analysis was undertaken via the sociotechnical system process, a formal approach to analyzing the technical part of the work and the social interaction part of it.

What Is STS?

Sociotechnical design, also known as STS (sociotechnical systems), a systematic approach to the design of work, involves a thorough analysis of both the technical (the tools and techniques used in the production or information flow process) and social (how work is divided and coordinated) components of a work system.

Typically, organizations tend to place more priority on one aspect at the expense of the other. STS seeks to avoid this imbalance, assuming that both aspects are equally important in controlling error (variance from standards). Controlling key variances is seen as the central challenge in producing a quality product or service at the lowest possible cost.

The approach, which differs from more traditional industrial engineering design, views meeting employee needs for personal control and autonomy as critical in controlling variance. According to STS, the best way for variance to be controlled is for the employee who performs the task to be aware of the variance and to make the necessary correction.

An in-depth analysis of the work system provides a complete picture of the environment, work flow, communication flow, technical problems, and other issues inherent in any modern work organization. When the analysis is done by people who do the actual work, their knowledge base increases substantially. Closer to the core work, they are able to use the knowledge to solve problems more effectively.

Figure C2.3-1 provides an overall picture of the major components of an STS design effort. It consists of three primary steps: an environmental scan, a technical analysis, and a social analysis.

The environmental scan, done first, includes reviewing the history, culture, goals, structure, and economic and marketing context of the organization. Inputs, outputs, and overall technology are also considered. The technical analysis, done next, breaks down the work flow into tasks, which are grouped into unit operations. Variances are tracked and recorded on a key variance control chart, and variances that a group inherits from the outside are separated from those that are produced internally.

Once key variances are understood, an analysis of the social system is conducted to see how those variances are being controlled. The social system review also addresses communication patterns and other organization climate issues. Finally, all these analyses are integrated into a new design recommendation.

This analysis is a demanding and challenging undertaking. Sufficient time must be allowed to accomplish it.

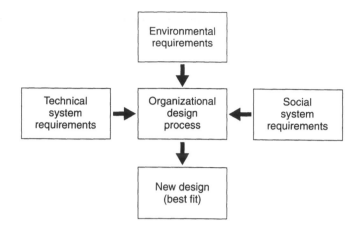

Figure C2.3-1 Sociotechnical systems design

How did management react to the fact that the design team took 8½ rather than 3 months? One of the steering committee members reflected, "By the time we got into the technical analysis, it was clear that we weren't going to get done in 3½ months. We really muddled through the technical analysis. That was probably the most frustrating phase. [But], we had to stick with it and go with it, because we didn't have any option."

One substantial roadblock was the issue of how the redesign efforts should deal with the existing system of measuring work output. A considerable amount of money had been invested in this system. According to one source, "This measurement system was designed by traditional industrial engineers according to classic industrial engineering principles." That is, the intent was to increase efficiency and enforce standards by implementing a high degree of control over the employees. The system, described by one organization member as an "automated tracking system" and by another as a "computerized electronic surveillance system," was a sophisticated automatic logging and data tracking system that measured each employee's work behavior to a remarkable degree. Certainly, individual employees were evaluated according to the numbers they produced.

The system had negative side effects. According to one member of the organization, "A core worker would not leave her post in order to solve a problem because it would affect her performance numbers. Customers would suffer because they would not solve the customer's problem." Job satisfaction was low and turnover was high.

The design committee initially wanted to scrap the system, but others pointed out the importance of the statistics that were derived from it, especially the notion that these statistics were necessary as feedback if the teams were to manage themselves. Eventually, the committee recommended that a modified form of the system be retained; most important, the main use of the system output would be for teams to manage their own system.

Another sticky issue revolved around the role of the quality assurance group, currently an external structure that functioned mainly for control purposes. The eventual recommendation was that most of these quality assurance personnel would be brought into the service teams.

Another factor that affected the amount of time the design team spent was the question of how much it should set minimum critical specifications and how much detail should be left to the teams. In retrospect, one member felt the design was overspecified:[3] "In hindsight, we have concluded that they spent too much time and effort and intensity of overstructuring, too much detail in terms of task. I think the teams could figure it out. Where do you draw the line between what the design team recommends versus the discretion that you give the team?" Another manager demurred, "But I think the level of detail was needed for the design team to have a deep understanding before they went ahead and tried to figure out a structure. Even though it wasn't used in a final design, all of that detail—they needed that."

Another post-hoc issue is whether the design team should have been assigned full time to the design process. One manager said, "I think the major mistake we made as a steering group is that we allowed this to be a full-time job for the design team. I'll tell you, you sit in a room every day, no matter how well you like somebody, five days in a row, three months straight, and you're into this analysis poop, I think you start questioning the meaning of life."

Another problem developed: a "we" versus "they" phenomenon between members of the design team and other members of the workforce. One design team member broached this issue: "There was some reaction to the design team . . . privileged and elitist. You were chosen; we were not."

Despite the difficulties, in the end, one manager commented about the design team, "(It) was a breakthrough for us . . . they became really empowered. They had a lot of power, and they knew it." The design team did indeed accomplish its objectives and produced a complete set of recommendations that seemed to be generally acceptable to various constituencies:[4]

1. Teams should be formed around customers/planners clustered within a geographical region.

2. Team members should be trained to perform multiple skills and tasks. That is, each team should have the ability to service virtually all requests made by clients and their planners.

3. Team size should be about 30 to 40 employees—large enough to handle regional volume and provide technical expertise, yet small enough to provide free-flowing communication and a sense of belonging. The notion of multiple skills was an important point of the recommendation. That is, a team will possess the skills and knowledge required to accomplish a wide range of tasks. It will have the capability to process transactions from start to finish.

4. The role of supervisor was to change to that of a team facilitator who would work with the team to establish goals and objectives, provide liaison with other teams and outside groups, project team volumes and staffing needs, participate in performance discussions, manage projects, and facilitate team building and conflict resolution.

5. An important recommendation was the reconceptualization of the manager's role in the division. The manager's previous role had been described as "fire fighters" and "watchers who watch the watchers"! Managers were described as "focusing their energy downward and inward—not out to the environment, nor forward into the future."

    The role of managers would change to strategic director, with primary responsibility for managing the interface with the outside world, dealing with long-term strategic issues, helping to create new systems, coaching team leaders, and coordinating across the organization.[5] At the time data were collected for this story, the changeover to the strategic director role had not been implemented. However, the current manager team had accepted the recommended change in management role. (An interesting aspect of this recommendation is that the subordinates of the managers had redesigned the role of these managers, and the managers had accepted this redesign.)

6. Information systems would be developed that would provide each team with the information it needs to operate efficiently as a small business. These included measures of quality and quantity of transactions.

The design team's timetable for change started with a single pilot team, formed around a specific geographical area. Later, the remainder of the employees would be formed into teams at a single time, popularly referred to as the "big bang," that also corresponded with a move of the physical premises.

The Pilot Team

At the time of data collection, the pilot team had been in existence for only a month, yet the enthusiasm of the members was obvious. "I've been on the team for about a month. I've made some significant contributions," said one member. The team consisted of about 25 employees (some from the design team) with two facilitators.

From management's point of view, an effective training program had been undertaken prior to the pilot team start-up, yet the employees did not see it this way. One month into start-up, one of the facilitators said: "The training needs have not been met. The people feel frustrated because they've been a file clerk or they've been a filmer, and they want to learn to be a phone rep or a letter correspondent or whatever, and they haven't had the opportunity to train. It all takes time." Also, it soon became obvious that a skills development opportunity was necessary. The team first conducted a skills analysis to identify what would be needed to carry out the expanded responsibilities. Next, an analysis was done, and a team facilitator helped to create and balance the skills among team members.

Clearly, the pilot team was in a mood for learning and experimentation. One member said, "If we were in an old unit, they might have said [about a suggestion for change], 'Well, we can't do it. It's not feasible. Forget it.' Now, they bring the idea to the team, and the team says 'Oh yes. We think this will work.' It's a chance to try ideas, and says, if they fall on their face, then that's the opportunity they had to do it. We're not going to say we're closing the door. You feel more important. You do what you can."

The feeling of control and authority was apparent: "I feel like I'm making more supervisory decisions than I've ever been allowed to before—as far as transactions are concerned. I can present myself as the authority in what I do, because I am." Another member said, "My definition of fun is: interesting. Also, being able to make a difference in what's going on, as opposed to sitting back and observing things."

The factor of teamwork came through loud and clear when pilot team members talked about their work. "When you're working in a very, very small group, you are accountable for how many calls you take and the quality that you put into your work, the amount of effort . . . you're going to find it's going to come back to you." One employee said: "We don't go to the facilitator and say, 'Can I have the day off' and expect them to find somebody to cover for us. We check it out with the people in our group."

Learning to work together as a team is not always smooth or without some difficulties. "Right now on the pilot team, we're experiencing some frustrations, some blockage points. There are some issues that we have to address—about how to make decisions or who has the responsibility to make decisions in certain areas." Differences in styles become apparent: "I like to get everything done quickly and get it out of the way. And some people need more time to deliberate. We're working through a lot of style issues. As a result, you're not going to see 100 percent of us happy." Overall, however, even at this early stage, the pilot team seemed to be experiencing some successes.

What Really Happened: Bumps Along the Way

Several issues seemed to be apparent during our visit. Among the problems were negative anticipation, the transition from supervisor to facilitator, anxiety from supervisors not yet on teams, and perceived decline in the status of senior clerks.

Negative Anticipation

Not all employees were looking forward to the team system. One employee described some co-workers as not wanting to change: "They don't want to have to learn these things. They say, "I hope they fall on their face because then we don't have to do that." Another said, "I hear a lot of negative feedback. Some people say, 'I don't even want to try it.' Either you are strongly for it or you are strongly against it." Indeed, there were very few in the middle. But it appears that much of this negative attitude is subject to change once the team system is actually experienced. One team member describes her initial reaction: "I hated the idea. I just despised it. I wanted to back out. I told my supervisor, 'I don't want anything to do with it.' Now that I'm active in it (the team), and participate more, I feel 'isn't this great?' "

The Transition from Supervisors to Facilitators

Two facilitators, both supervisors before the introduction of teams, were assigned to the pilot team. They found the team environment to be substantially different. As one of them noted, "We're finding that making decisions with 25 to 30 people is something that's completely different. Just getting to decide how the decisions are going to be made can be overwhelming as we experience it." She elaborated on this difference:

> In the traditional system it was clear that I had the final word, and right now it is not clear. That's different. Another thing that's different is that we have changed the tasks. It's one thing to be self-managing in your old room and doing the same function, but now we've put together 20 other types of jobs that we didn't know anything about, so instead of having one set of goals and objectives, we've got a variety of them.

> For example, I previously supervised a unit that processed new business. Now, the team has new business, redemptions, change of ownership, service—many different things—all of the functions that now revolve around a geographical area.

The other facilitator agreed, commenting on the need to become knowledgeable in a considerably enlarged area of service: "It becomes frustrating because you felt like you should be knowing it, but you don't, and yet we know that it's unrealistic for us to think at this point that we can know everything. We make it a learning experience, and it takes a lot of time to do that."

Facilitators try to instill confidence in the new team members as they undertake new responsibilities: "One woman expressed a need just to run exceptions by one of us. She probably has more knowledge than we do, but she also was not one who handled the exceptions in her former unit. When something comes up, she said, 'It would be nice if you were here so I can run it by you.' She's feeling that it's not traditional for her to do this and psychologically is not confident that what she decides would be accepted. She might be looking for a little bit of a security blanket."

Another example was cited: "Initially when she came and asked me the question, I said, 'What would you do if nobody else was available?' It's asking them to become independent. You have to spend the time with people to get them to that comfort level and to build up their self-confidence."

The system surrounding the team must change too. One facilitator said, "Some of the frustrations we have are really related to the transition . . . fumbling around with getting reports started up, system authorizations, and a lot of technical information because we've never done anything like this before. We're spending so much time on these start-up issues. Like right now, for instance, we don't even have some measures. We're just in the process of getting quality measure for some of the people."

Clearly, teams can learn through their mistakes, and the facilitator realized this, even to the point of allowing mistakes to happen occasionally. "Their first opportunity to display self-management was when they made the decision to have a person gone [leaving a station unmanned] when someone left the room. It was a small, minor thing, but it was a simple lesson. They made the wrong decision, and through that decision we learned, and we discussed it as a learning tool. We talked about the work flow and responsibility to cover their work and stuff. It was a valuable experience."

One of the pilot team members discussed the change in the supervisor's role: "There's an incredible redesigning of some of the power that goes with supervising people. Letting go of some of the responsibility and letting go of some of the control that you had previously is a serious deal, and I'm sure it's very threatening." "We don't really think of our facilitators as being supervisors. It's not 'you can do this no you can't.' They help us."

The motivation to be a facilitator is complex and not always immediately evident:

> The thing I've been struggling with is that there's nothing to call my own. Eventually, if they're truly self-managing, it's going to be the team that gets most of the recognition. And that part is going to be hard, because I think traditionally the recognition that the unit's doing good would start with the supervisor, and you'd feel like, "I really did something here on my own, an accomplishment." But now I get more satisfaction out of helping someone to do something rather than telling them to do it.

The second facilitator agreed with this perspective:

> I think basically we're all human, and where I would be very glad to have the team take the credit, nevertheless, my humanness says to me, "I really would enjoy it if just occasionally somebody would pat me on the back and say, 'Hey, you're doing a good job today.'" Sometimes you wonder if people you're working with realize the touchy position that the facilitator is put in because you have a strategic director up here expecting big things from you, and you have a whole team expecting their needs from you, and we're kind of like a pickle in the middle of a sandwich, and we don't know which side of the bread we should be on. Does the word "facilitator" really give credit where credit is due?

The traditional conflict of the supervisor as the person in the middle is still there with the facilitator role: "Right now, my strategic director is expecting some reports, and I'm finding some difficulty getting him the data that he needs, and, at the same time, the team has needs, and I'm feeling like I'm sitting in the middle here, and it's not a very good feeling."

In this early stage of the team development, the issue of goals and objectives was not yet resolved:

> In a traditional structure of supervision, you'd have goals and objectives—it was laid out. I always felt I knew what part of the path I was traveling on. Here as a team facilitator, so far I haven't felt that clarified yet, so I don't quite know where we're going. Part of the problem is the strategic directors, the persons we directly report to. After all this length of time, I think the strategic directors still do not have a real clear picture of how they fit into this, and this is kind of confusing to me. Before, it was the supervisor reporting to your manager, and your manager reporting to your vice-president and so on. Now, I kind of feel like there are several people out there giving input to what I should be doing and one day it may be coming from one person directly, but indirectly I sometimes feel like it's coming from several.

Another put it this way: "They listen to what we say and they can put in their input if they disagree, but if the majority of the team says 'it's gonna work,' then, we'll try it."

At one month into the pilot team start-up, the facilitators were probably at a point of maximum ambiguity and frustration. "The reorganization of the task and the structure of the task are one dimension, and the management style or the division of authority, if you will, is a different dimension." The facilitators seemed to be faced with a double-barreled change.

Finally, since the major changeover had not yet occurred, the change in the role of the managers to strategic directors had not yet taken place. We suspected that the managers, like the supervisors, would also be likely to experience some ambiguity, tension, and anxiety as their role changed over the next few months.

Supervisor Anxiety

Supervisors who were not yet on teams were anxious. "One of the first things I remember was, 'Oh, we're going to go on this team-based kind of operation and everybody's going to have to know everything.' I think that tended to spook people." Another question loomed large: "Will I lose my job as a supervisor? If the role of supervisor is going to change, does that mean some of us will be out of a job?"

Management made substantial efforts to counter the fear of loss of job security. One supervisor said, "They had several meetings to alleviate those fears and ensured everyone that they would not lose their job. Their role would change in many respects. People might be doing something else, but everybody's going to do something."

But some supervisors eagerly looked forward to "big bang" day, when all of the other departments would be changed over to the team system. One supervisor said, "I'm delighted. I think that it's going to make jobs a lot more interesting for people. I think there will be a lot more buy-in to decisions if it's a group decision than if it's mine." Another also expressed confidence and optimism: "Almost every week that passes, something tends to be cleared up. As we get closer and closer, 'Ah hah! So that's how it's going to be. That's great.' Weekly, we just feel more and more comfortable with it." Part of this optimism came from observations of the pilot team. One supervisor noted that "the pilot team is working. They're getting work done. Nobody's quit. They're not beating each other up. Things are going fine. The people that I've talked to who are on the pilot team said very positive things. Plus, we've been given a massive amount of training."

Finally, an interesting phenomenon seemed to be taking place: All of the attention surrounding the change seemed to be having an influence on the supervisors. Some supervisors were beginning to change their behavior even before being assigned to teams.

The Senior Clerks

Perhaps one group more than any other saw themselves as losers in this change to teams—the senior clerks. A senior clerk is a special problem solver—an hourly employee who has special knowledge and authority and a higher rate of pay. One senior clerk described the job in this way: "I investigate, I dig, I work on problem cases, I work with the supervisor on administrative things and attend different meetings, and I enjoy what I'm doing now."

In the new system, the position of senior clerk would not exist. All employees would be team members, and each team member would be expected to perform a fair amount of the work. As one supervisor put it: "Well, this is part of the senior clerk's problem. Right now, most senior clerks do not process. They don't write letters, they don't answer the phone, they don't process applications—only problems. So some of them have expressed distress that they're going to have to go back to processing than more of a consultant/training/question-answer problem solver. I'm not sure that's going to be resolved." Another supervisor said: "Now, they have a certain amount of prestige—they get more money. Everybody else can move up and learn a bunch of other things. The senior clerks are already up there."

One senior clerk directly addressed the issue in this way: "I'm going to be doing core work again, and I feel like it's a step backward. I took the training to be a senior clerk. And just as you learn and work toward certain goals and when you reach those goals, then you find out you're put into a team, and the goals and the titles you have achieved, they're no longer there. You're just like anyone else. It will be harder in a team." Uncertainty and anxiety among the senior clerks were high: "A lot of this stuff is still up in the air. If you are a senior clerk, you're losing out on that prior learning process. There's a lot of unknowns out there, and they can't really tell you because they don't know."

Senior clerks expressed skepticism about the team's ability to do error-free work: "Who's going to catch a mistake? It's really scary because there are so many different procedures involved in dealing with attorneys, documents. There's so many things to remember. I fear there may be more errors because I don't know who's going to be catching them." And another expressed doubt over the competence of ordinary employees: "They skim over things; they don't double-check everything. So the error rate goes up. They don't want to learn anything. Some of them are worried about going into the team because they just want to do the job they are doing. They need to get input from us. Further, "When you learn the job, it's a lot to learn. There's a lot to look for, a lot to check for. And there's sometimes a person that just can't cut it. Who's going to know?"

Preliminary Results

Since the pilot team had been underway for only a month at the time of our interviews, quantitative information about their performance was not yet available. Yet some changes were clearly taking place in several areas:

- Confidence for improvement: "We feel that we'll be able to increase our average speed of answer, and our 'abandon rate' (unanswered calls) will decrease proportionally."
- The idea of team ownership: "You feel that what you are doing is actually making money for your team. We are our own little company. Every time we loan

ourselves out to somebody, we know we're going to charge that other unit $35 an hour. It makes you feel better."

- The issue of quality: "You work more thoroughly. You want to make sure that you don't let the errors leave the unit. You also see where all the work goes. You feel more complete if you know the work is going to be done."
- Flexibility of operations: "One thing that I see as a really great benefit, even in the short term, is that we are able to be more flexible and respond to volumes quicker than previous. Our volumes fluctuate very heavily because of client whims and market fluctuations. I was spending a lot of time sitting, waiting for something to do. Now, we've arranged something where I can get work from other areas and help them while I'm waiting to serve my clients." Another supported this idea: "There's a high degree of flexibility that I don't think there was before. There are some jobs, such as mine, that it's critical that I be there when the phones open, because that's a client service element. I promised the client that I'd be there at 7 A.M., and I have to; I don't have a choice."

One result of the team implementation is that pilot team members were beginning to develop a more personal relationship with the financial planners in the field. Their contact with these planners is strictly through the mail or over the telephone:

I've never met them. I do speak to clients and planners on a daily basis. Now, since I have my own area, I speak to the same people many times a week. Now the planner knows you by name. Even though you've never met a person, you establish a rapport with somebody over a period of time because of repetition, rather than one of 10,000 or whatever. You can deal on a one-to-one relationship and establish that, yes, despite the fact that our planners are independent businessmen, they are also part of our team. We have already received a couple of letters, and it makes you feel, "Gee, I am really doing something for the people out there." And, they do appreciate what we are doing.

Sometimes pilot team members have taken on the role of informal trainer to field financial planners:

I find it easier to educate the planners when they trust you. There are some things that all planners don't necessarily know that would make it easier for them and their clients to do business. I don't say, "Hey, you're doing this wrong." That's not my idea of feedback. But if somebody is consistently doing things that are incorrect, just some feedback on that issue can prevent a lot of miscommunication or errors from happening. If I see the same planner do the same thing, you talk to them all the time, you feel like, "I think it'd be easier if you kinda went like this, or, you did that." I would help them. Now they say, "I know I can call somebody, and not just call a number and never know who you're going to get. I can personally ask for this person, and I can get this person. I know who you are. You've helped me." It makes me think, "Hey, maybe I can make a difference."

This attitude extends to the clients: "We've also suggested that we would like the clients' response also, not just the planners. We'd like the clients to say, 'Am I getting a better result now that we can call direct?'"

In the pilot team, the error rate was already beginning to decline, and the team members were very much aware of the output measure. "We had like 70 percent accuracy before. Now, it's always at least 99 to 100 percent every day. Now, we see that one day of the week we'll have one error, out of five days." Another team member said, "Yesterday it was 100 percent accuracy, and we were happy because nothing was out of our hands, and we felt really good because all these transactions went out error free."

With the team concept, the feedback loop to the team member was much more complete: "We used to have specialists. If you had an error on an application, you couldn't do anything with it, and we sent it to a specialist. From there on we'd never see the application again. But now, you hold it. You call the planner. It comes right back to you, so you see it. You started it, and now it's finished. We feel more of a completion. We don't feel like it's half done and it's still floating and you don't know."

The Big Bang

Following a trial period for the pilot team, IDS converted to a team organization in a single weekend. This "big bang" was undertaken in conjunction with a physical move to new premises.

Many expected a short-term decrease in quality and productivity. Others echoed the old refrain: "This is just not going to work." In fact, the opposite happened. Many of the quality indicators immediately shot up. Backlogs seemed to disappear. It was almost as if the teams were determined to show that this new organization was better from the very beginning.

One of the more interesting indicators was the difference between the way the organization handled a mini-crash in 1989 (after teams) versus the mini-crash of 1987 (before teams). Of course, a mini-crash is a precipitous falloff in the prices in stocks, mainly on the New York Stock Exchange. A mini-crash influences mutual fund operations by generating an extremely large surge in customer telephone calls, mainly requests for redemptions (customers want to withdraw funds before the market falls further). From an operations viewpoint, the traffic of incoming calls is increased suddenly and immensely, and the challenge to the organization is to respond to this surge.

During the 1987 market crash, the call volume to the organization quadrupled within one day, placing a tremendous load on the transaction system. The result, according to one individual, was chaos. Another called the day a disaster. (Remember that this gloomy event occurred under the old traditional/functional organizational system.)

In October 1989, subsequent to the change to the team system, there was another stock market crash of similar proportions. This crash occurred on a Monday, but movements in the market had presented some indications of impending trouble the previous Friday. On this particular Friday, the entire management group (now called strategy directors) was absent from the office, attending an off-site strategic planning meeting. Thus, they were not present to help plan for the anticipated surge in transactions.

One manager, who returned to the office about 5:00 P.M. on Friday, became aware of the potential situation for the following Monday. He also found that the teams had anticipated the possibility of a surge. Each, on its own, had implemented a plan of how to deal with a surge. For example, most of the teams had decided that several members should report early, they had arranged to work through their lunches, and they had made arrangements with other parts of the IDS organization for backup people to be immediately available to answer the telephones. When Monday came and the mini-crash did occur, people at IDS were very active and working hard, but it almost seemed like a nonevent—no panic, no hysteria, no confusion.

The following day, when the volume numbers were available, many were surprised to discover that IDS actually took more calls on Monday than it had in the 1987 crash.

For many, it didn't seem possible. Perhaps the strongest indicator of their strength was the average speed of answer, that is, how long it takes to begin to service a call. In 1987, the average speed was 7½ minutes (an indicator of information gridlock). In 1989, the average was 13 seconds! This comparison deserves a second look:

1987, before teams	7½ minutes
1989, after teams	13 seconds

One manager said, "This team concept really works!" We might say it a different way. Remember the absence of managers on the critical Friday, when the planning to handle the surge of redemptions was carried out by the teams themselves. This event was a classic example of effective teams. Today, the team system at IDS is alive and well. Most of all, the experience at IDS is one of the early examples that teams are not only appropriate for manufacturing environments, but will work with information workers as well.

Summary

Conversion of an existing organization to a team system is indeed a rocky road in the beginning. Many employees and managers are at a peak of frustration because of the uncertainty of how to get ready or how to react to the change. Yet the conversion to a team system yields obvious rewards. First, most workers seem to gain in status and perceptions of power. Despite initial difficulties in seeing benefits, managers also gain through greater productivity, better quality, and generally reduced tension and conflict at work. Thus, both managers and workers can benefit significantly and experience an increase in their own ability to influence the system and performance.

Many challenges emerge as well, and none is more central than the issue of the changing role of supervisors and middle managers, which we will discuss at length in Unit 3. Ambiguity and the threat of loss of status and control can make the transition difficult. The most important factor is to recognize the issue as a potential critical difficulty and to take steps to deal with it.

Our own observation is that many people can succeed in this transition to facilitator, but not everyone is capable of completing this emotional philosophical journey. In the end, some supervisors must be replaced because they are incapable of abandoning their previously learned behaviors. It is important to undertake this replacement in a humane, sensitive way. For example, some supervisors can be converted to technical specialists.

Team members are faced with major adjustments and challenges as well. One of the clear messages of the team approach is that employees are expected to use their head as well as their hands. They have a responsibility to try to make their job easier and better.

In any change to a team system, some people see themselves as winning; others see themselves as losing. Often the power base is knowledge. Knowledge has power. Sometimes existing knowledge is invested in the supervisors or in technical specialists, such as the senior clerks at IDS. People who currently have knowledge—the knowledge elite—may be reluctant to share it or facilitate making knowledge more widely diffused. Yet increasing the knowledge of the ordinary employee lies at the core of the team concept. Widespread knowledge is necessary for team success.

Despite the significant challenges in converting, team efforts can be very worthwhile. Employees at IDS were both excited and exciting. If you listen to their own words, you understand why a conversion to a team system can be a very constructive step. Despite being at a point of maximum uncertainty, the people at IDS were charged up about teams. They valued the strengthening of their linkage to the clients and realized that they could serve clients better. Most of all, they liked the fun of teams, and they realized that at last they could have an impact. As one pilot team member put it, "I really like the idea of being able to make a difference in what's going on, as opposed to sitting back."

Will the same desire for competitiveness drive service systems in the way that manufacturing systems have been driven in recent years? We expect so. The *Wall Street Journal* gave an advance indication of this trend with one article recently: "American Firms Send Office Work Abroad to Use Cheap Labor."[6] Work team systems, like the one at IDS, hold tremendous promise for improving competitiveness (as well as quality of work life for employees) in the service sector.

KEY LESSONS TO BE LEARNED FROM THIS CASE

1. Designing and implementing teams requires putting into place well-thought-out structures for designing change—for example, a steering committee, a design team, and so on. This means that teams can be an effective tool for facilitating an organization's transition to teams.

2. Sociotechnical systems (STS) analysis and design principles can be used to help guide team design. An STS approach offers important benefits but entails significant costs and is quite time consuming.

3. Special attention should be devoted to equipping supervisors and managers to make the transition successfully to the new role of leading teams. More about this critical leadership role will be presented in Unit 3.

4. Decisions about the design and implementation of teams inevitably result in winners and losers. Careful consideration should be given to how teams can be designed to make winners out of as many people as possible.

5. The road to designing and implementing teams is long and difficult. The people involved in the transition should have realistic expectations about the amount of time and energy required, as well as patience to allow the process to unfold.

6. Teams are not just for manufacturing systems. Introducing teams in offices in service organizations holds a great deal of promise.

NOTES FOR IDS CASE

1. All quotations are taken from interviews conducted with IDS employees during the summer of 1988. We acknowledge the generous cooperation of the IDS people and organization, Bill Scholz, former vice-president: Jim Punch, current vice-president, who was especially instrumental in making the interviews possible; and Becky Smith, who so competently transcribed the interview tapes.

   Barry Bateman is currently vice-president and partner of Block Petrello, Weisbord, Inc., Plainfield, N.J., a consulting firm specializing in whole system design.

2. The design team discussed whether the compensation system should be revised, but at the time information for this story was collected, this issue had not been resolved. As one member put it, "They are currently meeting on a regular basis to discuss compensation. The task force is made up of team members, management members,

human resources people. It's in discussion." Overall, the design team clearly was interested in a "wealth creation" model for the future.

3. The STS approach tends to invest design authority in the design team. Other types of self-managing implementations often leave greater latitude to the teams themselves, once they are underway.

4. This is a summary of the final recommendations. The actual final report was more detailed and complex.

5. At the time data were collected for this study, the change to strategic director had not been implemented, although the current manager team had accepted the recommendation for this change in role. An interesting aspect of this recommendation is that the role of manager had been redesigned by the subordinates of the manager, yet the managers had accepted the redesign.

6. *Wall Street Journal,* August 14, 1991, pp. A1, A4.

Team Processes: Developing Synergistic Team Relations

Unit 3 focuses on team interaction processes. A case description of the Fitzgerald Battery Plant first reports conversations and interactions among team members. A theory and research section then describes processes within teams by examining team development, socialization, power, influence, conflict, and leadership. Two additional case descriptions follow. One focuses on the interactions among supervisors as Charrette Corporation introduced teams into its warehouse facility. The other case examines how the introduction of teams in an insurance firm created social processes that reduced the individual autonomy of workers. Taken together, these cases and research summary provide insight into social relationships and interaction processes within teams.

CASE

Team Processes at the Fitzgerald Battery Plant

This case was written by Henry P. Sims, Jr., and Charles C. Manz.[1]

On a day-to-day basis, the interaction process of a team is expressed in conversations between members. In this case, we describe conversations within teams and how these conversations relate to processes that affect productivity and performance. In addition, we analyze team leadership, a particularly critical influence on team interaction processes. A facilitative leadership role was found to be more effective than a directive leadership role.

As discussed in Unit 2 (Case 2.2), the Fitzgerald Battery Plant of General Motors is designed around self-managing teams. These teams are relatively advanced in their level of team self-leadership; thus, team members rather than traditional managers complete many supervisory tasks. The process of internal coordination and self-leadership within these teams is highly visible in team meetings. We therefore observed several team meetings in order to learn about the internal relationships of these teams. We also observed how team leaders influenced internal team processes. In particular, we focused on how their actions differed from those of traditional supervisors.

Team Meetings

Team meetings proved to be a rich source of information about how team members interacted with one another. During these team meetings we explored what team members said, what they talked about, whether they dealt with serious productivity issues or just fooled around, and how their conversation was linked with the operations of the plant. By examining patterns of verbal behavior, we can gain some insight into the process that teams use to synergistically coordinate the efforts of team members.

Conversations about Rewards and Reprimands

Team members frequently exchanged verbal rewards—a compliment, thanks, or praise given in response to an action seen as useful or helpful. Sometimes the exchange was a one-on-one interaction: "Bobby, thanks for helping me with that No. 1 machine last night." At other times, verbal rewards were given in front of the whole team, frequently delivered by the team leader: "We owe a special thanks to Emily for making sure that the materials were ready last Monday. We would have had to shut down if she hadn't looked ahead and gotten what we needed." These conversations were particularly important in building team cohesion, cooperation, and esprit de corps. They reinforced helping behavior within teams and promoted the practice of working together to achieve objectives.

The counterpoint to verbal rewards is verbal reprimands, by which one team member directs displeasure or criticism toward one or more fellow team members. (Both positive rewards and criticism were technically designated as "giving feedback." A verbal reprimand was called "negative feedback.") We observed an especially dramatic incident of verbal reprimand at a regular team meeting after several items of routine business were completed. The team leader looked at one of the members and said, "Jerry, we want to talk to you now about your absenteeism." He went on to recount Jerry's record of absenteeism, referring to his record of dates on which Jerry had been absent, and then he asked Jerry if he had anything to say about the absenteeism. Jerry briefly mumbled excuses. The team leader continued by describing the effect of his absenteeism on the other team members; the others had to work harder because of Jerry's absences, and the absences were hurting team performance. He called Jerry's absences unacceptable and said, "We won't allow it to continue." One more incident of absenteeism, and Jerry would face a formal disciplinary charge that would be entered into the record. The team leader concluded by asking Jerry about his intentions. Jerry replied, "I guess I've been absent about as much as I can get away with. I guess I better come to work."

The question of discipline within the team is highly controversial. Many managers who have not had direct experience with self-managing teams believe that team members are incapable of disciplining their own members. Yet our example shows that self-discipline can take place, and in many ways peer pressure is the most effective form of employee control.

Conversations about Task Assignments and Work Scheduling

Teams used conversation to carry out the allocation of task assignments. Each self-managed team made its own decision as to who would perform which job. Some teams had relatively permanent task assignments based on seniority. Others traded assignments on almost an hour-by-hour basis, and still others on a daily or weekly basis, so that each person would have an equal share of both the "dog" tasks and the "gravy" tasks.

This exercise of control over their own tasks had a significant effect on employees' motivation. We sometimes observed employees negotiating with other team members about job allocation. Most of the time, they handled these negotiations without substantial conflict, but we observed one incident where emotions ran high. In this case, a six-man team was split across three shifts, and a dispute arose over which shift had the responsibility of completing a particularly dirty and physically demanding task. Finally, the coordinator virtually locked the team members in a room and demanded that they remain there until they worked out a solution. "I could make the decision for them," he told us, "but it will be a better decision, and they will do a better job, if they work it out among themselves."

This incident was atypical in arousing such intense emotions, but it was representative of the way role assignments and other issues were worked out. The usual procedure was to get those involved with a particular problem to sit down and work it out themselves. Hard feelings and bruised egos sometimes resulted, but solutions had a greater chance of enduring because they were agreed upon by the participants themselves and not imposed from the outside.

Many decisions revolved around issues of production scheduling. That is, which specific product should be produced at a particular time? Because of decreasing product demand, this plant had recently undergone a reduction of total production volume but without an employee layoff. One response to this crisis was a significant attempt to reduce in-process inventories. Less inventory also meant less room for mistakes and errors, less flexibility if a particular part was not ready, and, in general, a more intense problem of managing the day-to-day, and even the hour-by-hour, production.

We observed an interesting conversation revolving around this issue. One employee, vigorously complaining about the trouble caused by the lack of buffer inventories, asked why inventories had been cut so low. A fellow team member replied: "Do you know what the cost of interest is these days? For every piece that we have in inventory, we have to pay a finance charge, man! That comes straight out of profits. We have to keep inventories low if our business is going to make a profit!" He was referring to his own team when he used the word "business."

These conversations about production scheduling saved the company a significant amount of money, we believe. In a traditional plant, the scheduling role would be handled by forepersons and general forepersons. If a production section ran out of material or parts, it would cease operations until the foreperson got the necessary parts. In this plant, shortages severe enough to shut down production were rare because team members were able to anticipate problems and take corrective action in time.

Conversations about Production Goal Setting and Performance Feedback

The overall plant production goal for task performance is determined by corporate and division requirements. Therefore, for the most part, the employees do not participate in setting overall goals. Nevertheless, they are very much involved in deciding how these overall goals are to be achieved within their team. Teams are also involved in nonproduction goal setting. One conversation, concerned with making a weekly production quota, began: "We won't have materials to run [product X] on Wednesday. We won't be able to meet our goal this week." A reply: "Why don't we shift over to [product Y] on Wednesday and build up a bank for next week? We'll be short of [X] this week, but we can get a jump on [Y] for next week, and then we can make up [X] next week." The important factor here is that the team had discretionary authority to alter its roles and thereby shift product mixes within certain time limits, and it used its leeway to overcome short-term difficulties.

Goal setting also occurred in other areas, especially quality and safety. For example, "Our rejection rate last month was 5.8 percent. We need to get it down to below 5 percent for this month. How are we going to do it?" This problem was raised within the team and was not an exhortation from a foreperson or supervisor.

There was constant feedback to the teams—not only personal feedback but also daily, weekly, monthly, and quarterly quantitative feedback about their performance. Each team maintained charts of quantity, quality, and safety performance. Frequently, we heard reports such as, "We made 3,948 units yesterday. We got ahead about 10 percent." Another interesting comment was, "Have you heard about the safety results? The plant is now in the top one-third of the company."

Charts were everywhere. Formal charts posted on walls showed long-term trends in performance. Sloppier informal charts hung on hooks and clipboards and were posted near machines. Feedback was a critical aspect of the information shared within teams at this plant.

Conversations about Announcements and Problem Resolution

Routine announcements were part of the team conversation—for example, "The Holiday party will be on Monday. Give George three dollars if you are planning to come." However, significant conversations also related to the resolution of special problems. One incident revolved around the quality of an in-process product. A young production worker entered the quality control laboratory one afternoon carrying several production pieces. He said to the lab coordinator, "The color just doesn't look right. I'm going to check the chemistry." After doing a quick spot test on the pieces, he announced, "They're out [meaning out of control]. We have to see how much we're in trouble." During the following hour, the workers scurried about a great deal assessing the extent of the problem, and in the end it was determined that about one-quarter of a day's production of the piece was unacceptable. Adjustments were made to correct the problem and to remove the bad pieces. The worker who noticed the problem stayed two hours beyond his regular quitting time to help find a solution; he was compensated by early time off the next Friday.

This young worker did not have a special quality control role. He was a production worker within the team that worked on these pieces. He demonstrated significant initiative by spotting the problem early and by voluntarily acquiring the technical testing knowledge to make an informed judgment. Later a manager said to us, "You know, it's bad enough when we make a mistake and lose a quarter day's production on those pieces. But think how much more extensive it would have been if he hadn't caught the problem. We probably would have had to scrap several days' production of the full assembly."

In another incident, workers dealt with a different quality problem. A coordinator had called a meeting to discuss a certain deficiency. Four members from two different teams were present with the coordinator and a quality control technician. The coordinator presented the problem, citing statistics that showed a gradual rise in the reject rate over several weeks. He asked: "What's the problem? What can we do to correct it?" No one had an immediate solution. But the coordinator was patient, and he listened carefully, encouraging workers who spoke. After about five minutes, the meeting seemed to become more productive. Over the next half-hour, several causes of the problem were suggested and several "fixes" were proposed. Finally, the group listed the proposed solutions according to ease of implementation and agreed to begin applying them in an attempt to eliminate the problem. Afterward, we asked the coordinator whether he had learned anything new or was just going through the motions for the sake of participation. He replied, "I wasn't aware of many of the ideas they brought out. But most of all, they've now taken it on as their problem, and they will do whatever has to be done to solve it."

Both of these examples concerning special problems involved quality issues. Although the self-managing teams were not quality circles, they devoted considerable effort to solving quality problems.

Conversations about Interteam Communication

Conversations often dealt with issues between teams. For example, one team might complain about the quality of the product that another team produced earlier in the production process. One solution we saw was the temporary exchange of team members. Working with the other team for a week or so resulted in an improved shared understanding of why particular problems occurred, why certain procedures were important, and how negligence could affect other workers.

Conversations about Evaluation and Team Membership

Because team members rather than managers conducted performance evaluations for pay raises, conversations addressed this issue. For example, in a team meeting, a member said to the team leader: "How about running a performance test on the [Z] machine? I think I'm ready." The reply was, "O.K. I'll try to schedule it this week."

Teams also talked about entry to and exit from the team. We attempted to determine rules for assigning employees to teams but never discerned any. A typical answer was, "Well, we just work it out." One team meeting we observed addressed this issue. Because of lower production levels, this team had been asked to reduce its number by one person, who would be assigned to a role with a temporary construction team that was being formed to undertake repair and cleanup work. The team leader presented the decision issue to the group and asked, "How should we handle it?" The first reply was, "Well, unless someone wants to go we should do it by seniority." The man with the least seniority then spoke up: "Well, that's me, and I don't want to go." The team leader asked, "Does anyone want to go?" One person asked, "Would they be working outside? Is there any carpentry work?" Eventually this person volunteered to move to the construction team. He wanted to be outside and to do some craft work.

Team Leadership

The above examples describe how team members influenced one another through conversation. Another particularly important influence came from the teams' leaders. Teams at the Fitzgerald plant had two leaders. One leader, a within-group leader, is a member of and elected by the team. Another leader is external to the team and simultaneously coordinates several teams. We will refer to the internal person as the team leader and the external person as the team coordinator.

In this case we focus specifically on the role of the coordinator—the external leader. Coordinators are in a hierarchical position that in a more traditional production plant would be occupied by forepersons and general forepersons. Often some confusion surrounds the responsibilities of a coordinator in a team system. He or she is positioned over and is responsible for work groups that are deliberately intended to be self-managing, an inherent contradiction. The question, "How does one lead employees who are supposed to lead themselves?" represents this dilemma.

What do "coordinators" do? What behaviors and actions do effective coordinators display? If employee work teams are supposed to be "participative," or "self-managing," then how should coordinators attempt to influence team processes?

The coordinators are jointly selected by management and by the coordinator team. Many are former team leaders; others are selected because they have a desirable technical ability. Most do not have a college degree. The pay level of coordinators is roughly equivalent to that of forepersons and general forepersons in more traditional plants. Each team is assigned to a coordinator, who may have responsibility for one to three teams.

Traditionally, the appointed leader is a legitimate authority figure and therefore acts like a "boss." With self-managing teams, however, this fundamental assumption is largely rejected. At Fitzgerald coordinators of self-managing work groups do not use traditional legitimate authority and do not act as bosses. We thus sought to determine answers to a few questions. To what extent do the coordinators give directions, assign tasks, evaluate performance, and dispense rewards and reprimands as traditional bosses typically do? To what extent should they act as facilitators and communicators who typically do not invoke direct authority over the work team? Who makes the myriad decisions needed to carry out the group's daily tasks? Furthermore, how does the role of the external leader differ from the role of leaders who emerge from within the team? Finally, what behaviors differentiate effective leaders?

There are no formal guidelines regarding a coordinator's duties; rather, coordinator behaviors seem to be loosely defined according to social convention rather than any structured set of rules and regulations.

Role of the Coordinator

Our inquiry into the role of the coordinator was intended to answer the question, "What important behaviors can coordinators use in their work to influence teams?" We first posed this question to upper plant management and elicited the following answers (listed in order of importance):

1. Try to get a team to solve a problem on its own.
2. Help a team solve conflict within its group.
3. Tell people (teams and individuals) when they do something well.
4. Tell the truth even when it may be disagreeable or painful.
5. Encourage team members to discuss problems openly.
6. Ask for a solution to a problem rather than proposing (or telling) a solution. People promote what they create.
7. Encourage teams to set performance goals.
8. Provide teams with the information they need to run their business.
9. Anticipate future problems or situations (planning).
10. Encourage team self-evaluation.
11. Train teams in the philosophy of the plant.
12. Be a resource to a team.

The list provides some interesting insights. First, several of the behaviors, including the behavior obtaining the highest importance, reveal an emphasis on getting teams to manage their own efforts (for example, behaviors 1, 6, and 7). We also noted this emphasis on passing control to work teams during our numerous observations at the plant. Coordinators often purposely avoided providing answers or direction to employees even when they possessed the ability to do so, at times, to the extent of frustrating the workers. In one instance, an employee ran into a problem when welding a guardrail on a ramp and asked the coordinator what he should do. The coordinator responded by asking the worker what he thought he should do. The employee thought a moment, gave his opinion, and proceeded to act on it.

Another major theme of the behaviors is a focus on some form of communication (for example, behaviors 3, 4, 5). Observations indicated that communication—a coordinator's direct communication with team members, as well as efforts to facilitate communication within and between teams—is crucial, and most coordinators realized the importance, sometimes facilitating temporary exchanges of members between teams in order to improve interteam communications. Problems observed on the plant floor and discussed during team meetings often pointed to communication as both a cause and potential cure.

Finally, several behaviors indicated directly what many of the behaviors discussed so far have suggested indirectly: a coordinator should be a facilitator (behaviors 2 and 8). For example, in the incident already noted, employees asked a coordinator to make a decision and resolve a conflict over who should do a particularly unpleasant job. Instead of making the decision, the coordinator facilitated an energetic conflict resolution meeting that helped the team to make its own decision.

We also asked the elected internal team leaders—who were also members of the teams—to identify important behaviors for coordinators to use in their work. We got the following replies:

1. Ask for solutions to problems.
2. Be a resource to a team (concerning both technical and personnel problems).
3. Create an atmosphere of mutual trust and understanding between the coordinator and the team and within the team.
4. Provide honest feedback.
5. Communicate production schedule changes to teams.
6. Arrange problem solving and present possible solutions.
7. Get tooling, supplies, and materials for a team.
8. Provide backing and communication to the team leader.
9. Learn details about team operations.
10. Provide information to a team to solve its problems.
11. Help with interteam problem solving concerning quality control.
12. Try to get the team to set performance goals.
13. Recheck production schedule and inventory.
14. Help in the maintenance of equipment (e.g., get parts, needed personnel).
15. Support the team leader in the support group.
16. Communicate a problem solution of one team to another team that can help.
17. Keep abreast of new machines and processes (innovation).
18. Encourage a team to solve its own problems.
19. Maintain good communication between coordinators (to coordinate efforts throughout the plant):
20. Keep the team leader in the chain of communication.
21. Encourage a team to evaluate itself.

Team leaders seem to place especially high importance on the *facilitative* role as opposed to a *directive* role of coordinators. The two top-ranked behaviors support this interpretation.

Observations generally support the importance that internal team leaders place on the external coordinator's facilitative behavior and their apparent dislike of external direction. Views obtained from team members through discussion and observations (including those of team leaders) indicated that they often wished to be left to do their work on their own and solve their own problems. It was generally understood that teams resented overly directive coordinator behavior.

One team meeting we observed was convened and run by a team to solve an urgent quality problem. The coordinator was present but served only as an information resource. In another case, however, we observed a coordinator get impatient with the team's progress in solving a problem. Consequently, he essentially took charge and dictated a course of action to the team. Prior to his intervention, the team members were interested and highly involved in problem solving. The subsequent tone of the meeting, however, reflected their low interest and irritation. We thought that implementation would surely suffer because of this overly directive coordinator.

At the same time, however, some teams left totally on their own to solve problems became frustrated and dissatisfied with difficult situations in which a coordinator provided what they believed was inadequate direction. We concluded that there is a fine line between overdirection and underdirection on the part of coordinators. Team members placed a high value on independence to manage themselves, but sometimes they needed—and wanted—guidance and assistance. Coordinators must make a decision regarding the appropriate level of involvement based on each situation.

A second pattern of responses from team leaders concerns the degree of truthfulness with which coordinators deal with work groups. The suggested coordinator behaviors, "creating an atmosphere of mutual trust and understanding" and "providing honest feedback" reflect this type of behavior. Again observations supported this view. One team distrusted and disliked a particular coordinator who apparently had presented a work team's position to upper management differently from the way in which he had led the group to believe that he would. Both individual discussions with team members and observations of weekly team meetings indicated the strong value placed on having a coordinator whom the team could count on and trust.

The Paradox of Team Leadership

At Fitzgerald, there sometimes seems to be a contradiction between semantics and reality. The teams are regarded to be self-managing. Yet we are exploring and discussing the role of an appointed external leader to these groups. The essence of this dilemma can be captured by the question: If these groups are supposed to be self-managing, then why is an external leader needed at all?

First, upper plant management saw the coordinator's role as that of a facilitator to help work teams manage themselves. By facilitating the problem solving of team members and communication throughout the work system, coordinators can help to ensure that teams are working properly.

Team leaders see the coordinator's job as a balance between a facilitator who does not interfere with group functioning and a resource to provide some direction. This is a precarious position for coordinators. They must take action when needed but be essentially a backdrop for the team's activities when they are not needed. According to team leaders, truthfulness and trustworthiness are important characteristics for coordinators to possess in carrying out this role.

The ultimate question concerns what sort of expertise the coordinators should have in this type of work organization. Although technical expertise is useful and appropriate (especially to establish baseline credibility), the coordinator's social skills seem to be much more critical. In many ways, the coordinator acts as a counselor and a communication facilitator. Perhaps the most frequent type of coordinator verbal behavior that we heard was the reflective question, throwing the burden of judgment and decision back on the team leader or team member. Coordinators become applied day-by-day "organizational development" specialists, spending a significant amount of their time facilitating a team's capabilities to manage itself.

Overall, a new and sensitive role is prescribed for leaders of the self-managing. This role may initially cause uneasiness in its performers and inadvertently prompt a search for concrete tasks when compared to more traditional supervisory positions. The effective coordinator may be primarily a facilitator who relies heavily on communication and who carefully balances a hands-off and a directive style according to the requirements of each unique situation.

The Connection Between Teams and Productivity

Our investigation into intrateam processes yielded rich evidence of team members and leaders positively influencing the team. The conversations were particularly enlightening. While verbal behavior inevitably reflected some amount of self-concern and was sometimes trivial, the organizational commitment and motivation of these employees were among the highest we have ever observed.

What was the connection between effective team processes and the high level of motivation and commitment? How do team conversations and leadership get translated into bottom-line productivity results?

First, we should ask whether this plant was considered to be effective. Specific data are proprietary, but we did have access to internal data that showed good performance. At the bottom line, it had demonstrated the capability to produce products at a cost significantly lower than similar plants without innovative teams. The turnover at the plant has been extremely low. One manager listed on the fingers of one hand the people who had voluntarily resigned. Finally, overall attitude survey results showed that the levels of satisfaction in the plant were among the highest in the entire company, exceeding even those of many white-collar groups. Most important, many prominent people whom we talked to in the corporation regarded the innovative work structure at the plant as a success. This success has sustained itself over several years and through the transition of several plant managers. (General Motors is now attempting to extrapolate and apply throughout the corporation the lessons learned from this plant, although this issue of diffusion is another story and is not without controversy. Perhaps the success with the Saturn venture is a preliminary indication that General Motors has made significant progress.)

Once we assume productivity success, the next question focuses on the connection between teams and productivity. What is there about what team members and leaders say that gets translated into bottom-line results? Why is talk more than talk? Part of the reason that conversations get turned into productivity is the effect of information sharing, and part is influence on employee motivation to carry out roles.

Information Sharing

Ask any executive what his or her major problem is, and the chances are good that the reply will be something like: "Communication. Our communication is not what it should be. We just never seem to have the right information at the right place at the right time." Inadequate communication often means inadequate information sharing. More often than not, this problem is the result of a policy of secrecy: tell employees only what they need to know to do their jobs. But frequently a significant difference exists between what a manager thinks an employee needs to know and what the employee needs to know. The result is that the employee often lacks the optimal information needed to perform the job.

At Fitzgerald, management shared virtually all information that was not considered personal. The guiding belief was that only the individual employee and the team itself, not management, were in a position to know just which information was important. The net result was a climate of openness that we found virtually unprecedented in our previous experience. Furthermore, this information sharing provided a basis for employees to engage in roles consistent with proactive problem solving; they did not need to wait for management to present a problem for solution, instead discovering and correcting problems at a relatively early stage.

Individual Motivation

Conversations also seemed to affect productivity through their influence on individual motivation. Over and over again, we observed individuals positively affecting the team. If an individual performed well, the team as a whole was seen to be the beneficiary; on the other hand, when an individual fell down, the group was seen to be hurt. The net result was strong peer pressure to contribute to the efforts and performance of the team. Motivation and discipline came from processes within the team, not from management. This motivation and peer pressure were manifested mainly through positive group conversations.

The important point is that management's role was not to provide motivation and discipline directly to individual employees, as is the case in traditional plants. Instead, management created a climate in which motivation and discipline came mainly from within the individual employee and from fellow team members. In our opinion, this is the most effective form of motivation, and it translates into bottom-line productivity. In this case, people who wished to perform well and achieve seemed more likely to do so with the team system. Conversations within work teams are the means by which interpersonal influence was translated into motivation and, ultimately, bottom-line results.

We do not wish to leave the impression that the plant was a model of tranquillity and harmony. On the contrary, the members of the self-managing teams were tough and intense. We observed emotional conflict, but the prevailing mode seemed to be to deal with the conflict openly and directly. Overall, the level of motivation and commitment was high.

KEY LESSONS FROM THIS CASE

1. For a team to succeed, team members need to effectively communicate with one another. Through communication, team members control their interpersonal processes to coordinate effort and increase motivation.
2. Team members—including lower skilled employees—can effectively manage their internal dynamics when given the opportunity.
3. A facilitative leader can have a positive influence on team processes. This leadership role often includes asking the right questions rather than giving answers.

NOTE FOR CASE 3.1

1. We acknowledge the support of Richard Cherry, who helped to provide access to collect the data for this case and has served as a colleague and adviser over several years. We also acknowledge the exceptional helpfulness and cooperation of management and employees at Fitzgerald.

For readers interested in training, a training case based on the Fitzgerald story, "The Greenfield Case," is available from Organization Design and Development, 2002 Renaissance Blvd., Suite 100, King of Prussia, PA 19406, 213-279-2002.

Parts of this chapter were previously published as Henry P. Sims, Jr., and Charles C. Manz, "Conversations Within Self-Managing Teams," *National Productivity Review* 1(1982): 261–269.

TEAM PROCESSES

"Why did I agree to accept this job?" Sue mumbled to herself as she sat down and began to plan for the team meeting. Just last week she had accepted a new assignment to take over as leader of the Green Team—a project development team that had been formed a little over six months ago. She knew that this assignment was her chance to prove her value to the company. However, after meeting the team members and beginning her new responsibilities, she was beginning to rethink the wisdom of accepting the promotion.

The Green Team had started with high aspirations. Each team member had been carefully selected to ensure that all the required skills were present. The tasks and goals had been carefully laid out, and the Green Team was touted as a model for how teams would be designed in the future. Yet, the team never seemed to gel. Tom, the previous team leader, had asked for a transfer to a different division, saying that his job just didn't seem fulfilling anymore. Sue had heard rumors that several of the Green Team's recent meetings had ended in heated discussions, with team members blaming each other for the team's inability to progress toward its goals.

Sue's train of thought was disrupted by the sound of a knock at her office door. As she opened the door she was surprised to find Jan and George—two members of the Green Team. "We would like to speak to you about tomorrow's meeting," Jan said as she and George entered Sue's office.

George began to describe the history of the Green Team. "At first we were all really excited and it looked like we were going to make exceptional progress," he said.

"That was until we had to start making some tough decisions," added Jan.

"Yeah, and then we all looked to Tom—our leader—to tell us how to solve our problems and proceed, but he refused to do anything," George said.

Sue listened for awhile and then asked Jan and George to describe how team members currently interacted with one another.

"Oh, well it's not good," said Jan. "Everyone is always fighting."

"There isn't any real communication, and we just don't feel like a team," George affirmed.

"But believe it or not some of the arguments and fighting within the team have actually led us to new and creative insights," Jan quipped.

The conversation ended, and Jan and George left Sue to continue her preparations for the meeting. She began to ask herself if there was any hope for the Green Team. Was conflict really harming the team? Could she learn to effectively lead a team with such problems? How could she build camaraderie and get team members to work together?

The above case illustrates some common obstacles that many teams face. Even the best designed teams can only be effective to the extent that team members work cooperatively with one another. If team members do not work together in a manner that creates synergy (where the total effect is greater than just the sum of individual inputs), then the potential benefits of designing work around teams never accrue.

Unit 3 focuses on intragroup processes related to the various interactions between team members. First, we will look at the development stages that most teams pass through. An understanding of this development process provides insight into how interactions and intrateam processes change over time. We will also examine how socialization processes develop team identity and influence team members to sacrifice personal interests for the betterment of the team. This will lead us to a discussion about power, influence, and conflict within teams. We will then conclude this unit by focusing on how leadership affects team processes and interactions.

TEAM DEVELOPMENT

Imagine a team of product engineers who are called together to develop a new type of CD player. At first team members are reserved, and they approach group interactions cautiously, especially if they were not previously acquainted with one another. After a short phase of getting to know each other, the team will likely experience conflict. Differences in opinion surface, and members begin to disagree about significant issues. Team members then give and take until compromises are worked out. Agreements associated with the various compromises then provide guidance for how team members will work together to accomplish their tasks. The team builds on this cooperative foundation and moves into a productive phase where work is completed and the new CD player is developed. After the work is finished, the team may dissolve, and the various team members will move on to other teams and new assignments.

This example illustrates how processes and interactions among team members change over time. Even though each team is somewhat unique, most teams follow a pattern similar to the one described for the product development team. Of course, some teams are relatively permanent and do not dissolve, as their work is ongoing. Nevertheless, understanding the development process is critical for discerning how team processes and interactions evolve. In order to better understand this process of change, we describe a process of team development that is common to many teams.

The process of team development is usually summarized by five stages: forming, storming, norming, performing, and adjourning.[1] Although many teams seem to move chronologically through the five stages, the development process of other teams does not fit neatly into the categories. Teams may skip over a stage. The length of time in each stage may be different for each team. Some teams may experience the stages in a different sequence. Nevertheless, the basic process outlined by the five stages is common enough to provide a framework for understanding much of the process of team development.

Forming

The first stage of team development is forming. *Forming* occurs when a group of individuals come together and begin to think of themselves as members of a team. This initial phase is marked by apprehension. Team members are often becoming acquainted for the very first time. They are uncertain about how other members will react to them, and each person is unsure if he or she will be accepted by the team. Team members do not know exactly what is expected of them, and there is hesitation about how to proceed and accomplish the team's tasks.

During the forming stage everyone is generally on his best behavior, but there is an underlying tension that prevents team members from feeling comfortable and trusting one another. This tension begins to break down as members work together and share information about themselves and their expectations for the team. The personalities of the various individuals begin to express themselves, and members start to develop expectations for the behavior of their teammates. A sense of contentment sets in and group members begin to feel comfortable working together.

One of us recently experienced the forming stage of team development with a committee appointed to make some decisions about university curriculum. The Dean of the College appointed a group of professors to study the courses being offered and to make recommendations about changes that might help our school keep up with changes in the business world. All of the professors chosen for the committee knew one another to an extent, but most had not worked closely together on specific projects. At the first meeting most professors said very little. The person serving as the team leader described the committee's overall goal, and the members sat back and waited for others to express their opinions and make recommendations about how the work should progress. After several minutes of virtual silence, a few people began to assert themselves and make suggestions about how the committee might proceed. Yet, throughout the meeting team members were very careful about how they framed their comments, and nobody was willing to disagree openly with the comments made by another committee member.

Storming

The forming stage is usually followed by the emergence of conflict between team members. This stage is known as *storming,* which occurs as team members begin to disagree with one another. Being part of a team means that individuals may need to sacrifice many of their personal desires. Seeing areas where they might be required to sacrifice often leads members to resist the influence of others. Team members begin to argue with each other. Arguments about roles and procedures surface, and the pleasant social interactions of the forming stage cease. Team members often experience negative emotion and become uncomfortable interacting with one another.

The conflict that occurs during the storming stage may seem undesirable. However, most observers of team processes would agree that some conflict is beneficial, especially if it revolves around issues rather than individual personalities. Team members almost always have areas of disagreement. A moderate amount of conflict is needed to bring out these differences and begin the process of compromise. Too little conflict may lead team members to suppress their differences without resolving them. These differences frequently resurface at a later time, and the team is thrown back into the storming stage until it resolves these areas of conflict. On the other hand, too much conflict may permanently destroy social relationships and leave team members unable to work together. Effective storming results in the discussion of key differences among members and the establishment of working compromises. Once these compromises are developed, team members often feel closer to each other than they did before the conflict occurred.

The university curriculum committee mentioned above moved into the storming stage at its second meeting. Not long after the meeting began, the generally cordial atmosphere of the first meeting eroded into a rather serious debate. A somewhat controversial plan for accomplishing the committee's tasks was presented. Several committee members disagreed with it and argued that the committee should not proceed with the plan. Individuals expressed their fears that the proposed plan would lead to an improper emphasis in some areas and to overly costly changes in the curriculum. Other committee members supported the plan and saw it as an opportunity to effect real change. The two sides continued to express their opposing viewpoints, and it appeared that a compromise was impossible. At the conclusion of the meeting, it seemed as if very little had been accomplished. Many faculty members stated that they did not think the committee would ever be able to agree on an approach that was satisfactory for all members.

Norming

Most teams make it through the storming stage and enter the norming stage. *Norming* is the phase of development in which team members come together and begin to feel a sense of belonging. Unity increases and team members once again feel comfortable working together. Members feel a greater sense of belonging to and identity with the team. An increase in cohesiveness is perhaps the most significant outcome at this stage of development.

Cohesiveness is defined as a strong sense of connectedness between team members that causes them to work together to attain an objective.[2] Historically, there has been a great deal of debate about the desirability of cohesiveness. Some have argued that highly cohesive teams are dysfunctional because they force team members to give up their individuality. A potentially negative outcome of extreme cohesion is groupthink. *Groupthink* is a distorted style of thinking that leads to ineffective group decisions when high cohesiveness coexists with significant conformity within the group.[3] In some highly cohesive groups, each individual member censors her comments so that she will not be perceived as someone who is "not a team player." The leader in these groups is often someone who is highly charismatic; that is, group members willingly follow her comments without thinking through all of the alternatives. The group develops feelings of unanimity and invulnerability, which often result in a failure to explore the possible effects of their decisions. For instance, the faulty decision to launch the Challenger Space Shuttle in 1986 is often described as a result of groupthink. The ramifications of the decision were not clearly discussed, and many people on the team charged with making the launch decision had private reservations that were never expressed. The high cohesion of the launch team helped create a setting in which group pressure seemingly overwhelmed the better judgment of many individuals. The result was a life-ending disaster.

Others have claimed that group cohesion is good because it forms strong bonds between team members and thereby influences them to work harder to achieve the collective goal. The majority of evidence seems to support this claim, as highly cohesive teams seem to be more effective than teams without cohesion.[4] Effectiveness can be particularly high if teams vigilantly check the quality of their decisions, and strive to help team members retain their individuality. Helping teams successfully move beyond the storming stage and into the norming stage is therefore critical for ensuring their effectiveness.

A set of organizational development techniques known as team building can help increase team cohesiveness. Unit 4 will discuss some of these techniques and methods. A common purpose of the methods is to create interdependence among team members by challenging them with tasks like rope climbing that they must complete cooperatively. This necessity for cooperation builds relationships and teaches team members how to work together. Overcoming obstacles also builds a sense of accomplishment that helps develop camaraderie.

The norming stage is also important because it is during this phase that team norms develop. *Norms* are informal rules that teams adopt to regulate their behavior.[5] Informal rules develop in areas that are important to the team but not in areas that are unrelated to team activities. For instance, a basketball team is likely to develop norms about practice and discipline but not about the movies its members see. These norms provide cues for appropriate behavior and increase the predictability of team member behavior. A norm of practicing basketball during the summer provides individual team members with guidance about how they should act in order to remain a member of the team. The norm of practicing during the summer also provides team members with information that helps them coordinate their own actions with the actions of their teammates.

Norms increase the team's ability to stay together and accomplish its goals. A group of workers may establish informal rules about acceptable levels of productivity. These rules can have a positive impact when they encourage high performance, but they can also have a negative influence when they limit outputs. However, in either case the norms ensure that the team will accomplish its goal, even if its goal is to exert only a minimal amount of effort. Norms also help teams solve interpersonal problems. Rules develop about topics of conversation that should be avoided to reduce confrontation. They can also encourage compromise and define the roles of individual members.

One important source of norms—statements that team members and leaders make—was illustrated in the Fitzgerald case at the opening of this Unit. When team members consistently criticized someone for arriving late, a norm of arriving on time developed. Critical events in a team's history can also create norms. For instance, if a team of financial customer service representatives receives an award for exceptional service, the team may establish a norm to continue to go above and beyond the call of duty and provide great service to passengers. Norms are also created by the expectations members bring with them to the team. If a member has enjoyed open communication in a prior team, he might encourage his present team to adopt norms that encourage members to talk freely.[6]

Once norms are established, they are very difficult to change; hence, the early phases of group development are critical. Effort needs to be directed toward ensuring that statements from team leaders and members are positive and develop functional norms. Critical events should be monitored, and the positive norms that develop should be reinforced. If effective norms develop, the team is well on its way to achieving exceptional performance.

The norming stage did occur for the faculty curriculum team. Between the second and third meetings, several committee members with opposing views met in private and discussed their differences. These one-on-one conversations built personal ties between team members. A deeper sense of commitment to the task developed, and committee members began to agree that there must be a way to work out their differences of opinion. Team members began to refer to the whole team as "us" rather than to the one subgroup as "us" and the other as "them." A norm for listening and trying to understand the other side of issues developed. A norm also developed that encouraged conversation outside the formal meetings. Thus, much of the actual work of the committee was later accomplished as individual members met in one-on-one conferences and worked through issues.

Performing

The *performing* stage occurs when members work synergistically to accomplish their collective objectives. Not all groups arrive at this stage, but those that do are highly productive. Social relationships have developed, team members understand one another's roles, and a strong sense of commitment to the team exists. These factors drive the team toward high performance that exceeds the productivity of individuals working independently. Teams that maintain this phase over an extended period of time are truly exceptional. For example, Table 3.1 provides a summary of eight specific guidelines that can be used to help teams reach this point of development in terms of their management of time. Effective time management is an important part of being productive, and the table illustrates the kind of guidelines that might be identified for other areas as well. Another example would be in terms of a new perspective for enhancing group decision making. This new perspective is called "Teamthink." Some key aspects of Teamthink, as well as its contrasts with the earlier described detrimental effects of groupthink, are summarized in Table 3.2.

Research does, however, suggest that performance is frequently not consistent, even once the team has reached the performing stage. Teams tend to experience peaks of performance.[7] These peaks often correspond with dead-

TABLE 3.1 Ways to Improve Team Time Management

- Recognize that your team's time is scarce.
- Arrange your work area so that it is neat.
- Recognize and use time when you get the most work done (mornings, afternoons).
- Pace yourself by establishing a routine to help members be aware of what they need to do.
- Develop a plan that identifies your team's goals.
- Focus your team's energy on the tasks with the highest priorities.
- Effectively use pockets of time that result from things not going as planned.

Source: C. C. Manz, C. P. Neck, J. Mancuso, and K. P. Manz, *For Team Members Only: Making Your Workplace Team Productive and Hassle-free* (New York: AMACOM, 1997).

lines. As deadlines approach, teams that have developed effective norms are able to come together and exceed expectations for performance. This often means that a team spends a great deal of time preparing and developing critical relationships so that it can experience peak performance when time pressures arise.

The faculty curriculum team experienced the performing stage of development as it faced a deadline and felt increased pressure to perform. A faculty meeting had been scheduled at which the committee was expected to propose several changes for the curriculum. The team had overcome its initial conflict, and strong working relationships had developed. Committee members sacrificed many of their other projects to put extra effort into completing the proposal. Members who had once opposed each other now worked together on a plan

TABLE 3.2 Moving from Groupthink to Teamthink

To Teamthink	From Groupthink
Teams recognize and value member uniqueness.	Teams experience an illusion of unanimity.
Teams understand their limitations and threats.	Teams believe they can't fail.
Differing views are encouraged.	Social pressure impedes differing views.
The team recognizes the ethical and moral consequences of decisions.	The team has an illusion of morality.
Stereotypes are discounted.	Enemy leaders are perceived through stereotypes.
Team members openly express concerns and ideas.	Team members practice self-censorship.
Views outside the group are sought.	Mind guards screen external information.

Source: C. C. Manz, C. P. Neck, J. Mancuso, and K. P. Manz, *For Team Members Only: Making Your Workplace Team Productive and Hassle-free* (New York: AMACOM, 1997).

that appeared acceptable from all viewpoints. The end result was an innovative recommendation for curriculum change that was much better than had originally been offered by any of the individual committee members.

Adjourning

The final stage of team development (at least for teams that are not permanent) is adjourning. *Adjourning* takes place as the team begins to break up and individual members move on to other activities. Sometimes adjournment is planned, such as when a team completes its objectives and no longer has a reason to function. At other times, adjournment is unexpected, and the team breaks apart because members unexpectedly withdraw. Teams may also fade because members are unable to move beyond the storming stage. External constraints such as organizational mergers and downsizing can also cause a team to terminate before it completes its objectives.

The adjournment stage can be particularly stressful for some team members. Over time team members have melded their personal identity with the identity of the team. Many team members look to the team as a source for positive feelings of self-worth and personal achievement. As the team dissolves, members feel threatened and perceive a significant loss in their lives. One solution to this problem is to hold a sort of wake for the team.[8] During the wake, team accomplishments are highlighted. Members begin to look to the future and seek understanding about how their experiences with the team can aid them in their future endeavors. The wake can help team members deal positively with their emotions and provide a sense of closure for the team and its activities.

The faculty curriculum committee disbanded once their recommended changes were enacted. Although no formal meeting marked the team's adjournment, committee members who met in the hallways were often observed talking about the team's accomplishments. As individuals participated in other committees, they sometimes referred back positively to their experiences with the curriculum committee. Curriculum team members took the planning, management, negotiation, and conflict resolution skills they had learned and applied them to other teams.

SOCIALIZATION

A team influences the behavior of its members. The process through which this influence occurs is known as socialization. *Socialization* takes place as members learn the behaviors that are required for them to either become or remain members of the team. Similar to the team development process, socialization tends to occur in stages. The three stages are anticipation, accommodation, and acceptance.[9]

The first stage of socialization occurs before members actually join the team. This is the *anticipation* stage during which expectations about team membership are developed. Information about what to expect from membership is processed. An example can be seen in the process that occurs when a couple becomes engaged. In a sense, each person is joining the family of the other person, meaning that each must be socialized into the other person's family. Stories are shared before family members are introduced, and these stories provide information about what it is like to be a member of that family. Familiarity with the family helps the future spouse to understand the behavior that can be expected of family members, and communicates expectations about what behavior will be seen as acceptable from him.

The second stage is accommodation. *Accommodation* takes place as members become involved with the day-to-day activities of the team. This is the stage during which interpersonal relationships are developed. Team members are taught what it means to be included in the team, and basic expectations for behavior are communicated. Team members accept the group's norms and values and begin to intertwine their personal identity with the team's identity. Roles develop for the team member, and she must learn to balance those roles with the other roles that are a part of her life both internal and external to the workplace. In the marriage example, this is the phase that occurs just after the wedding. If the spouse is to be accepted into the new family, she must begin to develop relationships with family members. This means that she will internalize many of the family's values and begin a new role that defines how she interacts with the members of her new family.

The third stage is acceptance. *Acceptance* occurs as members fulfill their roles within the team. During this stage, a bond forms between team members and the team as a collective. Team members begin to feel like they make an important contribution to the team. They are committed to seeing that the team succeeds. Team members can take up to two years to arrive at this stage, but this is the point where they are fully integrated into the team. Acceptance in the marriage example occurs when the spouse begins to feel like he belongs to the family. This is largely psychological and might be manifested when a husband begins to refer to his mother-in-law simply as "mom."

The process of socialization can occur simultaneously for all team members when a new team is formed. Socialization can also occur when a single team member is added to the team. In either case, team members go through the process of taking on the values, beliefs, and norms of the team. Resocialization may also be needed if a team member starts to withdraw from the team. The process of resocialization is similar to that of socialization except the team and the member are trying to redefine their relationship rather than establish it.

In many ways the stages of socialization correspond with the stages of team development. Figure 3.1 illustrates these similarities. Just prior to forming, team members engage in anticipatory socialization that establishes expectations for performance. Once the team is formed, team members experience accommodation where they become integrated into the team. This causes conflict and corresponds with the storming stage. As members accept the values of the team and establish their roles, the team moves through the

Figure 3.1 Team development and socialization

norming phase. Performing is then possible because team members have been accepted into the team.

As described above, a critical lesson from both team development and socialization is the importance of the early stages of the team's life cycle. During the early phases of development, teams often use socialization to establish norms that guide their behavior throughout the team's existence. Successful implementation of teams thus depends largely on effective guidance and socialization of newly formed teams.

POWER AND INFLUENCE

Inherent in the process of socialization is the notion that team members influence one another. However, team members are not equally able to wield influence. One reason is that members have varying levels of power. *Power* is defined as the capacity to influence others. Power derives from a number of sources; however, five common power bases have been identified: reward, coercive, referent, expert, and legitimate power.[10]

Power Bases

Reward Power

Reward power comes from a team member's ability to provide other members with something they find desirable. This power is based on the capability to administer reinforcement. The idea of reinforcement suggests that people engage and persist in behaviors that are associated with desirable rewards. Accordingly, employees provide labor, at least in part, because of the compensation they receive from the organization. Historically, supervisors have held reward power. However, team members who are not supervisors can also possess reward power. This power may come through formalized mechanisms such as the use of peer ratings to determine individual pay levels, a practice that is currently being experimented with in some organizations. Reward power may also come through less formalized processes, such as a team member's ability to determine who enacts which roles within the team. Allowing peers to work on desirable tasks can be used as a reinforcer to influence the behavior of teammates. Recognition and social approval are other rewards that team members can provide to one another.

Reward power was demonstrated in the Fitzgerald teams (Case 3.1) when coordinators praised team members during team meetings. The leader's position allowed him to influence the meeting agenda and thereby determine who received special praise. However, because team members were consistently motivated by the positive comments they received from their peers, team members who were not formal leaders or coordinators also possessed some reward power at Fitzgerald.

Coercive Power

Coercive power derives from a team member's ability to give punishment. Parents often invoke this power base when they take away a child's privileges. A common example of coercive power in the workplace is the threat to terminate someone's employment. Similar to reward power, coercive power has historically resided with supervisors. However, the trend is toward more coercive power for team members. In particular, the Fitzgerald case described earlier illustrated how other team members can use coercive power by threatening a frequently tardy member with dismissal from the team.

Referent Power

Team members who are respected and liked by others possess referent power. Frequently, the personalities of these members are attractive to others, and in many ways teammates desire to become like the person who has referent power. An everyday example of this effect is the power of celebrities to influence others. People identify with celebrities and want to emulate their characteristics. Members of work teams with referent power may possess strong ethical values. They may also be hard working and intelligent. Often a team member with referent power is one who has received special recognition for his work skills or one who is connected with important people. Referent power can also exist when a team member is just plain likable so that others want to be associated with him.

Expert Power

Expert power is associated with knowledge, skill, and ability. A team member with this power is seen by others as having expertise that is superior to theirs in some area. Interestingly, it matters little if the person really has the expertise. The key is that others believe his or her relevant knowledge, skill, or ability is superior to theirs. Examples in work teams might include ability to operate a specialized machine, knowledge of legal issues, or skill at negotiation. Team members who are perceived to possess these strengths can generally influence their peers to agree with them and to carry out their agendas. Teams benefit when members recognize true expertise because it ensures that individuals will have influence in areas where they are best qualified to provide inputs.

In the Fitzgerald case, the young worker who noticed the quality problem and halted the production process had expert power. Because he had taken the time to train himself in a technical area, he had the power to influence other team members to alter what they were doing and to help him solve the quality problem. Without his expertise he likely would not have been able to influence the team to such an extent.

Legitimate Power

Legitimate power is based on formal authority. Supervisors have this power because they are seen as having a right to direct the actions of others. This right may come from an appointment or from an election. In either case, other members of the team usually accept the legitimacy of the role for the person who serves as leader and must do so in order for legitimate power to exist. The leader's ability to influence others comes not so much from his personal characteristics, but from the role that the group has given to him. While the leader may have reward and coercive power, legitimate power derives fundamentally from a sense of obligation to follow, meaning that others will follow even if the leader loses his ability to control rewards and punishments.

Self-leading work teams place a reduced emphasis on legitimate power; however, team coordinators at the Fitzgerald plant possess a sense of legitimate power. In one case a coordinator became impatient with a team's attempts to solve a problem. He asserted his legitimate power and dictated a course of action for the team. The long-term ramifications were harmful, for this action appeared to reduce team member motivation. In a more positive way, another coordinator at Fitzgerald used his legitimate power to facilitate conflict resolution. Rather than stepping in and taking control of team interactions, he used his authority to get team members to communicate and interact until they had reached a resolution themselves.

Influence Strategies

Another way of understanding how team members interact with one another is to examine the influence strategies that people use. Many influence strategies are associated with the power bases discussed above, for these strategies are often used to assert power. Common influence strategies include reason, friendliness, coalition, bargaining, assertiveness, higher authority, and sanctions.[11] Short descriptions of each strategy are provided in Table 3.3.

One way that these strategies differ is in their directness. Assertiveness and sanctions are direct strategies because the target of the influence attempt will surely become aware that he is being influenced. For instance, one team leader at the Fitzgerald plant (Case 3.1) used a direct tactic when he bluntly told a team member that "we won't allow it (absenteeism) to continue." Such direct strategies are normally used only if the influence initiator has a relatively strong power base such as legitimate, reward, or coercive power. In contrast, friendliness is an indirect strategy. A team member may use such an indirect strategy when she wants

TABLE 3.3   **Influence Strategies**

Reason	Using facts and data to support and develop logical arguments
Friendliness	Using impression management, flattery, and the creation of good will
Coalition	Mobilizing other people to join forces
Bargaining	Using negotiation through the exchange of benefits and favors
Assertiveness	Using direct force
Higher Authority	Gaining the support of higher levels in the organization
Sanctions	Using rewards and punishments

Source: D. Kipnis, S. M. Schmidt, C. Swaffin-Smith, and I. Wilkinson, "Patterns of Managerial Influence: Shotgun Managers, Tacticians, and Bystanders," *Organizational Dynamics* 12, no. 3 (1984): 58–67.

her intent to influence to remain concealed. Indirect strategies are generally used when a person has little power and must therefore rely on subtle influence.

Influence strategies also differ in the extent to which they are rational. Reason is a rational strategy that focuses on the use of logical argument and data. Bargaining is a rational strategy that focuses on the potential exchange of benefits. A team member using rational strategies might present an objective analysis that shows how the team could improve performance by changing a technical procedure. These rational strategies are most often used when the objective of influence is to benefit the organization as a whole. Less rational strategies focus on emotions and are often relied on when influence is being used to benefit an individual rather than the organization. One example is friendliness, whereby the creation of goodwill is used to influence another team member to take one's place on an undesirable shift because he or she does not want you as a friend to be inconvenienced.

Another way that influence strategies differ is in their incorporation of other people. Sanctions, reason, friendliness, and assertiveness can be carried out by a single individual. However, coalition building and appealing to higher authority require the cooperation of others before influence can be asserted. People with low power tend to use strategies that enlist the aid of others by essentially borrowing the power of someone else. For instance, a new team member may have little power but may be able to wield influence if she presents her ideas to a few individuals that form a coalition to support her attempts at changing a manufacturing process.

Every influence strategy has both potential benefits and potential problems. The effect of a particular strategy frequently depends on specific circumstances and on the norms that have developed for the team. Indirect strategies can be problematic when they establish a climate of distrust, whereas direct strategies often eliminate confusion because they are candid. Yet, direct strategies can also result in explicit confrontations between team members. As discussed in the following section, this confrontation can be detrimental unless team norms ensure that disagreements and criticism are directed toward concepts rather than toward individuals. Rational tactics are usually superior to nonrational tactics because they focus on improving situations rather than playing to emotions. Understanding and adapting to the emotions of teammates can, however, improve cohesiveness and ensure the development of strong interpersonal relationships. Strategies that can be carried out even if cooperation from others is absent are usually more efficient than strategies that require coordination. However, strategies that enlist the help of others provide an opportunity for low status team members to influence others.

CONFLICT

Here's an unusual team to think about: a congressional committee. For most of us this thought evokes an image of conflict. Members of the committee each have their own agendas (often driven by different party lines and constituencies), and the goals for some members can often be met only at the expense of the goals for other members. Thus, even though they are formed for the purpose of solving problems, many congressional committees experience strife and end up creating more problems than they solve. Yet, some congressional committees are able to work through their differences and arrive at creative solutions. Members of the committee influence one another to see issues differently, and the end result is cooperation. In either case, conflict and influence attempts greatly affect both interpersonal processes and outcomes of the team.

Although conflict may be less prevalent in work organizations than in political committees, employees in business organizations do disagree. Moreover, working in teams requires employees to interact more frequently than does working as individuals; this suggests that conflict can often be magnified in team-based organizations. Some of this conflict arises from the incompatibility of team personalities. This type of conflict is usually emotion laden and seldom beneficial. Other conflict in teams can be explained by understanding that team members have diverse goals both for themselves and for the team as a whole. Because this type of conflict can be beneficial to teams and deserves further attention, we explore the reasons behind conflict that goes beyond social incompatibility.

Sources of Conflict

In some teams, the goals of individual members may be different but compatible. One team member's goal may be to earn a lot of money. Another team member may have the goal to create a socially supportive work environment. Belonging to the same team may provide them with both financial rewards and social support. In such cases, a team can provide different members a common path to separate individual goals, and conflict arising from diversity in member goals is minimal.

At other times team member goals may not be compatible. As with political committees, the goals for some team members may seemingly be achieved only at the expense of the goals of other team members. This might happen in a work team where one member has a primary goal of job security and another a primary goal of expanding operations. The risk inherent in expansion may create a situation in which the interests of the two members are in direct opposition. Opposing individual goals can often lead to conflict and disagreement among team members.

Whether or not they are compatible, the achievement of a large number of team member goals is dependent on the interactions within a team. This need to rely on the team for individual goal achievement can create conflict between the team and the individual. A *social trap* occurs when an individual's goals, at least in the short run, can best be achieved at the expense of the team's collective goal.[12] For instance, an individual team member may desire a promotion. In order to obtain the promotion, he might perceive a need to stand out and appear to perform better than his teammates. This may lead him to focus on contributions that are clearly his and to thereby cooperate less with his coworkers. This lack of cooperation may allow him to perform some specific tasks better, and it may even help him to achieve the promotion. However, the lack of cooperation has a negative effect on the team, for cooperation is necessary for the team to reach peak levels of performance. A social trap is created because the team member's promotion may occur only if he maximizes his individual output at the expense of the team's overall productivity. The inherent trade-off between individual and team goals often fosters conflict.

A somewhat different effect occurs when teams force individuals to give up significant personal autonomy. Because teams require the coordination of inputs, they can often limit the discretion of individual members. For instance, a member of a computer programming team may prefer to take extended vacations and then work long hours just before a deadline for completing a project. This scheduling may be very effective when he works alone, but it can create significant coordination problems when he is part of a team. The need to coordinate with other team members reduces his ability to control his own schedule and can place his interests in conflict with the interests of the team as a collective whole. This conflict between individual autonomy and team coordination is illustrated in Case 3.3. When the CEO of the insurance agency desired greater coordination and standardization, he created teams. Although these teams were labeled "self-managing," they increased supervisor control and limited individual autonomy.

Types of Conflict

Not all conflict within teams is the same. Some types of conflict seem to be beneficial for a team, whereas other types of conflict appear to be detrimental. The most basic and useful distinction between conflict types seems to be between relationship-oriented conflict (sometimes referred to as affective conflict) and task-oriented conflict (sometimes labeled cognitive conflict).[13] Relationship conflict occurs when team members experience interpersonal incompatibility; task conflict occurs when team members disagree about the tasks that should be performed and how they should be accomplished.

Relationship conflict is generally detrimental to teams. For instance, team members may experience conflict because they differ in their preferences for communication and social interaction. This conflict is usually referred to in terms of personality differences and can take on a rather childish tone when team members bicker about things such as how others dress. Seemingly insignificant differences escalate into a negative spiral, with one person's negative comments eliciting equally negative responses from another. Breaking the cycle of negative reciprocation is difficult, and the team can be paralyzed by expanding conflict. Outside observers of the conflict usually agree that the source of the conflict is insignificant, but the negative cycle that is created can be immensely damaging. Such a cycle of negatively spiraling relationship conflict is often seen as the major cause of failure for perhaps the most common team in existence: a married couple.

On the other hand, task conflict can sometimes be beneficial for teams. This type of conflict centers not around interpersonal difference but around team tasks. Team members disagree about what tasks should be done and how those tasks should be carried out; yet issues don't become personal. A moderate amount of this type of conflict is beneficial because it leads teams to critical evaluation of what the team should be doing. This critical evaluation is especially important for creative teams that face nonroutine tasks. These teams succeed from looking at diverse perspectives of problems and developing creative solutions. In essence, these teams prevent groupthink from occurring. However, very high levels of task conflict can be damaging for teams, regardless of the tasks they must perform. When task conflict exceeds a certain threshold, it prohibits teams from cooperating and developing synergy. The result is less than optimal team performance. Thus, a moderate amount of task conflict seems to be optimal for teams, especially creative teams.

Both types of conflict occur in almost all teams. For example, the team of supervisors at Charette (Case 3.2) experienced both relationship and task conflict. Negative, relationship-oriented, conflict surfaced when a manager confronted the consultant and accused him of moving the organization in self-serving directions that would personally benefit the consultant. The manager was worried about his own survival in the organization and personally attacked others in order to thwart the group from accomplishing its goals. In contrast, the team of managers later experienced positive, task-oriented conflict when they discussed what they would do if the teams they supervised wanted to dismiss a member. Several different ideas and opinions were expressed, and the managers argued about their relative merit. In the end, a compromise was reached that incorporated many benefits of the different original proposals.

Conflict Resolution

Teams can have several possible reactions to conflict. One reaction is *avoidance*. This occurs when team members do not take steps to resolve the conflict. They try to ignore their differences and hope that they will not be required to integrate their positions.[14] Some evidence suggests that avoidance is an effective method of dealing with relationship conflict.[15] Teams with norms that require members to ignore interpersonal differences often perform better than teams with norms that encourage members to voice all of their likes and dislikes about one another. However, long-term avoidance can also allow conflict to build up to the point where team members become so angry with each other that they are unable to continue working together.

Another method of conflict resolution is *imposition,* whereby a team member is forced to concede his position. This may occur when a team member lacks a strong power base. For instance, a new team member may be forced to complete undesirable tasks because he has not yet developed the power bases that are needed to influence other members of the team. Imposition fails to acknowledge the interests of some team members and can often result in dissatisfaction and reduced motivation.

A third method of conflict resolution is *compromise.* Compromise requires that each side of a dispute make concessions. For instance, a team may need to decide if it will work overtime. Some members may desire the additional pay, while others may want to go home and spend time with their families. A compromise could be reached by the team agreeing to work a limited amount of overtime that would provide some additional pay, yet would not greatly impose on family time. Compromise ensures that diverse interests are accounted for but fails to find a resolution strategy that allows all team members to most fully pursue their interests and attain their individual goals. Relying too much on compromise may cause team members to get too comfortable with using it whenever conflict arises and thereby rob the team of the benefits of constructive disagreement and the potential to reach more optimal solutions.

A final method of conflict resolution is *integrative bargaining.* Integrative procedures bring together parties in a dispute and help them to search for a win/win solution. These procedures require trust and openness. Team members engaged in integrative bargaining work cooperatively to determine the source of conflict, and then explore alternatives that eliminate the conflict without significantly damaging the interests of either person. For instance, a marketing team that disagrees about the best marketing plan would examine the reasons why they disagree and then seek an alternative that maximizes the desirable outcomes of all perspectives. Integrative bargaining is the most effective method for resolving task conflict (although it can take more time and effort and may not be desirable to use in all—especially unimportant—situations). A key to integrative bargaining is assertive problem solving. In order to effectively deal with conflict, team members must know how to be assertive without being overbearing. Table 3.4 provides a list of five steps that can help team members to overcome task conflict with assertiveness.

LEADERSHIP

Perhaps the most pervasive influence on team process comes from leadership. A basic issue is whether teams (especially empowered ones) really need leaders. In fact, the term *leaderless teams* is popular in some circles. However, when one stops and thinks about the meaning of leadership, such terms are really inaccurate.

TABLE 3.4   Steps to Assertive Problem Solving

1. Communicate caring or empathy for the other person's situation.
2. Describe the particular problem area without being evaluative or judgmental.
3. Describe the effects of the problem area on the team, the task, or the mission.
4. Request a specific change in behavior.
5. Be willing to compromise.

Source: S. Bower and G. Bower, *Asserting Yourself: A Practical Guide to Positive Change* (New York: Addison-Wesley, 1976). The steps are discussed more thoroughly in C. C. Manz, C. P. Neck, J. Mancuso, and K. P. Manz, *For Team Members Only: Making Your Workplace Team Productive and Hassle-free* (New York: AMACOM, 1997).

One definition of leadership is the act of influencing others. This definition implies that any team member can exercise leadership and influence over her peers, meaning that the existence of a team without leadership is not possible, even though it may not have a formal leader. However, in this section we focus mainly on the role of formal leaders and how their actions can affect teams. We do this by examining different team leadership structures, forms of leadership influence, and effects of leadership behaviors.

Leadership Structures

Leadership structure addresses the following questions. How is the leader appointed (and, perhaps, unappointed)? Is the team leader a member and co-performer on the team or someone outside the team? And to what degree is formal authority given to the leader versus the team itself?[16] In response to these questions, team leadership structure may be expressed in one of three ways: an external supervisor, an external facilitator, or an internally elected leader. Note how these structures vary in the extent to which they encourage team self-leadership.

External Supervisor

The most common and well-known leadership structure is to appoint a traditional external supervisor or foreperson. This person, typically appointed by management, has legitimate power that stems from the position itself; this authority allows the leader to make job assignments, give instructions and commands, and allocate some rewards and reprimands. Control over the team's activities is vested mainly in this appointed leader rather than the team itself. Usually this person is not a team member and is at least one step removed from carrying out the work tasks.

External Facilitator

Another type of leadership structure occurs when a leader, often called a facilitator (or coordinator, counselor, or coach), is appointed to facilitate empowered workers. This is the role that coordinators fill in the Fitzgerald Battery Plant (see Case 3.1). A facilitator is usually not part of the team; he or she does not carry out team tasks, but rather offers advice and counsel on how the team itself might perform activities. A facilitator is usually appointed by management, similar to a supervisor, but the expected behavior or role of the facilitator is quite different. Whereas a supervisor retains a high degree of control and decision making, a facilitator typically attempts to encourage a team to undertake self-control activities such as self-job assignments or self-goal setting.

Internally Elected Leader

An internally elected team leader is another type of structure that might be utilized for team leadership. Teams at the Fitzgerald Battery Plant had this type of internal leader in addition to the coordinators. These leaders are usually team members who engage in most of the typical day to day activities of the team in addition to carrying out leadership responsibilities. They frequently come to the position as a result of some type of team election (or even team leader rotation) and thus might be considered an emergent leader. Of course, if the team leader is elected, some method of replacement must be devised to deal with turnover of the leadership role. A specified term of office may be invoked, at the end of which the leader may or may not be reelected. Other mechanisms might include a runoff to choose between alternative candidates or a vote of confidence in which a leader might be unelected or deposed. This approach is quite unusual, however, for elected team leaders who are having difficulty with the team usually volunteer to step down before an "unelection" is necessary.

A fellow worker who is also a team leader can have advantages and obstacles in terms of group norms, interpersonal relationships, and so forth that are not shared by external team leaders. For example, within-team leaders may be in a better position to contribute to the social well-being (group maintenance) of the group but face difficulties in emphasizing task performance because of personal relationships with other members. Moreover, an elected leader is empowered from below. That is, the elected leader acts to organize, motivate, and influence the team, but the power and authority to do so come from the very people the leader is attempting to influence.

The three leadership structures vary considerably in terms of the degree of team self-leadership that is established or, in other words, in terms of the amount of direct control that is vested in the team itself versus direct control retained by management. In the case of the traditional foreperson or supervisor, management retains virtually all control, since most of the power is vested in the supervisor, who represents management. Thus, these teams tend to be externally managed. On the other end of the spectrum, with an internally elected team leader, high team self-leadership is established as a great deal of control is vested in the team itself, which "delegates upward" to the elected team leader. The appointed external facilitator represents a role that falls somewhere in between in terms of empowerment, with the philosophy and practice typically moving in the direction of greater team self-leadership. A facilitator attempts to move more control into the hands of the team, although in reality management retains a great deal of control through the power to appoint or remove the facilitator.

Leadership Behaviors

Although leadership structure tells us something about how the leader's role fits into an organization's overall control structure, it does little to describe what leaders actually do. One way of thinking about leadership is to ask yourself what image you see when you envision a great leader. Is it an image of a "white knight" riding in to save his people by crushing and defeating their enemies? Is it an image of a football coach screaming at his players to motivate them? Is it an inspirational speaker who is effective at creating a vision for the people she leads?[17]

Although there have been numerous studies related to leadership, there is still uncertainty about which type of leader is most effective. The most consistent finding in leadership research seems to be that effective leadership must be adapted to the conditions and needs of specific situations. Perhaps this is best shown in leadership theories that suggest leaders tend to focus on either accomplishing tasks or building positive relationships, and that the appropriateness of the focus depends on the conditions present in the leadership situation.[18]

Our intent here is not to present a detailed description of each of the various theories of leadership; we leave this task to Organizational Behavior textbooks. Rather our purpose is to provide an overview of some common leadership behaviors and then examine their effect on teams. This limited focus provides insight into the question of how team leadership should be adapted to fit the conditions of certain teams, and therefore provides a team perspective of leadership.

We describe leadership behaviors by grouping them together into descriptive categories called archetypes. Each archetype represents a related set of behaviors. In accordance with common images and patterns of leadership behavior, we identify the following four archetypes: the Strongman, the Transactor, the Visionary Hero, and the SuperLeader.[19]

The *Strongman* pattern of leadership concentrates on command and instruction to influence followers. We acknowledge that this archetype label sounds sexist, but historically this type of leadership behavior has been associated more with men than with women. A strongman's source of power is the coercion that stems from the authority of his/her position. It is a top-down type of leadership that produces a fear-based compliance in followers. The behaviors most frequently used by this leader are instruction, command, assigned goals, threat, intimidation, and reprimand. One good example of this type of leader is the military dictator who uses sheer power to coerce his followers.

The *Transactor* leader enters into an exchange relationship with followers. Rewards are the major source of influence, with the follower displaying a calculative compliance with the leader's wishes, in order to secure rewards that are controlled by the leader. The behaviors most frequently used by this leader are the dispensation of personal and material rewards in return for effort, performance, and loyalty. For instance, a leader may offer a raise to her subordinates if they achieve the goals that she sets for them.

The *Visionary Hero* leader is a source of inspiration to the follower. This leader uses a top-down vision to inspire and stimulate followers, who make emotional commitments based on the leader's vision and charisma. This leader uses behaviors such as communicating a vision, exhortation, inspiration and persuasion, and challenge to the status quo. Other terms that describe the visionary hero are transformational leader and charismatic leader. Modern-day examples include politicians who focus on outlining agendas and programs designed to inspire people to improve society.

The *SuperLeader* focuses primarily on the development of the follower. Sometimes called an "empowering" leader, this leader has a strength that can be super because it is based on the strength of many followers. These leaders lead others to lead themselves. The SuperLeader models, encourages, and reinforces follower initiative, self-responsibility, self-confidence, self-goal setting, positive opportunity thinking, and self-problem solving. Power is more balanced between the leader and the followers. In contrast to the other archetypes that focus on the leader, this viewpoint seeks to focus on the followers. Expected positive returns include heightened follower commitment and psychological ownership, especially the development of self-leadership skills in followers so that they can provide leadership for themselves.

How Leadership Affects Teams

Building on the four archetypes of leadership, we can now describe how various leadership influences affect teams. Another way of grouping the various leadership theories is to focus on two broad dimensions that underlie most perspectives of leadership. The first leadership dimension is concerned with the leader's power orientation. Some leaders (e.g., Strongman leaders) are very autocratic and tend to use commands and threats to get followers to comply with their wishes. Other leaders are more democratic and allow their followers to have substantial latitude in determining courses of direction (e.g., SuperLeaders). The second dimension centers on leader involvement. Some leaders are highly involved in day-to-day activities, whereas others are more "hands-off" and allow their followers a great deal of freedom. Combining these two dimensions yields a typology of leadership that we will use to illustrate the effects of leadership on teams. The typology is shown in Figure 3.2.[20]

The cell labels in the typology do not describe the leader behaviors; rather, they describe how a team typically reacts to the leadership behaviors associated with each cell. Thus, overpowering leadership occurs when the team is overpowered by the leader, whereas powerless leadership leaves the team—not necessarily the leader—powerless. Examining the typology provides us with a link between leader behaviors and the way teams tend to respond.

Source. G.L. Stewart and C.C. Manz, "Leadership for self-managing Work Teams: A Typology and Integrative Model," *Human Relations* 48(1995): 747–770.

Figure 3.2 Typology of leadership's effect on teams

Overpowering Leadership

An active and autocratic leader spends a lot of time imposing his/her will on the team. Strongman leaders are usually overpowering, and they are actively involved in everything the team does. They see their way as the right way to accomplish things. These tendencies often lead to the use of threat and intimidation in order to get team members to perform. Active and autocratic leaders can be effective in situations that require team members to quickly respond to the leader's requests. An example might be a military team facing battle; a clear image is that of many of the character roles enacted by the late actor John Wayne. In his movies John Wayne frequently portrayed a leader who coerced the teams he led. He would threaten them with dire consequences if they did not obey his commands. He would also use his large physical stature to intimidate team members into performing as he desired. This form of leadership was often beneficial because the teams he led usually performed fighting tasks that required exact obedience and minimal deviation from the leader's plan. Modern examples of overpowering leadership include Frank Lorenzo at Eastern Airlines and Al Dunlap at Sunbeam Corporation.

Unfortunately, active and autocratic leaders can overpower the creativity and enthusiasm of teams. Team members have few opportunities to do what they think is best when the leader is closely involved in all team activities. This can be problematic in may business organizations, particularly when teams are expected to come up with novel approaches to work. Instead of exhibiting creativeness, team members are submissive and succumb to the leader. They fail to make intellectual and creative contributions of thinking power. Business teams thus run the risk of becoming overpowered when their leader is both active and autocratic.

Powerless Leadership

A passive and autocratic leader is perhaps difficult to imagine. This type of leader is not closely involved in the day-to-day activities of the team. However, he or she retains significant control over the team and ultimately determines how the team will function. Many of these leaders fit the transactor archetype. They appear to give a team a great deal of latitude to make its own decisions, but freedom and autonomy quickly disappear when the team's choices are not congruent with the actions the leader desires. The leader may intermittently step in and take control of team activities for short periods of time. The leader may also use subtle contacts and pressure points to quietly influence the team. Either way the leader is autocratic in that he uses reward power to ensure that his desires are ultimately carried out by the team.

The CEO of the insurance firm described in Case 3.3 is a good example of a leader who leaves a team powerless. The leader instituted "self-managing" teams with the underlying objective of reducing the individual autonomy of team members. He helped ensure the selection of team leaders who would carry out his personal agenda. He also used strict rules and policies to control the teams. In the end, the teams became powerless to make choices about their work, and many team members reported decreasing levels of job satisfaction.

A major problem associated with a "hands-off" approach to autocratic leadership is therefore its failure to allow the team to develop the skills needed to manage its activities. Moreover, team members are unsure about what they should be doing, so they spend a great deal of time and energy in trying to determine what the leader wants. The work climate for teams experiencing this form of leadership is often very political. Team members battle with one another to become the leader's contact and thereby gain power to influence the team. Team members also fear the possible sanctions that might be imposed if their actions are not in line with the leader's desires, even though those desires may not be known to them. In the end, the team is left powerless to actually perform quality work.

Power-Building Leadership

An active and democratic leader can be beneficial for teams, especially in their early development stages. This type of leadership encompasses elements of both the Visionary Hero and the SuperLeader archetypes, and to a lesser degree the Transactor archetype. These leaders provide guidance and teach important skills; yet, they are careful to allow the team itself to exercise substantial discretion in determining how work will be done. They delegate, encourage, reinforce, and cooperate. They help create a vision of successful team self-leadership, and their main focus is on helping the team develop power to lead itself. They do this by teaching technical skills, self-leadership skills like goal setting, and conflict-reduction techniques. Active and democratic leaders are often thought of as great teachers because they help others learn how to lead themselves. This requires a particularly difficult balance of freedom and direction for team members. This means that the leader will sometimes allow team members to fail and learn from their mistakes. Such learning is a critical part of building power so that the team can eventually become proficient at leading itself.

Facilitators at the Fitzgerald Battery Plant (Case 3.1) effectively used leadership to build power within teams. A good example is the leader who refused to solve the problems that team members brought to him. The employee needed encouragement and some initial guidance; however, the leader refrained from simply providing the employee with an answer that would solve the problem for him. This action had the long-term effect of helping employees believe in their abilities. As future problems arose, team members were increasingly likely to resolve them without relying on the leader.

A leader who is highly involved in team activities will, nevertheless, exert substantial influence over the team, even if her underlying style is democratic. The strategic direction of the team is likely to be set by the leader. This can be beneficial when the team does not have the expertise and skills needed to truly lead itself.

Empowered Leadership

A passive and democratic leader allows the team to design its own work processes and to determine its strategic direction. This type of leadership is consistent with the SuperLeader archetype. The traditional roles of the leader are carried out predominantly by the team. However, this does not mean that the leader is not needed. The leader's role changes to facilitator and coach. Perhaps most importantly, the leader becomes a living model of desirable behavior. Modeling is a passive form of influence that is often more powerful than active forms. The leader also becomes a resource for the team when it needs help. Rather than actively guiding the team, the leader usually waits until the team requests her inputs. The leader also helps coordinate the team's efforts with the efforts of other teams and individuals in the organization. This can be particularly beneficial, especially when the leader is an advocate who protects the interests and autonomy of the team.

To some observers, the actions of a passive and democratic leader may not appear to be leadership at all, but this form of leadership is critical for truly self-leading teams. Passive leadership will likely fail if the team does not have capability to lead itself. Therefore, active democratic leadership should usually precede passive democratic leadership in the earlier stages of team development. Once a team has developed the needed skills, however, it is ready to exercise its discretion and determine its own work routines. This freedom can allow the team to unleash its creativity and thereby pursue new avenues for accomplishing work. In many cases, such empowerment can radically improve how work gets done, as well as encourage a sense of ownership over team outcomes, thus helping teams with passive democratic leaders to be effective over extended periods of time.

Supervisor Resistance to Teams

As implied in the discussion so far, leaders are an important key to the successful launch of teams. However, in many cases team leaders, especially those occupying roles more consistent with the traditional supervisor position, can represent a barrier that makes it impossible for teams to succeed. Supervisors often see teams as a threat to their power and role as a leader. This resistance became clear when the Charette Corporation decided to implement teams (see Case 3.2). The first-line supervisors initially resisted the transition to teams but eventually embraced the concept and helped ensure success for the warehouse teams.

A classic theory of organizational development and change can be used to summarize a process for helping supervisors to overcome initial resistance to teams.[21] The theory suggests a three-step change process: unfreezing, changing, refreezing. The *unfreezing* stage requires a breakdown of current attitudes and behaviors. The key at this stage of the process is to help managers feel a desire to change. Providing them with information about the potential improvements associated with teams is one method of cultivating this desire to change. Benchmarking with other organizations that have successfully implemented teams can be particularly helpful. This occurred at Charette when the consultant pointed out the benefits of teams. The managers gradually came to believe that teams could make their work more enjoyable and productive.

The *changing* stage requires first-line managers to learn new behaviors. Throughout this unit we have described many of the new roles that a team leader must enact, but these roles are often difficult to learn. A great deal of training is required before change can occur. At Charette this training consisted of role-playing exercises that were designed to help supervisors learn a new set of leadership skills. This was a very difficult and time-consuming process, but it had to be done to guarantee that supervisors had the skills required for adopting the new leadership style.

The final stage of *refreezing* requires the development of systems that ensure that newly learned leadership behaviors will be transferred to the workplace. This can be done with compensation systems that reward managers for developing teams rather than solely for short-term profits. Although this step may not have been fully implemented at Charette, a follow-up four years later did find that leaders were continuing to use many of the skills they learned during the transition to a team-based work system.

Although the process of unfreezing, changing, and refreezing provides a nice framework for understanding dimensions of change, the refreezing step may not be applicable for many contemporary organizations. These organizations change so rapidly that continuous change and learning may be a more appropriate model. From this perspective, supervisor resistance can be decreased by creating a learning environment where supervisors are encouraged to continually search for new and better methods of leading teams.[22]

WHAT WE HOPE YOU LEARN IN THIS UNIT

After studying this unit, you should have a better understanding of the internal processes that take place in teams. Understanding these processes, and being able to apply them to work teams, can help you facilitate team effectiveness.

The first process that we examined is how teams develop over time. An understanding of the five development stages is critical for discerning the troubles that a team may be facing. The proper method for facilitating a newly formed team will of necessity be very different from the method for facilitating an established team. An effective member or team manager can significantly aid a team by helping it to move through the conflict stage. The norming stage then becomes critical, for events and statements made by leaders can have a significant effect on the team's long-term development and success. Teams that develop good norms and a sense of cohesion in this stage will be more likely to reach the critical stage of performing.

Our discussion about socialization also pointed out the importance of early events in the relationship between teams and individuals. Teams need to accommodate the individual requirements and desires of team members, whereas team members need to subjugate some of their own interests for the betterment of the team. Effectively managing this give-and-take process is one way to ensure that team members are not only gaining satisfaction from their interactions with the team, but are also equipping them to significantly contribute to performance.

In order to influence others, team members should possess a power base. Legitimate and coercive power are becoming less frequent in team environments. However, both individuals and teams can benefit from acknowledging expert power. If team members are able to influence others in areas where they have valuable expertise, then the team is better able to take advantage of diverse skills. Influence strategies should also fit the situation in which they are used. For the most part, teams succeed when they use direct and logical strategies that foster open communication and a reliance on relevant information.

Conflict, though perhaps inevitable in teams, is not always a bad thing. When conflict centers around tasks rather than people, it can have the effect of guaranteeing that all points of view are taken into account when making decisions. Usually the best method for accomplishing conflict resolution is to use integrative bargaining tactics, especially when addressing important issues.

Leadership has a particularly strong influence on team processes. Externally appointed leaders tend to exercise more control over a team than do internally elected leaders; thus, leadership structure should be matched with intended levels of team self-management. Specific leader behaviors also have varying effects on teams. A Strongman type of leadership tends to overpower a team. Ineffective use of Transactor leadership maintains a subtle form of leader influence that can leave a team powerless to establish its own direction. Visionary leadership can help establish a goal for the team to grow in its capacity for self-leadership but may interfere with team growth and development in later stages. SuperLeadership allows team members themselves to solve problems and set their direction. However, passive aspects of Super Leadership should not be used until a team has developed the skills needed to lead itself.

NOTES FOR UNIT 3

1. These development stages were introduced by B. W. Tuckman, "Stages of Small Group Development Revisited," *Group and Organization Studies* 2 (1965): 419–427.
2. See P. E. Mudrack, "Defining Group Cohesiveness: A Legacy of Confusion?" *Small Group Behavior* 20 (1989): 37–49 for a review of the cohesiveness issue.
3. The concept of groupthink is developed in I. L. Janis, *Victims of Groupthink*, 2nd ed. (Boston: Houghton-Mifflin, 1982).
4. A summary of these findings is presented by B. Mullen and C. Copper, "The Relation Between Group Cohesiveness and Performance: An Integration," *Psychological Bulletin* 115 (1994): 210–227.
5. See D. C. Feldman, "The Development and Enforcement of Group Norms," *Academy of Management Review* 9 (1984): 47–53.
6. See K. L. Bettenhausen and J. Keith Murnighan, "The Development of an Intragroup Norm and the Effects of Interpersonal and Structural Challenges," *Administrative Science Quarterly* 36 (1991): 20–35.
7. This idea of different stages of effectiveness is developed by C. J. G. Gersick, "Revolutionary Change Theories: A Multilevel Exploration of the Punctuated Equilibrium Paradigm," *Academy of Management Review* 16 (1991): 10–36. See also C. J .G. Gersick, "Time and Transition in Work Teams: Toward a New Model of Group Development," *Academy of Management Journal* 31 (1988): 9–41.
8. This concept of parting ceremonies has been developed by S. G. Harris and R. I. Sutton, "Functions of Parting Ceremonies in Dying Organizations," *Academy of Management Journal* 29 (1986): 5–30.
9. A good review of different perspectives on socialization, including its relationships with group development, is J. P. Wanous, A. E. Reichers, and S. D. Malik, "Organizational Socialization and Group Development: Toward an Integrative Perspective," *Academy of Management Review* 9 (1984): 670–683.
10. These concepts about power are taken from J. R. P. French and B. Raven, "The Bases of Social Power," in D. Cartwright (ed.), *Studies in Social Power* (Ann Arbor, MI: Institute for Social Research, 1959).
11. See D. Kipnis, S. M. Schmidt, C. Swaffin-Smith, and I. Wilkinson, "Patterns of Managerial Influence: Shotgun Managers, Tacticians, and Bystanders," *Organizational Dynamics* 12, no. 3 (1984): 58–67.
12. This concept was developed by J. Platt, "Social Traps," *American Psychologist* 28 (1973): 641–645.
13. These two types of conflict, as well as their effect on performance, are discussed by K. A. Jehn, "A Multimethod Examination of Benefits and Detriments of Intragroup Conflict," *Administrative Science Quarterly* 40 (1995): 256–282. A similar perspective is presented by A. C. Amason, "Distinguishing the Effects of Functional and Dysfunctional Conflict on Strategic Decision Making: Resolving a Paradox for Top Management Teams," *Academy of Management Journal* 39 (1996): 123–148.

14. The four strategies for conflict resolution are taken from D. R. Forsyth, *Group Dynamics,* 2nd ed. (Pacific Grove, CA: Brooks/Cole, 1990).

15. See K. A. Jehn, "A Multimethod Examination of Benefits and Detriments of Intragroup Conflict," *Administrative Science Quarterly* 40 (1995): 256–282. Also, J. K. Murnighan and D. E. Conlon, "The Dynamics of Intense Work Groups: A Study of British String Quartets," *Administrative Science Quarterly* 36 (1991): 165–186.

16. This section on leadership structure also draws extensively on H. P. Sims, Jr., and C. C. Manz, *Company of Heroes: Unleashing the Power of Self-Leadership* (New York: Wiley, 1996).

17. Different styles of leadership are extensively discussed in H. P. Sims and C. C. Manz, *Company of Heroes: Unleashing the Power of Self-Leadership* (New York: Wiley, 1996). And C. C. Manz and H. P. Sims, Jr., *SuperLeadership* (New York: Berkeley, 1989).

18. Although the specifics vary greatly, this general perspective is seen in several classic leadership theories including the following: P. Hersey and K. H. Blanchard, *Management of Organizational Behavior,* 3rd ed. (Upper Saddle River, NJ: Prentice-Hall, 1982). F. E. Fiedler, *A Theory of Leadership Effectiveness* (New York: McGraw-Hill, 1982). R. R. Blake and J. S. Mouton, "How to Choose a Leadership Style," *Training and Development Journal* 36 (1982): 39–46.

19. The four archetypes are taken from H. P. Sims, Jr., and C. C. Manz, *Company of Heroes: Unleashing the Power of Self-Leadership* (New York: Wiley, 1996).

20. This typology and much of the discussion are drawn from G. L. Stewart and C. C. Manz, "Leadership for Self-managing Work Teams: A Typology and Integrative Model," *Human Relations* 48 (1995): 747–770.

21. This three-step model was developed by K. Lewin, "Group Decision and Social Change," in E. E. Maccoby, T. M. Newcomb, and E. L. Hartley, eds., *Readings in Social Psychology,* pp. 163–226 (New York: Holt, Rinehart, and Winston, 1958). For a specific application of this model to supervisor resistance, see G. L. Stewart and C. C. Manz, "Understanding and Overcoming Supervisor Resistance During the Transition to Employee Empowerment," in W. Pasmore and R. W. Woodman, eds., *Research in Organizational Change and Development* 10 (1997): 169–196.

22. For an overview of the learning perspective, see P. M. Senge, *The Fifth Discipline: The Art and Practice of the Learning Organization* (New York: Currency-Doubleday, 1990).

CASE

3.2

Overcoming Supervisor Resistance at Charrette

This case was written by Charles C. Manz, David Keating, and Anne Donnellon.[1]

Success or failure of teams is often dependent on effective leadership. In this case we describe how managers of a warehouse operation prepared themselves to lead self-managing teams. The managers themselves formed a support team that aided them in their transition from traditional supervisors to team facilitators. They struggled with accepting and learning a new role for creating positive interactions between team members.

Charrette Corporation, located in the greater Boston area, is a nonunion wholesale distributor and retailer of architectural, engineering, and commercial art supplies and furnishings, with a current annual sales volume exceeding $50 million. It was cofounded in 1964 by the company's current chairman and its current president, who together totally own the company.

Our focus was on the organization's warehouse distribution center operation. The distribution center is broken into four basic parts: receiving/stocking, order filling, order packing, and shipping. The study centered on managers directly involved with the order-filling and order-packing workforce, approximately 65 persons.

The core management team consisted of seven persons: the director of operations, who is responsible for coordinating all aspects of the distribution center's four basic parts; the day and night managers who oversee all day-to-day operational details of order filling and order packing; and four day and night order-packing and -filling supervisors, who report directly to those two managers. The four supervisors handle all minute-to-minute concerns regarding workforce and production flow and because of heavy order volume, they often fill and pack orders.

Most of the core management team had been with the company for at least four years, about five times longer than the average worker, and most had come up through the ranks of order filling and order packing. The usual management style had been a traditional autocratic approach with a punitive emphasis. The typical perception of a good manager/leader in the organization in the past was one of doing "whatever it took" to get the job done, with a heavy emphasis on exerting tight control over the workforce.

The old management approach was not paying off. The operations efficiency and productivity levels were problematic. Current operating statistics on an annualized basis estimated absenteeism to be about 10 percent, turnover 250 percent, productivity utilization 60 percent, and errors at about 1.8 percent of all orders. Average cost of inefficiencies was estimated to be about 30 percent of earnings. Despite the clear need for change, the move to a self-managing team approach, decided upon by the CEO and a consultant, posed a direct conflict in management philosophy with the old management system and required significant unlearning on the part of the managers.

Several workforce characteristics made this an especially interesting organization to study in terms of the transition of management thinking. First, the average age of the employees involved in the change was 19, significantly younger than many other self-managed team applications. A majority of the workers were recent high school graduates or dropouts. Coupled with the relatively young age of the workforce were several other sources of tension and personal difficulties for the workers. There was some covert tension within the racially mixed workforce that consisted of approximately 73 percent white, 12.5 percent black, and 14.5 percent Hispanic employees. This tension showed up in hostile written exchanges on the bathroom walls and some uncooperative behavior during normal work operations. Often white male employees mocked the speech and behavior patterns of their minority counterparts. Rarely did white and black employees work together or socialize. In addition, several employees had been arrested for possession and dealing of illegal drugs.

All of these factors made an organizational change to the concept of worker self-managing teams particularly challenging for members of management. It was apparent to management that organizational change was needed to improve employee productivity and morale, but whether this young and troubled workforce could handle a self-managed team environment was uncertain. The managers' role in the transition and functioning of these teams would be critical to achieving a successful implementation.

Gathering Information

We used several methods for gathering information in studying the transition. First, the second author of this case (Keating) was a consultant to the company. He proposed and paved the way for implementing the transition to self-managed teams. (Enlisting the help of an outside consultant is not a necessity for introducing teams, but many organizations find the support and guidance of a consultant to be useful.) He worked with the company for a little more than two months. During this period, he analyzed the existing operating approach, proposed a self-managed work team design, and then worked directly with the core management team to facilitate their preparation for the change. This close work enabled very rich, first-hand observation and interaction with the management team during its transition toward a team structure. Detailed documentation was kept in a journal during this process.

In addition, multiple interviews and discussions were conducted with individual members of the management team from the time the proposed change approach was accepted until implementation was begun. Some of the key interactions of managers concerning managing in an employee self-managing environment were videotaped. The taping focused primarily on the role of managers as they began to practice and converse about managing teams of workers who were being encouraged and helped to be increasingly self-managing. The taping thus provided an especially detailed source of insight into the managers' thoughts, feelings and behavior during the transition to teams and self-management.[2]

Primary Themes of the Managerial Transition

Our study of the management team's struggle with the pending organizational change identified several primary themes. These episodes not only revealed the process but also seemed to provide the raw material for the construction and evolution of the change in management philosophy and action.

Theme 1: Initial Suspicion, Uncertainty, and Resistance

During the transition, the managers felt threatened by and resented the forthcoming change. They were concerned over having what might be viewed as past personal performance failings come to the attention of upper management. They also resented the idea that the change plan would be credited to the consultant, and they were sure that the new system would fail. In other words, they believed that an analysis of the system that revealed a need for change threatened to make them look bad. They also perceived that the new work design plan, even if it worked, would only enhance the image of the consultant and not the managers.

The day manager led the initial resistance. The existing system, he said, had "evolved over time" and was "designed for maximum flexibility" (that is, *his* flexibility in assigning orders to and maintaining control over the workers). He believed that if a team approach were instituted, orders would not be filled and shipped, since more of the decisions and responsibilities would be left to the employees and would be out of his control. He feared that missed shipments would cost him his job. In addition, gaining approval from senior management for the new system would require exposing the distribution center's inefficiencies, and he feared that this would cost him his job (especially precious because of a wife, a child, and another baby "on the way"). To overcome this resistance, the consultant had to ensure that this manager was insulated from senior management.

Senior management approved the new approach without firing the day manager, but he continued to resist the change. His response to the news that senior management had approved the change was to throw his cigarette lighter across his desk in disgust. Through the first several days of meetings, he displayed closed body language and offered little to group discussion.

At the end of one of the first days, he directly confronted the consultant with the argument that the design would mainly benefit him—the consultant. After the consultant pointed to the potential benefits to the organization, the manager again raised his accusation of personal gain for the consultant, which the consultant then acknowledged. (This manager later realized the positive possibilities of the new system and publicly apologized to the consultant. He began making excellent contributions to the change and was often instrumental in helping the core group develop a language for their new roles as facilitators. He was thus given the nickname "Wordman.")

A variety of comments made during these early stages of the transition indicated an attachment to the company's traditional style of management. One manager emphasized the inadequacies of the workers and pointed out, "We have to step in and solve the problem for them." Another manager revealed his impatience with the shortcomings of the workforce: "We can't be bothered by people that don't work." In general, the core group's behaviors suggested a belief that their workers were too immature and irresponsible to handle the change.

In summary, the initial responses to the change were suspicion, uncertainty, and resistance. Conversations during the early core management meetings placed a significant emphasis on these concerns. These conversations appeared to serve as a venting process for the internal pressure felt by some of the core management group members, and they seemed to be symptomatic of a last-ditch effort to stop the change.

Theme 2: Gradual Realization of the Positive Possibilities in the New System

The second theme was the managers' growing belief that the new system could work. This realization gradually emerged after hours of struggle and discussion about the possibilities and challenges of the team approach. The belief that the workers were competent and responsible emerged as the managers began to grasp the potential advantages of the new system. In addition, the core managers began to recognize that they had to assume a new role as facilitators, moving away from traditional thinking about management.

As they went through their transition, the core managers questioned and tested the boundaries of the new system. Questions ranged from "Can groups really facilitate themselves?" to such basic operational questions as, "Can groups train new people (a task previously assigned only to managers)?" These managers gradually switched from questioning their employees' competence to exploring ways of empowering them with the authority to perform management tasks.

In addition, the core group discussed a plan to have workers call customers for feedback on orders for which their group was responsible. The managers, recognizing that the company's success depends on courteous employees and accurate orders, voiced their concern that workers might be vulgar or unable to respond diplomatically to an angry customer. Nevertheless, they decided that it was an idea worth pursuing. This communication with customers would help build worker identification with and empathy for customers—a radical shift away from managers' previous belief that they should "keep the animals in the warehouse as far away from customers as possible!"

The core managers developed an understanding that the program's success depended on workers' placing significant value on group membership, that is, peer acceptance. This belief grew out of the managers' frustration over their inability to control absenteeism and unprofessional behavior. As they probed the issue with the help of the consultant, they realized that line authority over a worker does not necessarily equate to behavioral control. From this realization, the managers reached the conclusion that peer pressure often is more effective than managerial threats and that a worker would be less likely to call in sick if he or she had to face team members the next morning.

The core group came to realize that the new system might also change some enjoyable aspects of their old roles, such as identifying and developing rising stars. At first, they were concerned that their new role of facilitator was too indirect to be effective. Over time, they came to accept the idea that as workers became self-managing, they would have more time to develop key people, although in a new manner.

Finally, the core group developed an understanding of their new roles as resources to their teams, as well as a support group among themselves. Previously when workers were unsure of what to do, the managers would either tell them what to do or step in and solve the problem themselves. As the core group developed, they created and practiced techniques for facilitating worker problem solving. These techniques centered on asking questions rather than giving answers and allowing workers to make mistakes without reprimand as they struggled to solve problems on their own.

Throughout the whole process, the core group became a resource to itself. In the beginning, they doubted the value of spending so much of their time in discussion. "Well I'm off to group therapy," one manager would quip as he left for the meetings. By the end of the process, they were pleased with their ability to wrestle with complicated issues. They had solved problems that had stumped the department for years and attributed this success to the group process.

The group developed its own informal leaders and inside jokes. One member could always be counted on to supply candy during the three- to four-hour meetings. Other members used humor to break frequent tension. One member became known as "The Tower of Compassion," because of such statements as, "We can't be bothered by people who don't fit in (to the new program)." The group also occasionally engaged in storytelling about important accomplishments of the past.

Officially, they named themselves the Advisory Board. Their charter was to create policy and serve as informal judicial review for worker grievances. As a group, they took on increasingly more difficult tasks, including a multimedia presentation (proposing their plan for the new self-managed system) to the company's chairman and senior management.

In summary, conversations and interactions within the management team revealed their gradual realization of the potential benefits of the new system. During this shift in their beliefs and attitudes, the managers learned from and supported each other in a manner most members of the group felt to be more effective than any previous management training.

The final two themes reveal our findings from detailed analysis of some of these conversations, particularly the conversations captured on videotape. Our intent here is to show how the managers' interaction produced the new roles and behavior required for managing the self-managed.

Theme 3: Wrestling with a New Role

Throughout the process, the core management group wrestled with the question about their new role: What exactly is a facilitator? How is it different from or better than being a manager? In other words, they were asking, "How does the philosophy of team self-management influence managerial behavior?" This influence was seen in frequent references to the self-management philosophy as a guide to communication behavior. These references were mentioned by the managers of the core group, the consultant, and occasionally by the participating managers during role-playing. Whether the managers would grasp the full meaning of this philosophy and alter their image of their role ultimately would determine how effective they would be in managing the teams.

In role-playing about a team seeking to remove one of its members, one manager proposed to meet with each of the team members individually to determine the reasons for the request and the degree to which each person supported it. Recognizing this behavior as a violation of the team philosophy, one of his colleagues asked him to consider "what that will do to the group mentality."

Another manager, while practicing his new role as a facilitator, was reminded that "the facilitator's role is not to work with the individual but with the group." These managers did not overlook the challenge of managing both the individual and the team, as was obvious when one manager posed the dilemma: "What do we do if a person (whose teammates want him out) wants to stay in the group?" After much discussion of alternative responses, he stated the philosophy that was to guide all such communication with the teams: "So what we all agreed is, no matter what we do, we're gonna do everything on our part to keep the group intact." When another manager proposed dealing with team complaints about a poor performer by saying, "Maybe we say, 'Hey somebody's gotta baby-sit him; we'll do that on a rotating basis,'" he was quickly reminded that the facilitator role did not include baby-sitting.

The managers openly explored the motivation for adopting the philosophy of being a facilitator. One manager proposed that "the facilitator has a vested interest in making the group work." Other managers supported this argument by pointing out that the manager's motivation was more than monetary: "This group is his. If they fail, he fails. There's the psychological thing of 'I failed; I wasn't able to pull this group together.'"

Perhaps the most compelling evidence that the managers were consciously grappling with their new role was in the following statement: "They know you're in an uncomfortable role, and they're gonna push and push and push, and when you slip, they're gonna say, 'There he goes, acting like a son of a bitch again,' and that's gonna undermine the whole effort. They're gonna look at the whole thing as a manipulative effort." This manager clearly understands the challenge of the new role, and he implies that effective performance of the role will depend on the managers' genuine acceptance of the self-management philosophy.

Acting in their new roles as facilitators of self-managing teams, managers must be aware of what the new philosophy logically entails. Two such subthemes were discussed in the conversations we observed. One was the argument that the self-managing teams "can solve anything." The other subtheme dealt with appropriate styles of communicating within the team.

In scenarios that dealt with self-managing teams as potential sources of interpersonal conflict and coordination problems, these managers occasionally had to remind one another of an important aspect of the self-management philosophy: the teams were formed to be problem-solving groups. They proposed language that would remind the teams of this aspect of the new structure. During a role-play, the "facilitator" affirmed his team by saying, "We can solve it." When a member of the team apologized, the facilitator reminded him, "Apologies don't solve problems." Thus, they coached one another in the underlying philosophy of their new role and at the same time identified behavior that would be effective in such a situation.

The subtheme dealing with appropriate communication styles in the teams appeared to be more of a problem for the group of managers, particularly when serving as a guide to selecting and acting out effective behavior. On a number of occasions, the consultant responded to a role-play by asking the managers to critique and correct the language used by a management team member. A manager's response to one role-playing situation was the following:

> He just said he "snorted his paycheck," but that's not relevant. It doesn't matter why he's out; his absenteeism is the problem. You can't let anyone attack him. You've got to let just enough negative energy out to make him realize he's done something wrong that he needs to correct. And anything else is unnecessary and destructive. Insults are unacceptable.

The consultant argued that constructive communication is the goal of facilitation; the facilitator should counter destructive behavior and instruct team members in how to express themselves constructively. One manager, however, expressed concern about the potential for altering the language without solving the problem.

> I don't think that (saying he snorted his paycheck) was an insult . . . and I know he's got a drug problem. I've seen him, and it affects his work.

This interaction and others indicated the tension felt between working to foster open, honest communication of thoughts and feelings and working to block communication that could degenerate into emotional outbursts. The consultant put the problem on the table as a policy issue: "Is it going to be the role of the facilitator to say we're not going to use language that's inflammatory in this room, or do you feel it's the way they express themselves and you shouldn't inhibit that?"

The question of how to act when team members communicated negative emotion honestly was not directly posed or resolved by the consultant or the managers. However, guides to action were articulated, with the managers left to find their own motivation and produce their own responses: "That might be something to apply down the road," or "It would be unwise to inhibit them initially, they need to be able to swear to get loosened up."

Theme 4: Learning a New Language

The purpose of the training role-plays during the managers' transition to self-managing teams was to provide opportunities for the managers to rehearse appropriate behaviors for their new roles. The consultant told them, "We want you to have as many possible scenarios as could come up. We want you to be as equipped as possible so you don't sit there and say, 'Good grief I'm in this new role and I have anarchy on my hands,' and your first reaction is to pull out the fists and go back to being a supervisor again. When that happens, we've lost."

Preparing as a group, they experimented with the new ways of speaking and tested the effectiveness of this new speech with one another. For example, after one role-play, a manager offered the following critique to his colleague: "But doesn't that put me on the defensive again?" Another responded, "That sounds kinda hokey to me."

In these discussions of possible conversations with their teams, the managers and consultant produced action plans, or "scripts," for dealing with various contingencies. These discussions dealt with physical arrangements, word choices and sequences of dialogue, and even audience expectations and reactions.

Prompted by the consultant, one manager presented his plan of action for addressing team concerns about a member whose absenteeism was affecting their bonuses. The manager began by specifying that he would not have the accused person sit next to him, "just to make this individual not feel separated. If he's next to me, they'll be looking at me, and he'll feel their stares."

In the role-play of this interaction, another participant responded to the question of whether a person was entitled to a leave of absence by saying he would need to appeal to "the judicial board (a group created to deal with special issues such as this)." This discussion caused one of the managers to react negatively to the group's name: "'judicial board' is kinda strong. Doesn't that sound kinda scary?" Several other possible names for the body were proposed, including the "People's Board." (The interaction concluded with references to a popular television show, "The People's Court.") The managers realized that they needed to develop a name that commanded respect and yet was not intimidating.

In working to identify appropriate ways for the facilitators to communicate with their groups, the managers recognized that the team context heightened the importance of the words chosen to deal with workers. After one role-play, for example, one manager pointed out, "But three people (on the team) have a specific agenda they want addressed, and to just skirt around it and not get to the meat of it might be unwise." With this comment, he called his colleagues' attention to the fact that, in team conversations, the facilitator's words must be chosen with regard not just to the self-management philosophy or to creating the desired effect on the focal individual but to the audience of other team members as well. Another manager offered an interesting perspective on the team audience: "They've always seen authority figures, and they've never been invited to be a peer of that person. We're inviting them to be peers with us, and they're not gonna buy that right away." Obviously, he was concerned with the audience's expectations, which are based on prior experience and understanding of the roles each party typically plays. His words served as a sober reminder to his colleagues of the magnitude of change that self-managed teams represented in this company and the challenge of communicating effectively as a facilitator.

By this point in the process, all of the managers were convinced of the challenge they faced as team facilitators. They applied considerable energy to developing and practicing the verbal skills required for effective performance of the facilitator role. They had to establish the underlying motivation for their new role in their own minds, produce new plans to act out when confronted with difficult situations that they anticipated, and stop occasionally to reconsider audience expectations. Another obvious skill was to recall (or improvise) and deliver the right words at the right time.

The role-plays offered an opportunity to practice these skills. Dialogue lines that flowed from their newly developed language such as the following were quite common in the conversations: "I'm not here to solve the problem. I'm here to assist you in solving the problem." In the group training context, the role-plays also provided opportunities for feedback. For example, when, in the heat of dialogue, one manager used the line, "That's not up to me; it's up to you," he was reminded that the facilitator is also "part of the team, so you should have said, 'It's up to us.'" In self-evaluations, two of the managers said that they shouldn't have used the term "individual."

Although the bulk of their conversations was generally devoted to creating and practicing this new language, the managers and consultant also recognized the need for skill in improvising. As one manager pointed out, "They (the team) will push you. They know you're in an uncomfortable role, and they'll push you to react. It's gonna get heated, confrontational." Other managers proposed ways of developing the improvisational skill to deal with these pressures—for example, "Before you call a meeting, before you go to a meeting, it's up to the facilitator to assess the situation. You should know what's going on with your group; you should be able to assess what topics are gonna come up in the conversation and should come with all the ammunition." The consultant seconded this idea and advised, "Don't get thrown offguard, and if you are, don't get flustered. Throw it back to the group."

Summary

One of the challenging and often-overlooked aspects of implementing a change to teams, particularly self-managing work teams, concerns the transition from supervisor to facilitator. Frequently in the literature, the implementation of this innovative work design approach is viewed primarily in terms of the challenges and difficulties posed for workers. When supervisors and managers are considered, it is usually an afterthought—after the implementation has already occurred and when these individuals are trying to go about their business of managing. The initial transition of managers—after they learn about a self-managing team system but before it is actually implemented—is critical to the ultimate success of the team approach.

This transition for managers is challenging for two primary reasons: they experience a perceived loss of power and control as they realize that their subordinates are to become their own managers, and they recognize that their repertoire of management skills, often developed over years of experience and struggle, will become somewhat obsolete. Consequently, they are expected to learn a whole new set of managerial skills that they are not certain they can successfully master and apply. Managers' adjustment to these perceived threats and challenges was the primary focus of our study.

The warehouse distribution center of Charrette Corporation was a good one for examining the adjustments required of managers facing the transition to self-managed teams. The employees were part of a very young and perhaps troubled workforce. In addition, the dominant traditional management style used in the operation was autocratic, with an emphasis on punishment. Indeed, the managers we studied faced a significant challenge in establishing ways that they could act out a new role to help the system succeed in their organization.

The story examined here underlines the critical role that supervisory and managerial training fulfills during this sensitive transition. Managers can make or break a team implementation. Training is a critical element that helps to overcome initial suspicion and develop necessary facilitator skills and behaviors. In many ways, this transition might be described as the foundation for the future success or failure of the new work system.

Epilogue

Four years later, teams at the Charrette Corporation continued to achieve steady productivity improvements (approximately 10 percent per year), and the overall cost savings approached 10 to 20 percent of earnings. Quality levels averaged 99.8 percent of all customer items requested.

The management group, including supervisors, was still in place in the warehouse. The teams themselves had been reduced from five or six members per team to two members per team, but they retained their cross-functional nature; that is, one member picks items from the shelf, and the other packages them. This cross-functionality contributed to the high-quality levels being achieved. The management group decided to reduce the team size because of what they described as a need to reduce the communication needs inherent in larger teams. One manager noted, "Communication needs get in the way of getting the work done." This viewpoint and decision to reduce team size may indicate some lapse into the prior more traditional management style. Indeed, the transition to self-managed teams can be a very lengthy and stubborn process.

Nevertheless, the management group indicated that it could have neither achieved nor maintained the productivity, quality assurance, attendance, and turnover goals it has achieved without the system. The team system remained operational, effective, and supported by the implementation team, as well as senior management.

KEY LESSONS FROM THIS CASE

1. The transition to teams is very challenging for middle-level managers. Resistance by these managers often creates a stumbling block that inhibits team success.

2. Different constituencies of people (e.g., leaders, consultants, employees) often experience conflict with one another during the transition to teams. This conflict can be beneficial when it focuses on differences in ideas rather than personal attacks.

3. Teams must work through the conflict that is prevalent in the storming stage before they can perform effectively. In this case the conflict was resolved through direct and rational influence strategies.

4. Manager resistance can often be reduced by helping managers form a type of team where they develop positive interaction processes and support one another through a difficult transition.

5. Managers asked to lead teams are likely to experience four stages:

   Stage 1: Initial suspicion, uncertainty, and resistance

   The move to self-managing teams is frequently viewed as an indication of ineffectiveness in the managers' previous behavior. Also, teams are seen as benefiting someone else (e.g., the consultant) and ultimately destined to fail.

   Stage 2: Gradual realization of the positive possibilities offered by self-managing teams

   After hours of struggle and discussion, managers begin to see that teams offer many benefits that go beyond traditional management approaches: constructive peer pressure within teams, employee development of empathy for the customer, freeing up of managers' time for developing key people, and others.

   Stage 3: Understanding of their new leadership role

   Managers struggle with questions, such as, What is a facilitator? How does self-management influence managerial behavior?

   Stage 4: Learning a new language

   The managers develop and rehearse a new vocabulary and new communication scripts for leading self-managed employees. Through role-playing, the managers identify and develop the verbal skills that form the core of their new leadership role.

6. Training and learning opportunities to help middle managers through the transition to their new leadership role are a powerful method of encouraging team success.

NOTES FOR CASE 3.2

1. We sincerely appreciate the cooperation of Charrette Corporation and especially Lionel Spiro (chairman) in making this case possible.

    A number of sources were very helpful in preparing this case. These include Charles C. Manz and Henry P. Sims, Jr., *Superleadership: Leading Others to Lead Themselves* (New York: Berkeley, 1990) and Charles C. Manz and Henry P. Sims, Jr., "Leading Workers to Lead Themselves: The External Leadership of Self-Managing Work Teams," *Administrative Science Quarterly* 32 (1987): 106–128. Other helpful sources on the challenges that teamwork poses for professional employees, managers, executives, and organizations include forthcoming publications by Anne Donnellon: "The Meaning of Team Work," and "Crossfunctional Teams in Product Development: Accommodating the Organization Structure to the Team Process," *Journal of Product Innovation Management.*

2. For information on methods for analyzing conversations in organizations, see Anne Donnellon, Barbara Fray, and Michael Bougan, "Communication, Meaning and Organizational Action," *Administrative Science Quarterly* 31 (1986): 43–55.

CASE

$$\langle 3.3 \rangle$$

Using Team Processes to Decrease Individual Autonomy

This case was written by Charles C. Manz and Harold L. Angle.[1]

Do self-managing teams increase worker autonomy? This case addresses this question by illustrating interaction processes within two teams that work in an insurance firm. Although the teams were labeled "self-managing," strong external leadership was prevalent, and the introduction of teams actually reduced individual autonomy for many team members. Conflict existed between the interests of individuals and the interests of the group as a whole. Team processes deteriorated to the point were team members were coordinating their efforts through rules rather than through social interactions.

This case describes an independent insurance firm, specializing in industrial casualty loss coverage, that had recently introduced work teams. This story is especially interesting because the teams were seemingly designed with a high degree of team-level self-management. However, the insurance industry has historically intended to emphasize individual self-management. In this case, introducing self-managing teams had the effect of placing limits on individual freedom and control. The case addresses the question, "In an industry having a deeply ingrained cultural norm of individualism, can team self-management come to represent a loss of personal control?"

The Company and the Team System

The organization is an independent property and casualty insurance firm that employed 32 people at the time we studied it. The firm was founded in 1941—a time when the

independent operation, consisting of one or two agents supported by one or two sec-
retaries, was the industry standard. Typically, even when multi-agent organizations were
established, these tended to be loose associations of loners, each having a network of
highly personal relationships with clients. As a rule, there was little need for coordination, and each account executive operated within a set of rules and procedures, as a relatively independent agent.

In the mid-1970s, changes in the legislative environment led to strong competitive
pressures in the insurance industry. Efficiency (e.g., in developing client insurance programs, in collection policies) and synergy (optimizing combined efforts) in the efforts
of different persons within an agency became very important. Many of the single-agent
establishments were either forced out of business or forced to merge into multi-agent
organizations. Despite the economic pressures that made such changes necessary, this
move was frequently a difficult transition for agents accustomed to individual autonomy.

Less than a year before we began our research, a recently hired vice-president and
chief operating officer became acting chief executive officer (CEO). One of his initial acts
was to restructure the firm into a set of self-managing work teams. The team philosophy was explained to the employees when the system was introduced, and teams were
encouraged to make decisions and solve their problems jointly.

The work system appeared similar to designs used in self-managing team applications
in other industries. Within established company guidelines, work teams were expected
to be self-managing units that carried out the activities needed for cooperatively acquiring and servicing accounts. The CEO's apparent intent was to pass on what were formerly management responsibilities to the teams, with the intended result of more efficient
work performance. At the same time, the CEO felt that the company needed to increase
its organization and coordination of work efforts. He hoped that the teams would help
him achieve efficiencies that would boost the firm's profitability. Thus, although the teams
were similar in appearance to self-managing teams found in other work settings (in which
team members coordinate their efforts on tasks and work together to solve team problems and make joint decisions), they were apparently implemented with the ultimate objective of increasing the influence of top-level management.

Under the new system, three teams were created. The senior team consisted of the
more experienced sales producers (an industry term for agents who bring in premium
money), along with administrative assistants (referred to as production assistants) and
other support personnel. The junior team was similar in design except that its members
were the more junior producers in the firm. Finally, the small accounts team was made
up entirely of administrative personnel (no sales producers were included) and handled
all small accounts (those that brought in annual premiums less than $500). Our primary
focus is on the dynamics that occurred in the senior and junior teams following the introduction of the self-managed team system.

Organization Themes

The Research

Through a series of interviews, two group meetings with team members, a questionnaire,
and observation of the organization at work, we discovered several themes that reveal
how the internal processes of these teams led to decreased autonomy for individual
workers.

At two group meetings, one for members of the senior team and one for members
of the junior team, we asked, "Considering the recent change to the team system, how

has the change: (a) helped you, and (b) hindered you in accomplishing what you would like to in your job?" First, team members, independently and silently, generated written lists of answers to the question. After a discussion of the combined ideas generated from all the lists, each individual privately rated each item on a scale ranging from 1 (very important) to 5 (not at all important).

Interviews were conducted with employees at all levels of the organization. First, a series of interviews was conducted with the CEO over a period of about four months. The CEO was very articulate and appeared to be open and candid, as well as highly motivated to provide complete information during the interviews. Each interview session with him lasted about two hours and was kept flexible to focus on issues that emerged during the course of the discussions. Interviews were also conducted with seven members from the senior and junior teams.

Our observations of the work system during each of our visits to the organization led to a better general understanding of the team system and provided valuable insights that helped us to interpret the other information we collected. Finally, we prepared a questionnaire based in part on information obtained from our other study methods. The questionnaire focused on such issues as employee satisfaction, feelings of autonomy, degree of cooperation, performance, and quality of service to clients. Based on these sources, we discovered four primary themes.

Team Rationale: Self-Management—or Coordination, Efficiency, and Control?

Team processes did provide some distinct coordination and efficiency advantages. One junior team member noted that the work system "helps us to be more organized, especially for producers who do not follow procedures." Each team was expected to meet approximately once per week. Initial meetings often focused on company rules and procedures. Junior team members, in particular, told us that these first meetings had been badly needed and were quite productive. Given the diversity of job functions on each team (sales producers, production assistants, marketing personnel, and others), meetings provided a forum to discuss and coordinate work flow issues.

The junior team identified several organization and efficiency advantages: clarifying individual responsibility for work, developing a more uniform approach to account handling, facilitating system development and definition and understanding of responsibilities, and designating specific responsibility for special problems. The senior team identified similar issues, including providing more consistent customer service and developing greater knowledge of a smaller number of accounts. Similarly, the questionnaire indicated that interactions between team members helped make it clear who was responsible for what.

Efficiency was apparently a high priority of the acting CEO. Senior team members described him as "an efficiency man" and "the most organized man I know. He may be too organized." Junior team members indicated, "He helped me be more organized" and "Before he came, there was a low level of organization in both the people and the firm."

Over time, however, team interaction processes deteriorated and tension emerged concerning the emphasis on efficiency and organization. The agenda of team meetings continued to focus on procedural issues, a tendency fostered by the leaders of each team. (Both team leaders were administrators—a production assistant on the junior team and the marketing specialist on the senior team.) Their jobs were made easier when the producers in the team followed procedures closely. (The team leaders were selected by the teams, but the acting CEO significantly influenced this process.)

Many individuals expressed frustration with the perceived overemphasis on procedures, indicating on the questionnaire that the team system had resulted in "unnecessary paperwork." An obvious distaste was expressed for the firm's procedural manual, which some team members described as highly detailed ("our bible"). But when we examined this manual, we discovered that it was rather brief—almost an elaborated pamphlet—and limited to a small set of crucial procedural matters. We concluded that overstructuring may be in the eye of the beholder. Perhaps team members' perception of the amount of structure imposed on them was distorted by the frustration they experienced when their expectations and preferences for individual autonomy were violated.

The strong emphasis on rules and procedures in the team system appeared to threaten the sales producers' autonomy and discretion. Team members were pressured to perform a variety of activities dictated by the organization's approach rather than based on their own personal styles. For example, freedom to service small but loyal accounts—a high priority under the old system—was essentially removed. In fact, the questionnaire suggested that producers, particularly on the senior team, felt they had inadequate autonomy. The group meetings, interviews, and questionnaire responses indicated that if the company's procedures were rigidly enforced, individual autonomy for the producers would be limited. The boundaries placed on self-management would be seen as so restrictive that the remaining area of discretion would be perceived as inconsequential.

The interaction processes within these self-managing teams were operating as vehicles for limiting autonomy. One possible conclusion is that these were not self-managing teams at all but merely traditional groups falsely labeled as "self-managing." On the other hand, the external trappings appeared quite similar in design to self-managing teams in other settings. Even so, the team processes that were unfolding here were in many respects limiting rather than increasing the employees' freedom to manage themselves. A major reason for this outcome seemed to be the emphasis placed on using team interaction processes as a means of clarifying and enforcing rules and procedures rather than empowering employees. Another reason for the perceived decrease in individual autonomy may be the standard of comparison that the members brought to the teams. An individual's perception of autonomy is based largely on a relative, rather than absolute, standard of comparison. The producers who were members of these teams had been relatively autonomous under the old system, even though the agency itself was somewhat bureaucratic. Each producer, though not explicitly told that he was "self-managed" (all were male), was able to set his own priorities, work schedule, and the like, without first having to reach consensus with others.

Interestingly, the two teams appeared to perceive the team processes differently. The senior team members seemed to sense the primary threat to their autonomy as stemming from having to cooperate with other team members. The senior team leader described the situation in this way: "Senior producers are on a constant ego trip. Under the team system we have a democratic ideal. This is hard work. We have several different personalities. These people don't know how to cooperate." A senior producer told us in an interview that if he could change the work system, he would return to a system of independent producers with assigned support staff. He added, "The old system was like a profit center. You could do things."

The junior team seemed to be especially frustrated with the emphasis on rules and procedures. They tended to associate control pressures more with the organization (the work system) and with the personal agenda of their leader than with the processes within the team itself. The team was, in fact, viewed more as a source of support than a constraint. One junior producer described his team as providing a place to "compare notes [to share knowledge] with others" and a mechanism for bringing "different types [producers, production assistants, and marketing people] together."

The questionnaire (and our other information sources) provided support for this pattern of differences between the two teams. The junior team reported a greater feeling than the senior team of a "pressure to produce results" and "organization conformity pressure." It also reported a slightly lower "team conformity pressure."

Although these perceptual differences between teams are interesting, the primary theme remains the apparent trade-off between the self-managing team system and personal control. Most published studies of self-managing teams have dealt with occupations and situations in which the work prior to the teams was highly structured, so a change to teams caused an increase in autonomy. In many traditional manufacturing and service work settings, introduction of self-managing teams has led to substantial worker autonomy relative to the industry norm. In this organization, by contrast, the change may have been in the opposite direction. Visualize a continuum with one pole representing complete anarchy and the other total control. Somewhere in the middle range is the autonomy represented by self-managing teams. Whether teams represent autonomy to the participant depends on his or her prior location on the continuum. In this particular setting, to a large degree, team self-management was introducing a loss of personal self-management.

Reduced Customer Service and Organizational Unity

The emphasis on work teams in the firm had two other significant impacts—a loss of agency identity and reduced customer service on small accounts. Both problems were especially troubling to senior team members, and both can be traced to a lack of interaction processes that encouraged interteam communication and coordination.

Senior team members generally reported that the system promoted team unity, but they felt a sense of agency unity was lost. Outside their team, other sales producers would not possess the knowledge to follow up on a sales producer's accounts if he or she were absent. Team members reported that separation between units caused employees to lose sight of the whole; the system led to a loss of loyalty to the agency; no "young backups" were developed for older producers' accounts; and so forth.

In addition, the separation of all small accounts into a third team—one that had no sales producers—troubled senior team members. One member put it this way: "We've lost control and communications on small accounts . . . lost our purpose of serving clients better." A major reason that this bothered some producers was that some small account personal policies were owned by key contacts for large organizational policies. One producer recounted a story in which a policyholder was given notice of cancellation of a personal policy for being a few days overdue on his premium payment. This client also happened to be the company representative on a very large corporate policy (worth hundreds of thousands of dollars). Since the personal policy was handled by administrators in the small accounts team, no special effort was made to provide special service in dealing with this problem.

Team members jointly described the problem in the senior team meeting in the following (composite) way: "The system does not go far enough. It should not split one producer's accounts. Accounts should be divided by producer, not by size. With the system we no longer manage personal accounts as a spin-off from large ones; we lose coordination. We lose brother, sister, aunt, and uncle generated by personal contact." Overall, it was clear (particularly in the senior team) that the team system was constraining a number of sales producers from servicing small accounts in the way they would if they operated on an individual basis. Here, too, the attempt to achieve efficiency and organization within the system was limiting the discretion of sales producers.

Lack of Interteam Education and Training

Another primary theme concerned the education and training of younger sales producers. Both the senior and junior teams generally agreed that interaction with others enabled team members to learn from the members of their own team, a particularly important benefit for younger, less experienced sales producers. But a disadvantage of the team system was that it created roadblocks between junior producers and senior producers. Team members tended to be isolated from the activities of other teams.

In the senior team meeting, for example, two of the concerns recorded were "lose benefit of people in the other team . . . cheats inexperienced people of education" and "can't introduce young producers to senior accounts without crossing team lines." Similarly, junior producers were reluctant to go to the other team for help. As one senior producer pointed out, junior producers need "education, guidance, and motivation." His view was that the team system discouraged senior, experienced producers from helping junior people with these needs.

This concern with the education of sales producers demonstrates how personal freedom involves self-constraints as well as external constraints. The development of the young, inexperienced sales producers is important for providing them with the skills and confidence necessary for effective performance. Sharing ideas and concerns with fellow inexperienced producers in a team setting was viewed as being helpful in this regard. Separation of the senior, more experienced producers, who presumably have the knowledge junior producers need, was considered by many employees to be detrimental.

Leadership Practices

The fourth theme centered on leadership practices within the work system. The issue of team leader assignments was a special concern for the junior team. The acting CEO of the firm had made his desired choice for the position known, and this person was subsequently selected by the team. The team leader was generally respected for her work ability, but her concerns did not reflect those of the majority of team members. Two different sales producers, in separate interviews, said flatly that their team leader's conduct of the meetings focused on "the production assistants' concerns" (procedures). In contrast, the production assistants thought that the team system did provide individual freedom but too little attention to established procedures!

There was a natural conflict of interest between producers and production assistants in this regard. Producers wanted freedom from the red tape of procedures, whereas production assistants wanted procedures to be carefully followed to reduce their own hassles. The junior team leader apparently chose to focus on this latter concern in meetings, to the dismay of producers. In a team meeting (which included the team leader), one producer said the term of a team leader is too long and should be limited to three months. This was probably as negative a response as could be made in the presence of the team leader. One producer expressed confusion and obvious irritation about how the leader got the position in the first place. Over time, the meetings became shorter and shorter and, in the eyes of most participants, nonproductive. They also became less frequent as the incentives for attending were not sufficiently strong.

The acting CEO responded by putting pressure on the teams to be productive and by attending meetings and prodding members to participate—actions strikingly inconsistent with the principle of self-management. He took pride in his ability to get employees to do what he wanted them to do. For example, he stated, with satisfaction, that he could direct his employees to participate in our study. Although he stated that participation in the study should be voluntary, his offer to make it mandatory provided an interesting contrast. Along the same lines, our interviews revealed that the "self-managing" work system itself was instituted without the participation or consent of employees. Our extensive interviews with the acting CEO led us to conclude that he was sincerely committed philosophically to employee participation, but his espoused theory was inconsistent with his theory in use.[2] This contradiction supported our general impressions of the work system: the introduction of work teams was leading to a loss of individual self-management for employees.

As a result, senior producers, who did not need significant moral support from their peers (to develop confidence and skills), were not motivated to support the new system, and junior sales producers, who did need this moral support, were frustrated by their nonrepresentative, procedure-focused team leadership. Eventually, team meetings became infrequent and nonproductive. Interactions between team members became strained. Employee skepticism and apathy regarding the team approach rose, and efficiency and coordination plummeted.

The final piece of evidence that employees had developed feelings of reduced autonomy came from answers to our question, "How is the direction of the organization's activities established?" The responses could range from "democratically" to "autocratically." The average response was significantly above the midpoint toward "autocratically."

Implications for Teams

The story told in this case is especially interesting because it examines a setting in which an industry-wide reliance on autonomy and individual self-management is traditional. Our findings suggest a paradox: team self-management can sometimes result in a loss of individual control. Team processes related to leadership, group peer pressure, and a focus on rigid procedures combined to undermine individual discretion and self-management. This decrease in personal autonomy resulted in lower employee satisfaction.

It is important to view this case in light of the uniqueness of the organizational setting. In no way do we mean to suggest that the experience of one service organization indicates that self-managing work teams are inherently threatening to personal self-management. This particular situation contained a number of characteristics specific to this firm and to this industry—one in which individual autonomy has been a norm. The insurance industry has been forced to examine new ways of organizing to improve efficiency in the face of deregulation, tightening markets, and increasing competition. As a result, independent insurance salespersons have been confronted with some new restrictions on their freedom and autonomy. Against this backdrop, self-managing work teams have apparently served as a convenient vehicle for increasing control over employees and for gaining some advantages in efficiency. This represents a noteworthy challenge to the universal applicability of conventional wisdom regarding the impact of self-managing teams. These teams also developed several group processes that limited individual discretion. In the end, this case should be interpreted as an illustration of the idea that a "self-managing" team system may sometimes serve as a control mechanism that is more constraining than the traditional work system it replaces.

Our final meeting with the CEO (who had become president of the organization) provided a fitting conclusion. We asked if perhaps he had really intended to use the "self-managing" teams to extend and amplify his personal influence and control. He agreed: "Every reason for doing the team system was control." At least in this executive's view, there is no inconsistency in labeling such groups "self-managing"!

The implications of this story are compelling. Depending on the objectives pursued by self-managing teams, the nature of the setting in which they are put in place, and the way that they are implemented and maintained, team processes have the potential for undermining individual discretion, autonomy, and initiative.

KEY LESSONS FROM THIS CASE

1. The reason for implementing teams is an important consideration. If teams are intended to serve simply as a vehicle for enforcing company policy and procedures, negative interactions may result and individual autonomy is put at risk.

2. Individual interests may be at odds with the interests of the team as a whole. In this case individual autonomy was sacrificed for organizational efficiency. Conflict can emerge when individuals are pressured to subordinate their personal interests, and sometimes the interests of particular customers, to the interests of the team or organization as a whole.

3. The impact of leadership practices at both higher management levels and the team level will be strongly influenced by leadership agendas—for example, whether they are aimed at pursuing the concerns of management, the members, or the team leaders themselves.

4. Subtle forms of leadership are difficult to detect and can often appear to have little influence on teams, but in reality they can overwhelm a team's ability to exercise true self-management.

5. Incentives provided by the work system for team members to belong and to contribute constructively to their team's performance are important for work team effectiveness.

6. Communication and coordination across teams is critical to ensuring that teams are able to learn from each other. This lesson will be addressed further in Unit 4.

7. Different needs of employees in different job categories (e.g., sales producers versus production assistants) can lead to difficult interactions between team members. Recognition of the differences is a first step to resolving conflict.

NOTES FOR CASE 3.3

1. This chapter is based in part on material previously published in Charles C. Manz and Harold Angle, "Can Group Self-Management Mean a Loss of Personal Control: Triangulating on a Paradox," *Group and Organization Studies* 11 (1986): 309–334. The original research was partially funded by a grant from the Operations Management Center at the University of Minnesota. The authors are grateful to John Guarino and Rosemarie Orehek for their valuable assistance in data collection. Because of the sensitive nature of the information in this story, the name of the organization is confidential.

2. For more information on the tendency for views espoused by managers to be inconsistent with what they actually do, see Chris Argyris, "Leadership Learning and the Status Quo," *Organizational Dynamics* 9 (1980): 29–43.

Team Outputs: Accessing and Improving Team Performance

Unit 4 focuses on team outputs. A case description of the Lake Superior Paper Company begins this unit by presenting information about the successful implementation of teams in an industrial setting. A theory and research section then describes methods of measuring, understanding, and improving team performance. Two additional case descriptions follow. One focuses on the AES Corporation and describes how multiple teams coordinate and work together to develop organizational strategy. Another case description provides a glimpse of the future by explaining how W. L. Gore and Associates encourages teamwork without formally designated teams. Taken together, the cases and research summary provide insight into methods of assessing and improving team outputs.

CASE

Team Performance at Lake Superior Paper Company

This case was written by Charles C. Manz and John Newstrom.[1]

Teams are often credited with giving companies a substantial competitive advantage. This case tells the story of what has been described as the most successful start-up in the history of the paper industry. Teams helped improve the efficiency of paper production, and they were also credited with creating a highly motivated workforce. However, teams were not a magic cure-all. Some people were frustrated with what seemed to be a slow transition. Others felt that the team system was not beneficial for them personally.

This case is about the performance of teams during the start-up of a paper mill. Papermaking is an industry in which self-managing teams are rapidly becoming the norm, at least among new start-ups. The focus here is on the Lake Superior Paper Company, which began as a joint venture of a large American corporation previously involved in mill management and a major regional electrical power company. The new mill is located in Duluth, Minnesota, near plentiful timber sources, is not unionized, and is already the largest producer of uncoated, super-calendared (glossy paper used in magazines, newspaper supplements, catalogs, etc.) ground wood paper in North America. The mill is equipped with state-of-the-art technology and is designed to produce nearly a quarter-million tons of paper a year. It is a highly automated facility, with operations continuously monitored by skilled workers.

The mill has several distinct operations: receiving, washing, cutting, and debarking large wood logs; grinding the logs into refined pulp; converting the pulp into long, continuous sheets of paper; ironing and polishing the sheets to create the glossy finish; rewinding the paper and cutting it to desired sizes; wrapping and warehousing paper rolls; and using biodegradable by-products to fuel the steam plant that powers the mill's operations. Workers in the mill are organized into over 20 teams, including the wood yard crew, wood handling operation, pulp mill, paper machine, calendaring and roll finishing, laboratory, and maintenance areas on multiple work shifts. The plant also has a core of team managers and a design team (consisting of the president and vice-presidents) that spearheaded the initial mill design, start-up, and task assignments.

According to one of the mill managers, a self-managing team system was chosen for the new mill because "it would have been against the norm in the paper industry if we used a traditional work system in a new start-up operation." According to the vice-president for human resources, traditional management systems are not common in newer mills. "All of the last 10 paper mills built in the United States use some form of participative/sociotechnical system program," he added. Another executive explained, "We had a state-of-the-art mill in terms of technology. We wanted a state-of-the-art social system to go with it, not an old outdated kind of traditional system."

In the early stages of the mill's start-up and operation, all levels of management provided direction to the work teams. Typically, the mill managers had significant technical experience, while the majority of the workers had no prior experience in the paper industry. Thus, most actions in the start-up stages were intended to emphasize the technical aspects of the mill. Proper technical functioning (focused on the papermaking process, machines and equipment, computer systems, and materials) was seen as the primary avenue through which the mill could get off the ground and reach profitability at an early stage. Movement toward self-managing teams was expected to progress continuously but only as the teams and their members matured in both technical and social skills. The social system, in particular, required development and refinement of roles; mission, goal, and value statements; reward systems; career development procedures; justice systems; behavioral norms; and selection/placement mechanisms.

Because of the enormity of such tasks, each team still had a manager who was directly responsible for its supervision and support. As the teams matured, the direct role of these managers would gradually fade into the background, and they would assume different responsibilities, revolving around project assignments.

The development of truly self-managing teams was expected to take five to eight years. Initially, teams were under the direct leadership of the team manager with no rotation of member roles and responsibilities. Ultimately, self-managing teams are expected to have the requisite skills and abilities within the team, with members exercising control over their problems and rotating among various coordinating and scheduling roles. Figure C4.1-1 depicts the long-term evolutionary plan for team leadership, with team

STAGE 1: START-UP TEAM

Authority
Export
Teacher
Problem solver
Coordinator
Team supervisor
Mentor

STAGE 2: TRANSITIONAL TEAM

Shared authority
Monitor
Helper
Example setter
Teacher
Evaluator
Information provider
Link to other teams

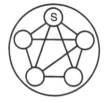

STAGE 3: WELL-TRAINED, EXPERIENCED TEAM

Manager of boundary
Auditor
Expert
Resource provider
Goal setting guider
Information provider
Protector/buffer

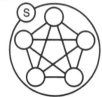

STAGE 4: WELL-TRAINED, MATURE TEAM

Boundary leader
Shared values
Coach
Champion
Counselor
Resource provider
Supporter
Shared responsibilities

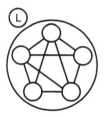

Figure C4.1-1 Evolution of team leader's role (S = Supervisor; L = Leader).

managers moving from direct supervision (stage 1) to positions of shared authority (stage 2) and to boundary managers and leaders (stages 3 and 4). The leader's role should thus move from external leadership to empowering leadership.

After its first year of operation, a company executive asserted that the mill had achieved "the most successful start-up in the paper industry's history and is already outproducing the best paper makers in the world." Objective measures of output included key performance indicators of average efficiency, speed, tonnage, job lot percentage, and waste. These indicators were more favorable than original (and even revised) forecasts based on comparative information from other mill start-ups. The mill even became profitable in its first year. This rapid success was unusual in the paper industry, where the art of papermaking entails a relatively slow learning curve for employee operators.

Company executives attributed the favorable early results to a combination of factors: state-of-the-art technology, quality of the workforce hired (both its overall work ethic and high average level of education), and the self-managing team system. A common view, expressed by management and workers alike, was that without the team system, the achievement level of the operation would have been significantly behind where it was at the end of the first year.

We discussed the work system in detail with many workers from many teams in the mill. We talked not only with employees, but also with team managers and design team executives. They told us about their experiences in the mill, their reactions, specific results, problem areas, and feelings about both team managers and the entire organization. They also discussed changes they desired to see take place in the young enterprise.

We reviewed company documents, covering descriptions of the design team plan, the organization's sociotechnical plan for improving productivity and quality of worklife, the team training process, the orientation program, and the demonstrated performance system (compensation based on certified skills). We toured the physical facility at several stages in the mill's development, and we were informally briefed by members of the human resources staff.

Ultimately, we came up with a series of conclusions that we sorted into two primary areas: (a) themes contributing to effectiveness of the teams and (b) problems impeding team effectiveness. From our examination of both the successes and struggles experienced in these groups, we derived useful lessons about team effectiveness.

Themes Underlying Success

Emphasize the Technical Side First for a Smoother Start-up

One of the most striking features of the mill's successful start-up was its focus on the most critical element for short-term survival and success: attaining satisfactory levels of production. One member of management explained, "Initial emphasis on the technical side helped the mill avoid the frequently typical performance dip [productivity below expected levels in comparison to more traditional operations] experienced in most self-managing team start-ups." Frequently, a new self-managing team system requires time to work out operations bugs and to allow workers and managers to adjust to self-managing teams. Consequently, in the early stages of start-up, an emphasis on the social or employee self-management side of the operation can cause the overall work system (including both the technical and social components) to underperform more traditional systems. This additional pressure requires considerable patience and commitment from the organization's management, even causing some to abandon teams before they have had a chance to mature and prove themselves effective.

This mill experienced no initial performance dip, largely, we believe, because of the strong commitment to refining the technical aspects of the system first. Extensive time and effort were devoted to facilitating the teams' technical skills, which meant that the highly experienced managers stayed directly involved in daily operations (consistent with stage 1 in Figure C4.1-1). Also important in the mill's early success was the decision to hire a significant number of workers (approximately 25 percent of the mill's workforce) who had prior technical experience in other papermaking operations. With this infusion of relevant backgrounds and expertise, a basic level of technical competence prevailed in the mill from its inception.

The social aspects of the system, on the other hand, were designed (and expected) to mature more slowly. The formal target was to achieve mature self-managing teams in about five years, with a gradual transition across the four stages portrayed in Figure C4.1-1.

In our interviews, most workers acknowledged that the evolution of highly mature teams would be slow, although almost all employees believed that their teams were slightly ahead of scheduled development. (Most members as well as team managers perceived that they were already in at least stage 2.) There were also hints at some discomfort with the imbalance between the mill's stronger progress on the technical versus the social dimension. (One worker commented, "There is a myth here that we have balanced our social growth with our technical growth.") This impatience, we sensed, may have been partially due to two factors. First, the workers may have believed that because they attained early technical goals so readily, they should have been able to accomplish the same dramatic results in the social domain. Second, many workers were probably unaccustomed to thinking about their work in five-year developmental time frames. Consequently, they may have implicitly abbreviated the team-maturity time line for their own teams.

Introducing Teams into a Greenfield Site Is Easier Than at an Established Site

Another cause of the predicted performance dip in many self-managing team experiments is the employees' difficulty in adjusting to new expectations and modes of interaction when a dramatic shift toward teams occurs. Since the mill we studied was new (a greenfield site) and many employees were new to the labor force, the majority of them were not required to adjust to an internal transition to a new technological system or to a new set of social relationships. However, the experienced technicians had to make a significant adjustment relative to their past work experiences.

All job applicants were rigorously screened in the hiring process in order to provide reasonable assurance that they would support the idea of self-managing teams. In addition, an extensive orientation process carefully exposed all new employees to the philosophy and operations of sociotechnical systems. Thus, the entire system was predisposed toward successful implementation. This is in contrast to other organizational change efforts where unlearning, as well as new learning, must take place.

Teams Can Lead to High Satisfaction and Commitment for Most Employees

Some of the most dramatic clues to the self-managing team system's impact on the mill's workforce were expressed in comments made by team members. One said simply, "I like to go to work here," with another adding, "They [mill management] treat you like real people." Even when workers expressed frustration with some aspects of the mill's operation (e.g., the unusually high number of meetings or management's reluctance to hire short-term staff to meet temporary work demands during start-up so as to avoid future layoffs), the comments were usually softened by modifications such as, "But here we have the power to do something about it."

Indications of employee satisfaction with and commitment to the organization (or, at least, a low level of desire to leave) as a product of participative orientation were reflected time and again in comments such as "I wouldn't work anywhere else." In fact, many workers stated that they had serious doubts about whether they would ever be able to work in a more traditional, authority-based system again because of the wasted human abilities they had witnessed and experienced. Employees related the story of a former co-worker who had relocated to another city; he had started a new job but just a few months later was seeking new employment. The clear reason given was that he could no longer tolerate an authoritarian style of management.

The employees we interviewed perceived that the participative work system was yielding positive results in terms of their own quality of worklife (as well as achieving efficiency, early profitability, very low turnover, and almost negligible absenteeism). They found company-related social functions like picnics fun to attend because people got along so well. The common feeling was that team managers were not opponents of workers but "more like team members." A pervasive sense of trust in and respect for the mill's top management team was conveyed, with one employee explaining that "they do everything they promise they will do." Weekly team meetings were seen as a useful process for cementing social relationships and opening up communication lines.

Finally, the participative selection process (team members were directly involved in selecting new employees) used to staff the mill provided a powerful sense of ownership for the workforce. Any member of the interview team could, with adequate justification, veto any applicant he or she believed should not be hired. As one employee explained with obvious pride, "It inflates your ego to have that kind of power."

Employee Learning Contributes to Constructive Empowerment

The paper mill established a generally favorable climate for employee learning and development. Workers were given a substantially wider range of responsibilities than in traditional manufacturing settings, typically working on multiple job assignments derived from work allocation decisions made within the team. Members also made many decisions and performed several functions that had traditionally been in management's domain. Consequently, learning new skills was critically important in this mill.

Concurrent with the timing of our interviews, a pay-for-knowledge/skill system (officially known as the demonstrated performance system) was being developed. This system was designed to provide employees with the opportunity (and to encourage them) to cross-train in a wide range of job functions (skill blocks) both within and across mill teams. When employees believed they were ready to be certified as capable on a new skill block, they were tested in order to assess whether they had the adequate knowledge, could apply the skill effectively, and could get results. As skill blocks were added to an employee's repertoire, he or she received advanced technical ratings resulting in salary base increments ranging as high as 22 percent for each advancement in grade.

The introduction of this pay system sent a powerful message to the workforce that learning was needed, expected, and integral to the mill's long-term success. The pay increments were attractive to the employees we interviewed, but they also seemed to value the opportunity to improve themselves and help the organization. One worker explained, "I like the idea of pay increases, but I also just plain like to learn."

This theme—a positive emphasis on learning—was consistently echoed by several team members and managers. One team manager explained that the workers "are learning much quicker because they are being allowed to learn." Another added that "the mill would be years behind schedule" if it was based on a traditional system. The organization's emphasis on learning was best exemplified by one of the team manager's transitional roles, the teacher. One manager summed up his primary role at this time as to "first teach and then allow them [the workers] to do." In effect, empowering workers in this mill involved more than just giving them more responsibility and involvement in decisions. It was also aggressively helping them to acquire the skills and knowledge to contribute successfully.

Problems Remaining to Be Resolved

Reactions to the concept of self-managing teams often range from showing complete skepticism to their embracing them as a cure-all. This diversity of responses may stem from a variety of reasons—ignorance of the approach, philosophical differences, biased or unsubstantiated reporting, or unique (idiosyncratic) experiences with it. Actual performance results with teams appear to fall somewhere between the two extreme possibilities of unmitigated success or total failure. Although some half-hearted and misguided attempts have clearly failed, other applications have proven successful. But even the road to success is often filled with roadblocks and other obstacles, and this was true of this mill's experience as well.

Lake Superior Paper was successful through its early stages of operation, from both a technical and a social perspective. Nevertheless, many significant challenges remained, and mill employees at all levels seemed to recognize this reality.

Support for Team Managers in Their New Role

Supervisory positions were historically fraught with conflict; supervisors were often caught in the middle, trying to satisfy the demands of management from above and the expectations of workers from below in the organizational hierarchy. One manager described her primary role as a kind of buffer that "gets it from both ways." It got to the point that she occasionally wished that she could just turn toward one group or the other and say, "All right, you do it."

As discussed in Unit 3, self-managing teams present additional challenges that make the team manager's role even more difficult. First, many of the managers obtained their work and supervisory experiences in more traditional organizations, where directive modes of leadership were the norm. The transition to a team system called for not only a new set of roles but also an entirely different managerial philosophy for the treatment of employees. This could create internal conflict for team leaders. Second, a clear organizational plan was in place for the evolution of team leader roles from start-up mode to those ultimately required for supporting a well-trained, mature team (see Figure C4.1-1). Consequently, the team leader's role was in a constant state of flux. The issue was compounded by the fact that some teams in the mill were progressing at different speeds on their own paths to maturity. Therefore, the roles required of team managers were somewhat different across teams within the mill.

Third, many of the mill's employees were drawn from work backgrounds in traditionally managed firms. Therefore, initially, they lacked unreserved trust in the new system and also required development of social (teamwork) skills. These circumstances provided additional challenges for team managers.

Finally, there was a haunting, if not always stated, fear among some of the team managers that they risked managing themselves out of a job. If they were to be truly successful, their team would become self-managing and appear not to require a team manager any longer.[2]

In general, however, the team managers seemed to value their new roles despite the many challenges. A manager who had previously worked in a more traditional mill for 12 years explained, "I could never go back. I saw all that wasted potential there. Here, if you ask if someone will do something, you get three people stuck in the door volunteering for it. They're really gung-ho." Other team managers supported this view with their comments. Although they had little difficulty identifying flaws in the system (e.g., dealing with a dozen different opinions from team members all at once; unrealistic expectations from employees regarding their own rate of advancement through the skill blocks), most of them expressed significant satisfaction with their positions.

The team managers brought out other issues. One explained, "Technical operations in the mill are a piece of cake, but developing the team will keep you awake at night."

Some of the specific issues they faced in team development included the frustration of waiting for the team to come up with its own solution to a problem (while the team manager withholds a solution in order to facilitate the team's growth), being "kind of a psychologist" so as to pay attention to workers' feelings and needs, and ensuring that team members were not too tough in managing themselves (a rather unique situation). For example, if a team member failed to pull his or her weight on the team (e.g., was chronically absent), the manager may have been required to "take the (figurative) lynching rope out of their hands" (a rich metaphor offered by one team leader) and try to fashion a peaceful settlement rather than mete out the more traditional punishment.

Aside from intrateam challenges, the team managers were most concerned with the ambiguity surrounding their own future roles. The persuasiveness of this uncertainty was exemplified by one team member's flat assertion: "We know our team manager won't be there forever. Eventually we intend to phase him out, and then we'll be managing on our own." Despite strong assurances from upper management that the team managers would ultimately shift their focus to special projects and boundary-spanning functions, the message had not yet sunk in. It was not clear whether it was simply the ambiguity inherent in what would eventually constitute their new leadership role or the lack of job security that concerned them the most.

One clue to the depth of their worry came from the positive anticipation with which they viewed the mill's possible expansion in the near future. Team managers realized that new teams of workers would need a new set of team managers. If they were successful in moving their existing teams through the first two or three stages of team development, they might be able to bypass the uncertainty of struggling with stage 4 team leadership roles by being selected for team management positions in the new section of the mill. This revealed a curious irony: After doing their job well and struggling through the reportedly sleepless nights of developing strong and independent teams, they looked forward to going back and starting over again. (Note that this would mean going back to a stage that required stronger leader directiveness.)

Emerging Feelings of Inequity for Employees Who See Themselves as "Losers"

Most organizations have employee groups who perceive that they are disadvantaged at one time or another. Lake Superior Paper Company was no different. Certainly this was true of the team managers, who perceived the possible loss of their jobs as the teams matured. But they were not the only ones who sensed they might be treated unfairly. The most notable class of paper mill employee who appeared vulnerable to perceptions of loss were those who were hired specifically because they possessed considerable prior technical experience in the paper industry; we refer to them as "techs." To expedite the technical start-up of the mill, the managerial design team hired a substantial number of employees with papermaking expertise. The use of these techs expedited the start-up from an operational perspective, but it also produced some disadvantages. First, many of the techs came from more traditional work systems and faced not only the problems of mill start-up but also adaptation to a sharply different social system and an unlearning of prior attitudes. Movement for the techs along the path toward trusting the new form of management was slower. One inexperienced worker noted that the techs still displayed a lot of skepticism, clung to previous mill traditions, and expressed a lot of reservations ("I'll believe it when I see it").

The techs' feeling of inequity apparently stemmed from two sources: performance of tasks that they viewed as beneath their status (and this offended their dignity) and the

more rapid acquisition of increased status (and income) by other, inexperienced workers. As the inexperienced workers progressed and learned and performed higher-skilled
and higher-status jobs, the techs, who were hired at level 7 of the nine-point pay scale,
increasingly had to perform a variety of lower-status jobs (like hosing down the floor).
They would have escaped such menial chores in a more traditional system with narrowly
defined job tasks for each level. In addition, under the demonstrated performance pay
system in the new mill, they would soon (within 18 months) be required to acquire the
knowledge and demonstrate the skills consistent with the seventh level of pay (e.g., learn
an entire process and be able to function anywhere within it) regardless of their previous background and experience. To some, this appeared to be a regressive step.

Even more visible than loss of status was the techs' perception of inequity in terms
of financial rewards. Although they started at a salary level roughly double that of the
inexperienced workers, the latter group was in a position to receive much larger relative, and absolute, increases in salary as they became certified on new skill blocks. The
techs foresaw the day (probably several years away) when newer employees would catch
up to their own salaries and match their status from an earnings and expertise perspective. Although the techs would be losing nothing in the process, it was hard for them to
watch others gain more.

When our interviews touched on the pay-for-knowledge/skill system that was being
phased into the mill, the employees' reactions indicated that this was a controversial
topic. (The pay system provides increases in worker pay contingent on learning and
being certified on multiple jobs, or essentially more pay for more job knowledge.) "You've
hit a raw nerve there," was the representative response of one employee. Inexperienced
employees viewed the certification process very favorably ("I like to learn, and the money
is motivating for me, too"); the techs seemed almost unanimously opposed to it.
(Progression from their current level to the top of the salary scale, two steps away, would
bring about only a 5 percent salary gain for them.) This created a powerful dilemma for
mill management; the pay system was viewed as integral to the mill's progress toward
self-management, yet it created perceptions of winners and losers. To the credit of mill
management, the salary scale was revised to allow a two-step gain amounting to over
18 percent.

Impatience with Slow Development

The evolution and development of mature self-managing teams are not smooth processes,
despite occasional claims of instant success. On the contrary, unrealistic expectations or
simplistic assumptions that the achievements of teams can be quick and painless can
sabotage the long-term chances of success. The demands and rewards can be great for
members and leaders alike, but if the participants are not emotionally prepared, patient,
organizationally supported, and carefully trained for the challenges, disillusionment is a
real danger. (This may represent an especially serious obstacle in countries whose cultures have not traditionally prepared first-level employees to assume significant self-
management responsibilities.)

Lake Superior Paper Company did not escape the frustrations surrounding the pace
of change, the demands made on workers, the time frame required for maturation of
teams, and the fragility inherent in intrateam (and interteam) relationships. Mill employees had been carefully informed that progress toward team development would require
time, patience, and hard work, but differing perceptions of the actual and desired pace
of change nevertheless resulted in some frustrations. Some workers indicated that "we're
moving too fast . . . I feel like we're on a runaway train." Almost all expressed concern

over the number of meetings they had to attend. "I've got a meeting before and after my shift every day this week," one employee reported.

Other employees countered with complaints of moving too slowly. One employee with prior experience in a self-managing system in another industry talked wistfully of the past pleasures of working on a mature self-managing team and of his occasional frustration in this mill because of the seemingly slow progress toward team maturity. Another worker, recognizing the frustrations of others with the slow pace, responded that he was confident that "the whole design would be really great for workers in the long term, but in the short run what was needed was a little more patience."

American cultural perceptions of time frames hold one key to this pacing dilemma. It was undoubtedly difficult for U.S. mill workers to think in terms of time horizons of five years for meeting a long-term goal of mature self-management. This was especially true given the presence of daily and monthly production goals. An example was shared by a team manager who explained how all of his team members had already targeted a particularly high-skilled and prestigious job in a control room as their major career objective. He admired their strong motivation to progress rapidly in their careers but noted ruefully, "They all want to have that job by next year." His concluding remark revealed a curious but very real paradox: "The opportunities for these people are unlimited, but there's a limit to it." (In cultures where employees are accustomed to slower promotions, this self-imposed pressure for job advancement may not represent a serious problem.)

Another source of pressure for team members arose from the perception that they were temporarily short-handed in some areas of the mill. "We're lean . . . pushed to the limit," complained one employee. He pointed out that corporate resources were available for new equipment and supplies but that top management was reluctant to hire any more workers. Their rationale, which he understood and accepted, was that further hiring now would require that some people be released later (a practice inconsistent with an apparent goal of no layoffs). This explanation was valid, since he realized that as workers became cross-trained, they would increasingly be able to help out other workers who were experiencing problems on any given day. Thus, in the future, slack human resources would already exist through the cross-training program and could be allocated wherever help was needed.

Ironically, however, working hard and keeping the mill operating well without added personnel made it more likely that additional workers would not be hired. (Why should management fix a problem that doesn't really exist?) But to the work system's credit, it was apparent that the mill's long-term success was more important to the workers than their immediate comfort. They conveyed feelings of pride in the mill and their work, and they seemed willing to pay the price for success.

Team Setbacks and Growing Pains

Initially, self-managing teams were fragile, vulnerable entities. Members and leaders realized that they had almost no opportunity to rest on their laurels. One employee stressed that "working in the system is great, but it can be very fragile." He explained that "one moment a team can be really clicking, with things going really well, and the next moment things can be in turmoil, with people hollering at one another and a lot of hard feelings produced."

This reality reflected one element of the organization's mission and philosophy statement, which suggested that "conflict is inevitable" but must be resolved in a "timely and equitable manner." Team members were learning that disagreements would arise and voices would be raised, but consensus decisions within the teams had to be reached and supported for the team to move ahead. Teams experienced both successes and failures, and overall progress took a lot of work. Without continuous effort, the tremendous investment of time and effort in team development would quickly be destroyed as group members discovered that group cohesiveness is a fragile entity.

In summary, even in highly successful self-managing team operations, expectations are raised and sometimes not fulfilled, and workers become frustrated. Employees receive a lot of flexibility, responsibility, and variety in their work and yet simultaneously face a heavy training load and numerous time-consuming meetings. Team members gradually come to help one another in significant ways but in the short run may find themselves feeling they belong to an understaffed organization. These challenges, combined with the ambiguity and threats that team managers often feel in a new work system, make for some tough times. Add to this the reality that some classes of employees see they are losing importance and status as others are gaining influence and involvement, and the road to continued progress can seem rocky.

Overcoming Obstacles to Achieve Success

After one year, self-managing teams at the paper mill were apparently thriving, despite some growing pains and imperfections. Some employees were more enthusiastic than others, but in general, the mill's workforce was highly committed, involved, and satisfied. Early data for mill efficiency and profitability indicated that they were sharply ahead of even their most optimistic projections.

The decision to emphasize the technical aspects had some clear advantages. Mainly, this approach offered more optimal utilization of the technology in the beginning. Nevertheless, a significant disadvantage should be noted. The decision to use a high percentage of managers and experienced workers from other traditional organizations may have been an impediment to the social development of self-managing teams. In some ways, Lake Superior had characteristics of a "retrofit" launching of teams rather than a pure "greenfield" launch. Managers and workers may have hindered the development of teams because they would not relinquish preestablished attitudes.

The pursuit of effective self-managing teams is still viewed as a radical work design innovation in most countries and industries, even though it is rapidly becoming the norm in new U.S. paper mills. The logic for using teams in this mill seemed clear—matching state-of-the-art machinery with a state-of-the-art managerial system.

Perhaps the most challenging question raised by this study is why other firms in other industries have not moved as rapidly toward the use of self-managing teams. They can represent a major competitive (yet socially responsible) strategy. Employees at all levels of the mill seemed to be saying, "We couldn't compete, let alone excel, in this industry with a traditional work system that stifles worker contributions." One worker summed up the situation: "I'm amazed that manufacturing hasn't done this earlier. It totally baffles me that America has gone this long without it. Sometimes I wonder how we ever made anything." The insights gained and lessons learned may help other organizations in many countries recognize the value and avoid some of the problems associated with the use of teams.

KEY LESSONS FROM THIS CASE

1. An emphasis on the technical aspects of work can improve effectiveness in the early stages of team development. Social aspects are important but can be viewed in a longer time frame and be brought along more slowly.

2. Initial team success can be facilitated by hiring workers who have requisite skills. These skills can be either technical or social.

3. Teams that are introduced in greenfield sites have a better chance of being effective. These teams do not have to break down many of the barriers that exist in established organizations.

4. Employees working in participative teams can experience high commitment, satisfaction, and loyalty. However, not all employees will have these feelings.

5. Some employees are strongly concerned about equity in their work relationships. When team members feel that they are not being equitably rewarded for their inputs, they are likely to oppose teams and possibly inhibit team success.

6. Effective transitions to teams require the management of expectations by communicating probable long time frames, differences in maturation rate across teams, and other difficulties.

NOTES FOR CASE 4.1

1. Sincere appreciation is extended to Ted Smith and Fred Zambrowski, who were instrumental in providing extensive organizational and operational background information and facilitating the scheduling of interviews that formed the basis for this case. We also thank the numerous team members, team leaders, and design team members of the paper mill for sharing their time and candid comments with us. This case is also based on published material: Charles C. Manz and John Newstrom, "Self-Managing Teams in a Paper Mill: Success Factors, Problems, and Lessons Learned," *International Human Resource Management Review* 1 (1990): 43–60.

2. For more information on this issue, see C. C. Manz and H. P. Sims, Jr., "Searching for the Unleader: Organizational Member Views on Leading Self-Managed Groups," *Human Relations* 37 (1984): 409–434, and C. C. Manz and II. P. Sims, Jr., "Leading Self-Managed Groups: A Conceptual Analysis of a Paradox," *Economic and Industrial Democracy* 7 (1986): 141–165, and H. P. Sims, Jr. and C. C. Manz, *Company of Heroes: Unleashing the Power of Self-Leadership* (New York: Wiley, 1996).

TEAM OUTPUTS

Jack parked his car at corporate headquarters and walked toward the main entrance. He was a bit nervous about the presentation he would be giving in a few minutes. The tire manufacturing plant that Jack manages had made a transition to work teams about a year ago. As part of an evaluation of his plant's performance, top management had asked Jack to report on the success of the teams. Trying to figure out what to say had been difficult, but late last night he had finally put the finishing touches on what he hoped would be a successful presentation.

As he arrived at the front door, Jack was greeted by Al, who was the corporate vice president responsible for directing the region in which Jack's plant is located. "Are you ready?" Al asked as they entered the building.

"Well, I'm not sure," Jack responded honestly. "In many ways we are ahead of where we planned to be. The employees seem satisfied with their jobs. The overall quality ratings for our tires have steadily increased. However, the transition has not been without setbacks, and I'm not sure that all of the teams have established long-term relationships that will help them to remain productive. In some ways it just feels like the system might be getting ready to explode at any minute," he concluded.

"So is that what you are going to tell the executive committee when you make your presentation?" inquired Al.

"Yeah, believe it or not, I think I will. I think I should try to paint the most accurate picture that I can. I don't see a need to try and make things sound any better or worse than they really are," responded Jack.

"That's the right approach," Al assured him.

As they entered the elevator, Jack decided to see how Al would react to one of the more negative things he would bring up in the presentation. "You know one major problem seems to be that the teams don't share information with each other. They tend to compete against one another as if it were some kind of contest to prove who is the best team."

"Wow! That is a problem. Why do you think that happens? What are you going to suggest that we do to help them work together more? I hope you have some suggestions," Al interjected quickly as they were entering the meeting room.

Upon entering the room, Jack felt his stomach start to turn. He did have a plan and some suggestions for beginning to deal with the problems, and he really did believe in the team concept. However, he knew that the future of teams in the entire corporation might depend on his ability to convince top management of their merit. Moreover, from both Al's comments and the direction he had received from other members of the top-management team, Jack knew that he needed to present a sound plan for resolving the problems his teams were encountering. Did he really have the right measures of team success? Did he truly understand the most important problems his teams were facing? Was his plan for resolving team problems on target?

This short case illustrates several important issues related to team outputs. Perhaps the most fundamental question is what constitutes team effectiveness. Most people who study and observe teams agree that effectiveness has many dimensions, and a thorough evaluation of a team's outputs requires analysis from several perspectives. After introducing some of the more common perspectives of effectiveness, we begin to examine ways that team effectiveness can be improved. Part of this description focuses on getting teams to work together with other teams. For an organization to be successful, teams must work cooperatively rather than engage in destructive competition. Getting teams to cooperate, as well as a host of other methods for improving team effectiveness, often relies on some type of training and development program. We present a model of team analysis and evaluation that provides a framework for understanding when training is needed, as well as for determining whether training helps the team become more effective. We then reexamine some of the case examples to determine common problems that impede team effectiveness, along with a list of fundamental requirements for team success.

DETERMINING TEAM EFFECTIVENESS

The 1995–1996 Chicago Bulls won more games in a single season than any other professional basketball team in history. They were the dominant team throughout the season and tournament. In the 1996–1997 and 1997–1998 seasons the Bulls repeated as champions. At times the team seemed to be invincible. Throughout the three seasons, many sports commentators were asking whether this was the greatest basketball team ever. Interestingly, the answer was not consistent. Some so-called experts claimed that the Bulls were far and away better than any other team. Others argued that the competition was just weaker and that former teams had been superior. Analysts argued about the specific strengths and weaknesses of the Bulls and other teams. The skills of individual team members were discussed, and the "chemistry" of different teams was compared. In the end, each person was left with his or her own perception, and there was no definitive answer about the greatest team of all time.

This example taken from the sports world shows that measuring the performance of teams is a very difficult process. The process is often even more elusive in the workplace where objective measures are difficult to obtain. What then separates a successful team from an unsuccessful team? Should the Chicago Bulls be considered the best basketball team simply because they won most of their games? Should other factors like their record over several seasons be considered in this assessment? Similarly, should one work team be considered better than another simply because it produces more output? Does it matter if they cannot sustain that output over an extended period of time? Should other factors like satisfaction of team members be taken into account? Should the work be done by a team, or would it be more efficiently and effectively accomplished by independent workers?

We can begin to answer questions about measuring team success by presenting a multidimensional perspective of team effectiveness. A multidimensional perspective indicates that work team effectiveness should be measured not only by the products or services a team produces but also by the ability of the team to remain intact and the extent to which the team satisfies the individual needs of each member.[1]

Goods and Services Produced

One dimension of team effectiveness concerns the goods and services produced by the team. These outputs can sometimes be measured quantitatively by tallying the number of objects produced or the number of clients served. However, objective indicators are not always available. More importantly, objective measures may sometimes present an inaccurate picture of performance. For instance, consider two manufacturing teams that are both producing dishwashers. One team is assigned to use state-of-the-art equipment, whereas the other is assigned to use older equipment that is unreliable. Examining only their production records would lead to the conclusion that the first team is superior. However, the second team may be contributing more when their constraints are taken into account. This illustrates the inadequacy of using only objective indicators of output to assess team performance.

The most common method of assessing team output when quantitative measures are flawed or unavailable is to measure the satisfaction of those who receive or review the product or service. These people can be clients or employees and supervisors who are internal to the organization. Their assessments of team effectiveness are particularly important because it is often these output receivers that determine both if the team will continue to function and if it will receive additional resources. These assessments are largely subjective and can sometimes be biased. The fact that they are subjective does not, however, mean that they cannot provide valuable insight into the team's productivity. Combining subjective indicators with any objective measures that do exist tends to be a more optimal method of assessing team outputs.

The combined use of objective and subjective measures was demonstrated in the Lake Superior case (Case 4.1). Objective performance indicators included measures of speed, tonnage, job lot percentage, and waste. For these measures numerical values could be obtained from organizational records. Overall profitability was also determined and compared to similar mills. These objective indicators were, however, sometimes difficult to link directly to the performance of a particular team. Thus, both managers and team members supplemented objective measures with subjective judgments.

Team Viability

In addition to the services and goods produced, assessments of team effectiveness should include measures of team viability. *Team viability* is concerned with the team's capacity to continue working together. Teams with high viability have developed effective social relationships that allow them to work cooperatively for extended periods of time. Even though teams without positive relationships might be able to complete short-term, focused projects, they are generally unable to excel over the long run.

Both team members and outside observers such as supervisors can make assessments of viability. The team members themselves often have a good perspective of viability because they are very familiar with the team and their relationships with its various members. Yet, outside observers sometimes have less emotional attachment and can therefore see a broader picture of the numerous social relationships. In either case, the focus should be on understanding how well team members get along and work together, for performance will generally decrease over time when social relationships are not positive.

Team viability appeared to be exceptionally high for the teams discussed in the Lake Superior case. Many of the difficulties in creating viable teams were circumvented by introducing teams at a start-up plant as opposed to an existing plant. Job applicants were screened to ensure that they had the skills needed to work in teams, making it less likely that teams would experience negative conflict that would prevent them from developing effective working relationships. Weekly team meetings also provided an avenue for teams to resolve any conflict before it escalated to a point where it harmed performance. Teams at Lake Superior Paper Company also exhibited willingness to learn. Openness to learning helps ensure that new skills will be developed, which in turn increases the likelihood that a team can overcome the numerous challenges it will face over an extended period of time.

Member Satisfaction

A third criterion for team effectiveness is the extent to which the team satisfies the needs of its members. The team may be ineffective if it imposes high costs in terms of individual sacrifice and disillusionment. Each team member has his or her own reasons for wanting to belong to the team, and the team is not as effective as it could be unless the needs of each person are being adequately fulfilled. Thus, part of assessing the effectiveness of a team is determining the extent to which members are happy with what the team is providing for them as individuals. This can usually be determined through an anonymous survey (such as a quality of worklife survey) that asks team members to provide feedback about how satisfied they are with what the team is providing for them in terms of rewards, growth, and motivating work.

Satisfaction was high for members of the teams working at the Lake Superior Paper Company. Team members reported that they liked to go to work and that the team system helped make them feel like "real people." They reported that they would not be comfortable going back to a traditional work structure that did not incorporate empowered teams. Much of this satisfaction seemed to stem from perceptions of employee ownership, as team members felt like they—rather than top-level management—had primary responsibility for the work process.

TEAM EFFECTIVENESS POTENTIAL

A team's effectiveness should also be judged in relation to its potential. Actual team performance is affected not only by team inputs and processes but also by team potential, which is dependent largely on the tasks the team is performing. Because team performance is influenced by a team's tasks, a taxonomy has been developed to classify group tasks in terms of their relation to potential effectiveness. This taxonomy can help establish how high expectations should be for team performance.[2] The taxonomy also helps illustrate areas where effort can be directed to increase effectiveness.

A Taxonomy of Team Potential

In a broad sense, tasks can be classified along two dimensions. One dimension concerns the extent to which tasks can be divided and completed by different people. *Divisible* tasks can be subdivided so that each team member can complete a part of the whole. *Unitary tasks* cannot be divided, and the task must be completed by the collective group. For instance, the task of lifting a heavy object is unitary because the lifting cannot be done by a single individual, but rather requires the combined effort of all team members. In contrast, the task of assembling an automobile is divisible because one person can bolt on the bumpers, another person can apply the paint, and someone else can mount the tires.

The second dimension concerns the type of output that is desired. *Maximizing tasks* seek output that is measured by amount produced. An example of a maximizing task is the work of a sales team given the primary goal of selling a large number of insurance plans. *Optimizing tasks* seek output that is measured in terms of quality. A marketing development team has an optimizing task because the expected output is a single marketing plan that will be judged primarily on its quality. Variation in both divisibility and type of output is illustrated in the following three task categories.

Additive Tasks

Additive tasks pool the inputs of team members, and the group outcome is the sum of each individual's contribution. One example is a group of lawn workers trimming weeds. The task is divisible because each person can trim some of the weeds. It is also maximizing because the desired output is defined more by the amount of area trimmed than by the quality of the trimming (although quality below a certain threshold might indeed be problematic).

The performance of a team on additive tasks should always exceed the performance of any individual team member. Thus, teams are often effective for completing additive tasks. However, if the group outcome is divided by the number of team members, the output per person may be lower than if workers completed the task individually and were not aware that their inputs were being pooled. This is because additive tasks make it difficult to link contributions to individuals, which can result in people exerting less than maximum effort on a group task. Nevertheless, the team performance on additive tasks is equal to the sum of individual inputs, and its performance can be improved by focusing on increasing each individual's performance.

Disjunctive Tasks

Disjunctive tasks address a common question or a challenge and require the selection of a single answer to represent the group's performance. These tasks are unitary and optimizing. An example would be a quiz for which the group must come up with a single answer for each question. In the workplace this might be a task that requires the team to provide a specific forecast. Individuals cannot provide separate answers, and the end goal is to come up with the best answer rather than a large number of answers.

For disjunctive tasks, group performance is often equal to the performance of the best member, because it is he or she who provides the correct response. If some kind of synergistic process occurs, group performance may exceed individual performance. However, group performance may be less impressive than individual performance if the rest of the group convinces the highest performing member to accept a suboptimal solution. The potential for high performance of disjunctive tasks is, therefore, largely dependent on high-performing individuals. Performance of the group as a whole can be enhanced by focusing on the inputs of these high performers, as well as on creating group processes that ensure that the group will recognize and accept an optimal answer.

Conjunctive Tasks

Conjunctive tasks require everyone to provide some input. The classic example is an automobile assembly line that requires each person to complete a part of the overall process. These tasks are usually divisible and can be either optimizing or maximizing.

The group's performance for conjunctive tasks is often constrained by the lowest performing member. For maximizing tasks, the constraint might be a bottleneck in the production process. An example is an automobile manufacturing employee who is so slow that the rest of the team spends a great deal of time waiting for that person to complete his task. For optimizing tasks, the constraint might be the provision of faulty inputs. An example here might be a budgeting team in which each member is required to provide data. If one person provides bad data, the entire budget is affected and will be less than an optimal solution. Thus, team performance on conjunctive tasks can often be improved by focusing on increasing the quantity/quality of inputs provided by the lowest performing individual team member.

Social Facilitation

Another issue related to a team's effectiveness potential concerns the extent to which tasks are performed better by people working in groups rather than as individuals. Some insight might be found in your own study habits. Do you like to study when other people are around, or do you like to study in private? Is your answer the same for all subjects you study? Would all your friends have the same preferences? The answers to these questions are not always simple, and you may probably find yourself saying, "It depends. . . ."

Issues related to performance in the presence of others have been examined by researchers interested in social facilitation. *Social facilitation* occurs when individuals perform tasks better in the presence of others than when they are working in private.[3] Members of a team can sometimes choose to physically separate themselves when they perform tasks. Research related to social facilitation does not, therefore, directly speak to the issue of whether work should be organized around teams or individuals—the issue that was addressed in Unit 2. The concept of social facilitation does, however, provide some guidance about the expected performance potential of employees physically working together in teams. It also helps explain how teams might approach their tasks in order to maximize performance.

Much of the early research into social facilitation was not conducted with people. One of the more interesting studies used cockroaches as subjects.[4] The researchers wanted to know if cockroaches run faster when they are in the presence of other cockroaches. They used glass to design a research apparatus consisting of a long tunnel lined with several individual compartments. A cockroach was then placed in one end of the tunnel with a bright light. Because the cockroach's natural instinct is to run away from the light, the researchers timed the cockroach to see how long it took to run from one end of the tunnel to the other. In some trials the individual compartments lining the tunnel were empty; in other trials the compartments were filled with live cockroaches that observed the runner. Interestingly, cockroaches ran more quickly when they were observed by other roaches. Similar support for social facilitation was found in other studies using people as research participants. In one case, participants were given a word and asked to write as many associated thoughts as possible. Writing in the presence of others—even when competition was downplayed—resulted in more associated thoughts than did writing in isolation.[5] These results imply that people (and cockroaches) perform better when they work in the presence of others.

Other research studies, however, found opposite results and concluded that the presence of others impairs performance. An example of these opposite findings occurred when the researchers studying the cockroaches changed the research apparatus slightly. Instead of having the roach run straight, they placed a bend in the tunnel so that the roach had to make a turn in order to escape the light. With the new apparatus the results were reversed so that cockroaches got to the other end of the tunnel faster when others were not present. Results for people also frequently reversed as the task changed. For instance, one study found that people could memorize nonsense words more quickly in isolation than when working around others.[6] Why would this be so?

The answer to the question of why cockroaches ran faster in the presence of others in the first instance but not the second (and the larger question of social facilitation) is found in the difference between the tasks. In the first instance, the roaches were running in a straight line, which is consistent with their natural instincts. In the second instance, they had to negotiate a turn, which is not something that comes natural for cockroaches. The same is true for studies involving people: we tend to excel in the presence of others when we perform dominant tasks—those that are natural and instinctual, but the presence of others can harm our performance when we work on novel tasks that are difficult.[7]

A number of theories have been developed to explain why social facilitation occurs for simple but not complex tasks.[8] One theory suggests that having others around increases arousal. Arousal is beneficial for performing simple tasks because it focuses attention and increases effort. However, too much arousal can be harmful when someone is trying to complete a difficult task that she is uncertain how to accomplish. Another theory focuses less on arousal and more on the distraction created by others. When an audience exists, people tend to pay attention to the audience and focus less on the task at hand. This can facilitate performance of dominant tasks because these tasks require automatic responses and too much thought can get in the way of effective performance. In contrast, paying attention to people rather than the task impedes performance on novel tasks that require high levels of concentration.

Although theories of social facilitation have generally been supported by research, issues related to individual differences of people have not been studied extensively. It seems reasonable that some people with certain characteristics (perhaps extroverts) would have higher performance in the presence of others than people with different characteristics (such as introverts). Future research will probably address this question, but to date little is known about the extent to which social facilitation occurs for some people and not for others.

In summary, social facilitation research suggests that a team can maximize its performance when its members physically work together to complete simple tasks. The presence of others can provide a motivating environment that facilitates high performance. However, when the team members perform complex tasks, performance may be higher if they complete their work in physical separation. Doing difficult work tasks alone may allow team members to focus and individually excel before combining their efforts into a team product. This may be impossible for some teams that operate under reciprocal technology (see Unit 2); thus, other factors associated with technology should be taken into account when seeking to maximize the performance of a work team.

INTERTEAM COOPERATION

In order for a team to be truly effective, it should also work cooperatively with other teams. Cooperation among teams is often difficult to facilitate, however. This difficulty has been observed over and over when people who are friendly with one another are separated into groups and labeled by their membership. In most instances, cohesiveness increases within the new groups, whereas the people in different groups who were once friends begin to compete with and dislike those who are in another group. This phenomenon tends to occur regardless of group size. Once the boundaries have been drawn, something happens to people. Individuals who up to that point got along well with each other begin to compete. Why does this happen? Is there a way to get groups to cooperate rather than compete?

To help explain interteam cooperation, we first explore theories that have been developed to explain why groups tend to compete with each other. We then describe some methods that are useful for increasing cooperation.

Social Identification

Once people are placed in a group, they begin to define their self-concept in terms of that group. They develop a sense of responsibility for the group and define their personal success and failure in terms of group success and failure. In short, they gain a social identity from the groups to which they belong.[9]

Because we gain social identity from groups, we prefer to see groups that we belong to in a desirable light that enhances our personal value as individuals. We begin to interpret the actions and outcomes of our own group positively and thereby increase our personal feelings of self-worth. Yet, because our social identity is also developed in relation to others, we often tend to discount the positive actions and outcomes of other groups and individuals. This process helps us to see ourselves in a relatively favorable light and can be very adaptive, but it also encourages us to see the world in terms of group memberships.

The act of viewing the world in terms of group membership can help us make sense of information. Our minds have limited capacity and cannot process all the information that we receive.[10] We thus tend to simplify and categorize our environments. Simplification and categorization are beneficial because they provide us with a way to sort through large amounts of information about people and retain data that are helpful. Unfortunately, this process can be problematic because it encourages us to remember things about groups of people rather than about individuals. By placing someone in a group and associating them with the characteristics of that group, we are able to remember a great deal about them in a general way without remembering anything about them as specific individuals. This process is commonly known as *stereotyping*. The problem is that the stereotypes we develop are often inaccurate and members of a group seldom exactly fit a stereotype.

Stereotyping accentuates differences between members of groups. Some of these differences may be meaningful and perhaps even beneficial, such as when we stereotype a team of mechanical engineers as mathematically focused. The stereotype is based on a work-related characteristic, and it may provide some general guidance regarding how to interact with the engineers. Yet, other stereotypes may be less accurate and less useful. For instance, members of one team may stereotype another team's members as lazy. They will then tend to reinforce the stereotype by paying attention to all the instances in which members of the other team failed to work diligently. They would ignore cases in which members of the other team worked hard. Each individual within the team would be seen as lazy, regardless of how hard she worked. This in-group and out-group process would feed on itself, and a cycle of perpetuating stereotypes would occur.

Harmful stereotyping can often occur in manufacturing plants where teams have divergent goals and backgrounds. For instance, a team of engineers may have expertise in designing and building products, and a team of sales personnel may have expertise in marketing and selling those products. Both manufacturing and selling are critical for the firm's overall success; however, functional differences between the two teams may lead to undesirable stereotyping. The team of sales representatives may believe the engineers are out of touch with customers, whereas the team of engineers may perceive the sales representatives as out to make a quick buck. If the two teams begin to treat each other in accordance with these stereotypes, a sense of distrust is likely to develop. The perception of hidden agendas may even escalate to the point where the two teams purposely do things to fulfill their own agenda at the expense of the other team's agenda.

One effect of creating teams in work organizations is therefore that people begin to identify with the teams to which they belong. Their sense of personal worth starts to depend on the performance of their team. Although this in itself may not be harmful, it can create conditions whereby teams begin to compete with each other. In order to enhance their own self-identity, team members may sabotage the efforts of other teams, meaning that the very act of creating teams may in some cases be a step toward decreased cooperation within an organization. Whether overall cooperation decreases or increases depends largely on other conditions in the work environment. Fortunately, a number of methods exist for facilitating cooperation and thereby counteracting negative competition. After reviewing sources of competition, we discuss some of the most prominent methods.

Conditions That Foster Competition Between Teams

Some competition between teams can motivate them to work hard and strive for success. But competition can be harmful when it promotes infighting and undermines the efforts of other teams. Here we focus on this negative type of competition.

Competition increases when members of a group perceive a lack of equity. *Equity* is the perception of balance between inputs and outcomes relative to other groups. Team members evaluate the fairness of the rewards they receive from the organization by comparing those rewards with the rewards that members of other teams receive.[11] If a team perceives that its rewards are about the same as those of other teams that provide similar input to the organization, then the team will experience feelings of equity. However, if the team feels that it receives fewer rewards for similar inputs, then it will experience feelings of inequity. These feelings of inequity can lead the team to engage in competition with other teams that it feels are receiving higher rewards relative to inputs. Perceptions of inequity between groups can thus trigger competition, suggesting that effective team leaders strive to approach team interactions with fairness.

Another source of competition is scarcity of resources.[12] When resources are scarce, teams begin to perceive that their success is dependent on the failure of other groups. For instance, an organization may say that its financial situation will only allow it to provide a total bonus of 5 percent of net income for a year. If the bonus distribution is to be based on team merit, then a team's bonus can be increased by making sure that the performance of other teams is so bad that it does not receive a portion of the overall bonus pool. Another example of scarcity might concern the allocation of desirable projects. If an organization has a limited number of interesting and rewarding projects, teams will naturally compete for the best assignments. Scarcity could also revolve around issues such as determining which team a desirable individual is assigned to as a member, allocating work space where the team will carry out its tasks, and assigning sales customers and territories. In each of these cases, success for one team requires another team to experience a degree of failure. Scarce resources can thus encourage teams to try to get ahead at the expense of other teams who work for the same organization. Thus, an organization's reward system must be carefully planned and developed to make sure that success for one team is not come at the expense of failure for another team.

Other contextual events can also trigger competition between teams. A seemingly unimportant event can escalate into an issue that boosts negative competition. For instance, an off-hand remark by a member of one team may provide an impetus for the other team to feel that they are not respected. This may cause the team members to try and show their superiority over the team that they feel does not respect them. Similarly, a transfer of leadership in the upper echelons of an organization may cause a team to feel threatened and thus compete with other teams. Perhaps another triggering event might be a labor surplus and fear of downsizing. If teams feel that positions in the organization may be eliminated, then they are likely to compete and try to ensure that it is the jobs of another team, not theirs, that are eliminated. Each of these events brings perceptions of inequity and scarcity to the forefront of team member minds and can thereby serve as the episode triggering a destructive competition mode. Effective team leaders thus seek to resolve issues as soon as they occur rather than after they have festered into much larger problems.

Encouraging Team Cooperation

Since teams often move toward a state of competition, organizational leaders should be encouraged to use a variety of methods to encourage cooperation.[13] Perhaps the simplest method is to encourage members of different teams to interact with each other. Simply having contact between members of different teams can begin to break down in-group biases and correct false stereotypes. As they associate with people from different teams, they begin to see their co-workers as individuals rather than as members of another team. This helps break down biases and allows them to see that the needs and desires of other teams are similar to theirs. AES Corporation (see Case 4.2) uses this strategy when it requires top-level managers to visit and interact with teams working in its production plants. The result is greater understanding and increased cooperation.

The strategy of encouraging interaction can backfire if teams have already developed intense animosity toward one another. In these instances, interaction fuels the fire of hostility and in extreme cases can escalate into physical confrontations. This, however, seems unlikely in most business settings, particularly if steps are taken to ensure that competition between teams does not get out of hand before team members have a chance to interact. Work organizations can therefore benefit from encouraging teams to interact with other teams as soon as they are formed. This can be done by designing plants that guarantee that teams will have to work in close proximity to each other. It can also be done by scheduling both formal and informal times when members of various teams can meet together and get to know one another, even if they work in different locations.

Perhaps the most effective method of encouraging cooperation is to develop some type of shared goal that can be accomplished only when numerous teams work together. This is illustrated by an interesting experiment conducted in the 1950s.[14] The experimenters invited several young boys to attend a summer camp. With permission from the boys' parents, the experimenters then formed the boys into two different teams. The two teams were brought to the camp separately and initially resided in separate areas. Campers were encouraged to work with their own team on several projects, and strong ties formed within each team. The peaceful camp continued until the teams discovered each other. They then asked if they could compete to find out which team was superior. Competitions were arranged, and relationships between the two teams deteriorated to the point that camp leaders had to constantly separate the two teams to prevent their fighting.

The camp leaders then designed a number of crisis problems that could be solved only if the two teams worked together. At first the boys resisted working with their "enemies." However, over time they learned that they needed help from each other in order to solve problems such as restoring the camp's water supply. As they worked together, they found that many of their biases about the other team were misinterpretations. They began to see the two teams as having mutual goals that required cooperation. Most importantly, they began to communicate and find ways of involving the other team in their activities. In the end, the boys asked if both teams could share a bus home so that they would not be separated.

Although there are several dissimilarities between teams of boys at a summer camp and most business teams, a similar process can be used to encourage cooperation among business teams. One key is to make sure that the teams have a shared goal. This is sometimes done by developing an overall mission, or set of values, for the organization. By defining a common goal, a work organization can communicate how its various teams must work together in order to achieve something larger than each team's unique set of goals. A statement of purpose for the entire organization also helps new employees and teams to understand the importance of working together with other teams.

Work organizations can also create a common enemy, such as a competitor, that becomes the focus of team competition. This approach provides a new target that is the focus on which in-group biases are based. Consequently, social identity will tend to develop based on membership in a team within an organization rather than simply based on membership within a team. Although the primary loyalty may still be with their specific teams, employees also develop a sense of loyalty to the organization as a whole. This loyalty encourages them to avoid sabotaging the efforts of other teams who are seen as helping them in the fight against a competitor—their common enemy.

Another means for developing cooperation among teams is to create a compensation plan that merges the interests of teams. These compensation plans tie team and employee rewards to performance of the organization as a whole. They often include *gainsharing* and *profit sharing*. Gainsharing bases rewards on gains in improvement and quality, whereas profit sharing returns some of the organizational profits to employees within the organization. The common theme is that they both base rewards on organization-wide performance. Part of any individual's compensation is therefore based on the performance of other teams in the organization. This can help discourage undesirable competition between teams.

At any rate, preventing competition is usually easier than reducing it once it has begun. The process of conflict reduction is very time consuming. The best solution is therefore to design a team system so that competition will be minimized and cooperation between teams enhanced. The AES Corporation (Case 4.2) has adopted such a proactive strategy. A shared vision helps unify teams and encourages them to work together. AES's onion skin structure nests teams within teams, so that numerous teams are encouraged to work together. Moreover, plant managers and team leaders are members of more than one team, which allows them to play a linking role that can facilitate interteam coordination. In the end, a cooperative culture begins at the top and filters down through AES.

IMPROVING TEAM EFFECTIVENESS

It is easier to be a critic than a composer; this saying certainly applies to teams. For instance, think about your worst student group experience. Now ask yourself the harder question, "If I had to do it over again, what would I do to make that group experience more positive?" Often students work in groups and wish that their experiences were more productive; yet, they seldom take steps to improve these groups. Why? Part of the answer may be that they know student groups are only short term; that is, they will not be required to work with the group for an extended period of time. From this perspective, it might be easier to "just live with" the problems rather than to try and solve them. Another reason may be that they simply don't know what to do to solve the problems facing their groups. Both answers are unfortunate because groups enable students to learn important skills that can serve them well as they begin to work with teams in business organizations.

Businesses spend billions of dollars each year on training and development activities. Many of these activities are aimed at improving teams and teamwork. Although some are well planned and carefully implemented, others are simply reactions to what other companies seem to be doing. Without careful planning, little thought goes into either assessing the appropriateness of plans for a particular training program or evaluating its effectiveness. In order to aid the planning process, we now present a model that can serve as a foundation for organizations that desire to use training and development to systematically improve their teams. This systematic process helps shift effort away from mere criticism toward specific actions designed to enhance team effectiveness.

Overview of the Training Cycle for Teams

Training is a continuous process that is best described as an ongoing cycle.[15] This cycle is shown in Figure 4.1. The first step is to analyze the situation and determine the needs of teams and employees. In this information-gathering phase, research is performed to determine what is impeding team effectiveness. The second step is to develop a training intervention. This intervention should be designed specifically to address the needs uncovered in the analysis. The third step is to conduct the training. This is the only step that occurs in many organizations, but it is largely ineffective when it is not built on the previous steps. The fourth step is to evaluate the effects of the training and development that were carried out. This evaluation feeds back into analysis, creating an ongoing loop of training and development.

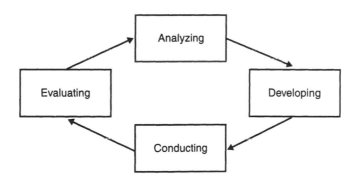

Figure 4.1 Training and development cycle

Even though this text focuses specifically on teams, it is also important to point out that the training cycle can be applied to different levels of organizations.[16] At the individual level, the cycle can be used to determine how to improve the knowledge, skills, abilities, and attitudes of particular employees. At the team level, it can be used to increase the cooperation and synergy of team members. The cycle can also be used to improve ties and relationships between teams and thereby improve overall productivity for the organization as a whole. The three levels are largely interdependent, and a solution to performance problems at the team level might be found at the individual or organization level as well as the team level. Specific examples of this interplay between the various levels will be pointed out in the following discussion.

Analyzing Training Needs

Analysis is a critical step that is often overlooked not only for teams but also for individuals and organizations.[17] However, problems must be identified before they can be solved; therefore, organizations that skip the analysis phase may be wasting their training dollars. Sometimes analysis may be reactive and focus on problems that already exist. In other cases, analysis may be proactive and focus specifically on barriers that keep performance from being even better. Proactive analysis is a hallmark of many quality-oriented programs that stress continuous improvement. It is generally considered to be more effective than reactive analysis since it does not wait for problems to occur before it begins to solve them. Effective analysis can also determine which needs can be met through training and development, for some problems may require other interventions such as restructuring.

One method of analysis is to conduct performance appraisals. An effective performance appraisal asks the rater to provide information about multiple dimensions of team performance, which highlights specific areas where improvement is needed. Performance appraisal data can also provide information about the inputs of each team member. For instance, appraisals can be used to identify team members who do not have the necessary technical skills, as well as members who do not carry their fair share of the workload. Although these assessments cross over to the individual level of analysis, they can definitely provide information about how to improve team performance.

Another method of analysis is to carefully examine the specific tasks that the team carries out. Historically, this process has been known as job analysis and is frequently performed at the individual level. However, similar analyses can be performed at the team level. One example is the technical analysis that took place as part of the sociotechnical approach that was discussed in the IDS case of Unit 2. This process looks at the overall tasks for the team and seeks to determine improvements that can be made in physical layout, and in coordination of tasks between team members and with other teams.

Employee surveys also provide data that can be used in the analysis process. Individual reports about ability to work together with other team members can provide insight into the team's capacity to continue working cooperatively. These surveys present a forum for employees to report deficiencies that they see in the current work process. Such surveys were beneficial in helping the Lake Superior Paper Company know that its start-up was on target and that its employees perceived the new plant as a success.

Another important vehicle for analysis is team meetings. Team meetings provide teams with the opportunity to discuss issues that might be impeding their effectiveness. Observations of team meetings at the Fitzgerald Battery Plant revealed numerous issues in relation to scheduling, conflict resolution, and problem solving. However, for team meetings to be successful, team members should be trained in how to hold effective meetings. Teams should also be encouraged to develop procedures ensuring that the team systematically discusses methods of improving its quality and productivity. More importantly, teams need to learn to use action items so that the issues discussed in the meetings are addressed with actions. Otherwise meetings can become "gripe sessions" that provide little new information that can be used to improve effectiveness.

Developing the Training

Development takes place once analysis has uncovered areas where a gap exists between actual performance and desired performance. The first step in development is to establish objectives. These objectives specifically define what the training will accomplish, and they can illustrate how the effectiveness gap will be closed. Although the required specificity of these objectives may vary from setting to setting, the key to good training objectives is that they clearly outline how things will be different once a training intervention has taken place.

Once objectives have been established, the next step is to design a curriculum. What specific components will the training include in order to meet the objectives that have been set? Perhaps the first decision is the context in which the training will take place. In many instances the training will be most effective if it is carried out as part of on-the-job activities. In other cases, it will be better to hold the training off-site in order to ensure an uninterrupted block of time when participants can focus on learning the material rather than performing their jobs.

Lesson plans can then be developed to spell out how the training will proceed. These lesson plans should be adapted to the specific situation and can include an outline of how the training will proceed as well as who will carry out specific assignments. Lectures and experiential exercises can be developed for delivery of the training content. Training materials such as workbooks and texts can also be chosen to support the instructional content. A viable alternative for many organizations is to hire an external consultant to design the curriculum and present the training. This is what occurred at Charrette Corporation when the consultant was hired to meet with supervisors and help them develop and learn new leadership behaviors. The important thing to remember is that the design and presentation should be based explicitly on both the needs uncovered during the analysis phase and the training objectives.

Conducting the Training

A great deal of research has been done to determine methods for facilitating adult learning. Some of the most important findings of this research suggest that adults do not learn very well in the traditional, lecture-oriented classroom. They learn best when they are actively involved in the learning process. Learning can be facilitated by making sure that the material is relevant to the trainees in terms of helping them solve problems they currently face or believe they will face in the near future. Adults also tend to learn best when they can see how new material fits with things that they already know and do. Because they are adults, responsibility for learning ultimately resides within themselves and not with the training facilitator.

As implied above, adult learning theory suggests that lectures may not be the best method of training.[18] Alternatives include simulations and direct experiences, as well as case discussions and experiential exercises. A common example of such a high-involvement learning tool is the group decision-making survival experience that requires a group to make decisions while imagining that they are lost in a wilderness, desert, or other survival setting with only limited supplies. Working together, the group must decide what it will do to survive. This usually provides the team with a captivating learning experience. However, careful planning and implementation are necessary in order to make sure that training objectives are met. Another example of a high-involvement learning method is the role-play described in the Charrette case. Supervisors role-played both their new leader behaviors and the new behaviors they expected from the employees they would be leading. This helped them to see areas where change was needed, as well as to learn new scripts for communicating with workers. Such exercises can be used to facilitate change at both the individual and team level.

Perhaps the most common training intervention involves a set of intervention tactics that have come to be known simply as team building. *Team building* is training that is specifically targeted at building the relationships and capacities of the team to work together.[19] Examples include activities such as outdoor obstacle and rope courses. Such interventions are generally used to develop trust and team efficacy. Team building thus provides a specific intervention aimed at the team as a collective rather than at the skills of individual team members.

Another innovative method for training is to let team members teach themselves.[20] Often, team members are given training materials and allowed to work at their own pace. Other team members or supervisors then test them to make sure they have learned the material. This can facilitate the training of individual team members and can in turn improve the performance of the team.

Evaluating the Training

Training can be evaluated in several different ways; the most common approaches are shown in Table 4.1.[21] The reaction method focuses on measuring the reactions of the learners. This approach makes sense in many cases because those who receive training should be seen as customers who can provide valuable

TABLE 4.1   Methods for Evaluating Training

Method	Description
Participant Reactions	People who receive the training complete surveys that describe how satisfied they are with the training. Student evaluations of professors fit this category of assessment. Participant reactions are frequently used because they are relatively easy to obtain.
Participant Learning	People who receive the training are assessed to see if their knowledge has increased. Paper and pencil tests are common methods of assessing participant learning. Final exams given to students are an example.
Behavioral Changes	People who receive the training are assessed to see if they can perform certain behaviors. This might include role-playing, where training participants are observed to determine if they have learned the skills necessary to perform a particular behavior. However, the most effective measures are those that actually assess on-the-job behaviors. For instance, a student could be observed in her first month of employment to see if she could really perform the tasks she was taught in a class.
Outcomes	Outcome assessments focus on results. One example is profitability. Another might be the scrap rate in a production plant. These assessments are perhaps the most critical indication of whether training is effective. However, they are relatively difficult in practice. For example, measuring the outcome of student training might require an evaluator to compare the on-the-job productivity of students who had taken a particular course with the productivity of students who had not taken the course.

input into the evaluation. The next method assesses the learning that has taken place and might include tests or other evaluations. The third method is an assessment of behavioral change. Can the trainees apply what they have learned to behave differently than they did before the training? Finally, an assessment can be made about the results and outcomes associated with the new behavior. Do productivity and satisfaction increase when teams complete the training?

A logical extension of the evaluation process is to provide feedback that serves as analysis information when repeating the training cycle. If participant reactions were not positive, then better methods of conducting the training might need to be developed. Improved training methods may also be necessary if assessments suggest that the objectives were not obtained. If reactions, learning, and behaviors are improved but outcomes are not, then the objectives themselves should be reexamined to determine whether their focus was appropriately directed toward significant needs. The analysis step is broadened if the training was successful, which then helps to focus on ways of improving future performance.

COMMON CHALLENGES TO TEAM EFFECTIVENESS

The cases described in this book suggest a number of common challenges teams face. In this section we summarize and review several of these challenges in order to highlight areas where training and development activities are especially important for facilitating team effectiveness.

Organizations Tend to Expect Too Much, Too Soon

When it comes to teams, managers sometimes expect too much, too soon. Recall the original expectation of IDS executives who thought that the design for team implementation would take three and a half months. In fact, the design took eight and a half months. Fortunately, IDS management had the patience and the staying power to absorb the frustration of this extended planning period. Their patience paid off with a very successful start-up. Managers who severely underestimate the effort necessary to launch teams successfully are setting up their organizations for failure. Training can help provide managers with more accurate expectations for teams.

Things Often Get Worse Before They Get Better

As is true of any other innovation, teams undergo a learning curve. It is not unusual for organizations to suffer an initial reduction in effectiveness as teams begin, and it may take a year simply to regain former performance levels. Significant increases in productivity may not become evident for 18 months or more. This decrease in productivity may occur as team members learn new behaviors and new responsibilities and struggle to find the path for a team-based organization that works best for them. The Fitzgerald case describes a set of specific behaviors that workers functioning in teams need to learn. However, many employees have no practical experience with self-management strategies, such as self goal setting, self-feedback, and designing their own information system, so they must learn how to go about these tasks. Training in these skill areas is therefore critical. The Lake Superior case also illustrates the need for an initial emphasis on technical skill development.

Managers' and Supervisors' Sense of Power and Control Is Threatened

Frequently, middle managers and supervisors feel that they are the big losers in a transition to team systems. In one sense, they are right; the number of managers and supervisors is typically reduced with a team system. One of the major sources of savings that derives from a team system is a delayering of management and supervisors.

A more insidious and difficult challenge, which was described in the Charrette case, is dealing with the psychological loss of control that supervisors and middle managers sometimes experience. Frequently, supervisors have grown up under a system in which the manager is a boss who gives orders and employees carry out those orders. This means that these leaders do not know how to behave in a team system. A great deal of training, including role-plays such as those described in the Charrette case, can help supervisors learn new skills.

Some High-status Employees Initially Feel Like Losers

Just like supervisors, some other employees also feel like losers. The "techs" at Lake Superior Paper and the special clerks at IDS believed they had more to lose than gain from the introduction of teams. From these examples we can generalize some characteristics of employees who are likely to have negative feelings about a change to teams. Employees who enjoy some privilege because of seniority may feel the loss of that privilege. Teams tend to reward and value people more on the basis of performance and contribution rather than seniority. Also, employees who have achieved a special position, such as specializing in a job with a degree of prominence that derives from a particular knowledge or experience, are more likely to feel a loss. With teams, knowledge tends to be spread more evenly throughout the entire team, so that specialized knowledge becomes a more common commodity.

Resentful employees who feel a loss because of the introduction of teams can be dealt with in several ways. Bluntly forcing the change on them can create lasting problems. Sometimes these employees leave the system, and sometimes they cause distress to the team implementation. A better approach is to involve them in the transition planning process and attempt to deal with their concerns. Sometimes their special status or pay might be grandfathered into the new system. Most of all, management must realize that not all employees will see a transition to teams as a winning proposition and that these employees can cause considerable damage to the transition.

Employees Need Expanded Technical and Behavioral Skills

Added responsibility and expanded autonomy mean that both the technical and behavioral skill repertoire of employees must be expanded. One of the fundamental changes typically accompanying a team implementation is the notion that a team member becomes capable of most, if not all, of the tasks required of a team. Typically, task- or technical-oriented training is required to ensure that team members develop these skills.

Perhaps more important, and not as well understood, is the idea that team members must develop individual and group self-leadership capabilities. They need to learn organization, planning, interpersonal, and self-direction skills. As shown in the Fitzgerald case, training can help them learn how to set goals, interpret feedback systems, lead and participate in meetings, resolve conflicts, and initiate problem solving on their own rather than automatically shifting the burden to a supervisor.

Team Implementation Requires Planning and Organization

Although none of the cases in this book reports such a drastic action, we have heard of organizations that have formed teams by removing the supervisor and making a grand pronouncement that henceforth the work groups are teams. This approach—with no training, no design, no organizational change strategy— is usually a sure recipe for failure. The general logic behind this implementation strategy is that self-managing teams will also be able to self-manage the implementation. The flaw in this logic is provided by the rubber band metaphor.

A rubber band can absorb a limited amount of stress by stretching; if it is pulled too much, too soon, however, it breaks. Teams can also break.

Typically, failure comes because teams are given total responsibility without the necessary technical and social knowledge and skills. As shown in the IDS case, a great deal of planning is necessary before teams are implemented. Teams need to be trained in the fundamental social processes such as how to lead a meeting, generate creativity, conduct a problem-solving session, engage in conflict resolution, and, most of all, develop leadership skills.[22]

"Greenfield" Sites are Easier Than "Retrofit" Changes

In "greenfield," sites the team system is tightly integrated into the organizational structure from the very beginning.[23] The Lake Superior case describes a greenfield site. A "retrofit" (or "brownfield") means an organizational change in which an existing traditional organization is changed over to a team system. Charrette, IDS, and Texas Instruments Malaysia represent retrofit sites.

In a retrofit change, the challenges of implementation are considerably more intense. First, a significant amount of "unlearning" must take place before the new learning can replace the old. As illustrated in the case of Texas Instruments Malaysia, this "unlearning" may take years of gradual change. One of the main issues for change is the behavior of supervisors. Many supervisors have years of experience with a particular pattern of leadership—typically, top-down. To become a facilitator or coordinator, a supervisor must act in ways that are directly contrary to what has been learned over the years of experience. Yet, in a greenfield situation the managerial tool of selection is available. That is, the management team can devise tests and selection mechanisms to evaluate an applicant's cooperation and team skills.

The potential difficulty of implementing teams in existing work systems should not, however, be interpreted as suggesting that there is no hope for changing existing organizations. There are many examples of successful retrofit applications. Indeed, many examples are included in the cases throughout this book. However, it is important to accept the reality that change is difficult, and then develop and hone training interventions so that a retrofit to a team system becomes a more certain and routine exercise.

FUNDAMENTAL REQUIREMENTS FOR TEAM EFFECTIVENESS

As we have seen, the teams described in our cases faced several challenges. Each of these challenges presents a specific area where a training and development intervention can occur to improve team success. These cases provide a real-world background for many of the ideas we have discussed throughout this book. Therefore, a review of some fundamental requirements for team success is appropriate now.

Teams Must Begin with a Fundamental Philosophy

A fundamental belief in the capacity of humans is necessary. To some degree, this relates to the old Theory Y/Theory X viewpoint. Theory Y describes a set of assumptions that articulates that people will generally respond in a responsible way if given the opportunity and the resources. Thus, people are capable of performing creatively and effectively within their repertoire of skills without close external supervision and direction. Theory X, in contrast, assumes that people are inherently lazy and irresponsible and will choose to behave badly if not monitored and controlled. Many of the cases and theories we have presented suggest that a fundamental philosophy which is optimistic about the human capacity to respond constructively to opportunities for greater responsibility and empowerment is an important prerequisite for a successful launch of teams.

Teams Will Require a Change in the Management Information System of the Organization

Teams increase employee responsibility. A great deal of information is required for them to be able to make effective decisions and to perform successfully. Many of the case examples suggest that teams will demand information systems and design their own if needed.

Continuous Training Is Required

The training requirements for teams cannot be overestimated. Training must include technical and task training, as well as sophisticated interpersonal and social training.

Outside Facilitation Is Extremely Helpful

Outside help need not come from an expensive consultant. For large companies, an internal facilitator from a staff department or from some other unit may be more appropriate. The main point is that an outside consultant (which might be an internal facilitator) can provide an objective viewpoint that will help to overcome the bumps and challenges that invariably arise with teams.

Patience, Patience, and More Patience— Remember the Learning Curve

We typically think of a learning curve when we are adopting a new technology; yet the development of new social skills that are inherent to self-managing teams also requires a learning curve. Many mistakes will be made; the way is laden with difficulties. Yet successful organizations think of teams as an investment. Patience is the key.

Teams in the Future May Be Different

It is hoped that this textbook has provided you with a solid, realistic overview of contemporary work teams. Given the widespread use of teams in organizations today, this knowledge can be an important part of your repertoire for a successful work career. Although our recommendations apply well to relatively clear and concrete teams, teamwork in the future will likely involve situations in which people work together without relatively permanent or clearly defined teams. In this spirit, and as a look toward the future of teams in organizations, a final case (Case 4.3) presents the highly successful story of W. L. Gore and Associates. You might think of the Gore case as a peek into the future to see how effective teamwork might be used to foster positive organizational and employee outcomes without relying on formally created, long-term teams.

WHAT WE HOPE YOU LEARN FROM THIS UNIT

After studying this unit, you should have a better understanding of team effectiveness. Being able not only to measure but also to improve team effectiveness is critical.

The multidimensional perspective of team effectiveness shows that measurements of team success should include a variety of assessments. One effectiveness dimension relates to the quality and quantity of team output. In some cases, this output can be measured with objective indicators that yield numerical values. However, objective performance measures seldom provide the whole picture and are normally supplemented with subjective assessments from the people who use a team's goods and services. Another effectiveness dimension relates to the team's capacity to continue working cooperatively. Highly effective teams develop positive social relationships that increase team viability. The third effectiveness dimension concerns the satisfaction of each team member. Teams are considered most effective when they fulfill the needs and desires of team members.

Teams have varying potential for effectiveness. One source of variation is a team's tasks. When teams perform additive tasks, the inputs of their members are essentially summed together. Team performance will therefore always exceed that of any individual team member, and effectiveness can be increased by helping each individual to become more productive. When teams perform disjunctive tasks, the team must work together to develop a single solution to a problem. In these cases, team performance potential is often equal to the performance of the best individual team member, as long as the team as a whole is able to recognize an optimal solution when it is presented. Effectiveness for disjunctive tasks is thus facilitated by developing the abilities of high-performing individuals, as well as creating group processes that ensure the identification and acceptance of optimal solutions. When teams perform conjunctive tasks, each team member must contribute something before the team can accomplish its objective. In these instances, team effectiveness potential is often constrained by the lowest performing team member. This suggests that development efforts should focus on improving the performance of the least skilled team member.

Research into social facilitation shows that people perform routine and natural tasks better in the presence of others than in private. The opposite effect holds for creative and nonroutine tasks. This suggests that teams have the potential for higher performance when they physically work together on easy tasks and physically separate to accomplish difficult tasks that are divisible.

Teams naturally move toward a state of competition, unless efforts are made to ensure cooperation among teams. Successful methods of cooperation enhancement include developing a sense of equity, providing organization-wide incentives, encouraging contact with members of other teams, and developing an organizational mission that aligns the interests of various teams.

Team effectiveness can be improved through a four-step process. The first step is to analyze the needs of organizations, teams, and individuals. Analysis helps pinpoint areas where improvement is needed and allows a training program to be developed to resolve specific issues. The second step in the process is to develop the training. This includes development of clear objectives that define how things will be different once the training is completed, as well as the creation of lesson plans and identification of essential training resources. The third step is to conduct the training. Generally, team members learn best when they are actively involved in the training, and when they can draw direct connections between their jobs and the training material. The final step is to analyze how well the training intervention has resolved the concerns identified at the beginning of the process. Without evaluation, organizations can never be sure whether they are getting a return for the money they spend on training. The analysis phase can also provide information that can be used in future analyses as a start for repeating the four-step process.

The cases throughout this text also illustrate a number of specific areas where training can facilitate teams. Much can be learned about teams by looking at both the successes and failures of organizations that have adopted team-based work designs.

NOTES FOR UNIT 4

1. This model is the work of J. R. Hackman, "The Design of Work Teams," in Jay W. Lorsh (ed.), Handbook of Organizational Behavior, pp. 315–342 (Englewood Cliffs, NJ: Prentice-Hall, 1987).

2. This taxonomy is taken from I. D. Steiner, *Group Process and Productivity* (New York: Academic Press, 1972).

3. For an excellent review of facilitation, see Robert S. Baron, Norbert L. Kerr, and Norman Miller, *Group Process, Group Decision, Group Action* (Pacific Grove, CA: Brooks/Cole, 1992).

4. This study is reported by R. B. Zajonc, A. Heingartner, and E. M. Herman, "Social Enhancement and Impairment of Performance in the Cockroach," *Journal of Personality and Social Psychology* 13 (1969): 83–92.

5. This study is reported by F. H. Allport, "The Influence of the Group upon Association and Thought," *Journal of Experimental Psychology* 3 (1920): 159–182.

6. This study is reported by J. Pessin, "The Comparative Effects of Social and Mechanical Stimulation on Memorizing," *American Journal of Psychology* 45 (1933): 363–370.

7. A quantitative review of findings is reported by C. F. Bond and L. J. Titus, "Social Facilitation: A Meta-analysis of 241 Studies," *Psychological Bulletin* 94 (1983): 265–292.

8. See Baron, Kerr, and Miller, *Group Process,* for a review of these theories.

9. See H. Tajfel and J. C. Tuner, "The Social Identity Theory of Intergroup Behavior," in S. Worchel and W. G. Austin (eds.), *Psychology of Intergroup Relations,* pp. 7–24 (Chicago: Nelson Hall, 1986).

10. R. Lord and K. J. Maher, "Alternative Information Processing Models and Their Implications for Theory, Research, and Practice," *Academy of Management Review* 15 (1990): 666–681.

11. Equity theory is developed by J. S. Adams, "Toward an Understanding of Inequity," *Journal of Abnormal and Social Psychology* 67 (1963): 442–456.

12. See Baron, Kerr, and Miller, *Group Process.*

13. A good review of methods for encouraging cooperation among groups is found in D. R. Forsyth, *Group Dynamics,* 2nd ed. (Pacific Grove, CA: Brooks/Cole, 1990).

14. M. Sherif, O. J. Harvey, B. J. White, W. R. Hood, and C. W. Sherif, *Intergroup Conflict and Cooperation: The Robbers Cave Experiment* (Norman, OK: Institute of Group Relations, 1961).

15. The training cycle is presented by Tom W. Goad, *Delivering Effective Training* (San Diego: University Associates, 1982).

16. See Nicholas S. Rashford and David Coghlan, *The Dynamics of Organizational Levels* (Reading, MA: Addison-Wesley, 1994).

17. See Gordon E. Mills, R. Wayne Pace, and Brent D. Peterson, *Analysis in Human Resource Training and Organization Development* (Reading, MA: Addison-Wesley, 1988).

18. The ideas about adult learning theory are based on the work of Malcolm Knowles, *The Adult Learner: A Neglected Species,* 2nd ed. (Houston, TX: Gulf, 1978).

19. Additional information can be found in William G. Dyer, *Team Building: Current Issues and New Alternatives,* 3rd ed. (Reading, MA: Addison-Wesley, 1995).

20. The concept of self-directed learning is presented in Charles C. Manz and Karen P. Manz, "Strategies for Facilitating Self-directed Learning: A Process for Enhancing Human Resource Development," *Human Resource Development Quarterly* 2, no. 1 (1991): 3–24.

21. These are taken from D. L. Kirkpatrick, "Evaluation," in R. L. Craig (ed.), *Training and Development Handbook,* 3rd ed. (New York: McGraw-Hill, 1987).

22. See Charles C. Manz, *Mastering Self-Leadership: Empowering Yourself for Personal Excellence* (Englewood Cliffs, NJ: Prentice-Hall, 1992), for a description of how to teach self-leadership skills.

23. For a training case that addresses this issue, see "The Greenfield Case," available from Organization Design and Development, 2002 Renaissance Blvd., Suite 100, King of Prussia, PA 19406.

CASE

4.2

Coordinating Teams at AES

This chapter was written by Kenneth A. Smith and Henry P. Sims, Jr.[1]

In addition to carrying out day-to-day tasks, teams can be used to create organizational strategies. This case focuses on a network of teams that has emerged throughout a company in order to develop business strategy. Strategy is created through a bottom-up process of interlocking teams. A core set of values helps ensure that various teams are working toward a common goal. Coordination among teams is also enhanced through annual executive visits to plants where top managers "stand in" for a wide variety of employees.

This is a story of how teamwork is used as a critical element in framing and carrying out the overall strategy of a business. We focus on a network of teams that has emerged throughout a company because of the team's commitment at the top—the executive team. Teams and teamwork are an important part of this story, although the company does not routinely use the term "team" in connection with strategy making. Nevertheless, relationships and communication both within and between teams are important parts of strategy making. Cooperation among interlocking teams is an important element that helps the company to succeed.

This company emphasizes the importance of shared values, which both define the company's culture and contribute to the teamlike atmosphere. We have also observed that shared values are major drivers of strategy making in this company.

As we begin, let us clarify what we mean by the phrase "strategy team." In reality, there is no single group at AES to which we might attach this label. Rather, the strategy team is a network of individuals and teams who collectively define strategy.

AES Corporation: The Company

AES Corporation, formerly called Applied Energy Services, Inc., is an independent power producer; it develops, owns, and operates electric power plants and sells electricity to utility companies. All of its current plants are cogeneration facilities, a power generation technology in which two or more useful forms of energy, such as electricity and steam, are created from a single fuel source, such as coal or natural gas.

AES was cofounded as a privately held corporation in 1981 by Roger W. Sant (chairman of the board and chief executive officer) and Dennis W. Bakke (president and chief operating officer). Previously, Sant was assistant administrator of the Federal Energy Administration (FEA) for energy conservation and the environment from 1974 to 1976 and then director of the Energy Productivity Center, an energy research organization affiliated with the Mellon Institute at Carnegie-Mellon University, from 1977 to 1981. Bakke served with Sant as deputy assistant administrator of the FEA and as deputy director of the Energy Productivity Center.

AES was formed in response to certain legislative and business environment changes in the regulated utility industry. In response to the energy crisis of the 1970s, Congress passed the Public Utility Regulatory Policies Act (PURPA). As a result, a significant market for electric power produced by independent power generators developed in the

United States. AES was an early entrant to this market and today is one of the largest independent power producers.

AES's stated mission is to help meet the need for electricity by offering a supply of clean, safe, and reliable power. It has pursued this objective by creating a portfolio of independent power plants, all of which use cogeneration technologies. Prior to obtaining financing for its first power plant, most of AES's revenue came from providing consulting services focused on least-cost energy planning for utilities, governmental agencies, and others interested in energy markets. AES still provides these services, although they no longer represent a significant portion of revenues. According to Roger Naill (vice-president), consulting serves as a way to stay on the cutting edge of economic and technological developments.

The company now operates five plants, with two more facilities under construction, and is pursuing additional projects in the United States and overseas. The combined capacity of the five plants is approximately 860 megawatts of electricity and approximately 400,000 pounds per hour of process steam. The two plants under construction have a combined capacity of approximately 430 megawatts and 280,000 pounds per hour of process steam.

Pursuing a strategy of operating excellence, AES has established high standards of operation and has been a leader in environmental matters associated with independent power production. All of the solid fuel projects it owns and operates employ the very best "clean coal" technologies available, such as scrubbers or circulating fluidized-bed boilers. AES facilities emissions have been recorded at levels considerably below those allowed under environmental permits, thereby exceeding the federal performance standards mandated for such plants under the Clean Air Act. AES has also offset carbon dioxide emissions by funding projects, such as the planting of trees in Guatemala and the preservation of forest land in Paraguay. AES has also established a better-than-average safety record for the electricity-generating industry.

In July 1991, AES went public, selling approximately 10 percent of the company in an initial public offering. In the same year, the company generated $333 million in revenues on $1.44 billion in assets. By mid-1992, its market value reached $1.7 billion. AES has since been ranked on *Fortune*'s list of America's 100 fastest-growing companies. Clearly, the market considers AES a substantial success.

Core Values as a Strategic Driver

An important underlying framework for AES's strategy is its four core or "shared" values.

- To act with integrity
- To be fair
- To have fun
- To be socially responsible

These values emerged over time, mainly from the founders and officers, and have now been articulated to the degree that they are written and were published as a part of the prospectus for the company's initial stock offering. According to Bakke, "The only thing that we hold tightly as to what has to be done are the four values." These values permeate AES and serve to unify the company as it pursues its objectives. They also foster a strong team spirit.

Bakke describes integrity as "it fits together as a whole . . . wholeness, completeness." In practice, this means that the things that AES people say and do in all parts of the company should fit together with truth and consistency. "The main thing we do is ask the question, 'What did we commit?" At AES, the senior representative at any meeting can commit the company, knowing that the team will back him or her up.

Fairness means treating its people, customers, suppliers, stockholders, governments, and the communities in which it operates fairly. Defining what is fair is often difficult, but the main point is that the company believes it is helpful to question routinely the relative fairness of alternative courses of action. This may mean that AES does not get the most out of each negotiation or transaction to the detriment of others. Bakke asks the question, "Would I feel as good on the other side of the table as I feel on this side of the table on the outcome of this meeting or this decision with my employee or supervisor or customer?"

Bakke also says, "If it isn't fun, we don't want it. . . . We either want to quit or change something that we're doing." Sant agrees: "It just isn't worth doing unless you're having a great time." Thus, fun is the third value. AES wants the people it employs and those with whom the company interacts to have fun in their work. Bakke elaborates: "By fun we don't mean party fun. We're talking about creating an environment where people can use their gifts and skills productively, to help meet a need in society, and thereby enjoy the time spent at AES."

The fourth value is social responsibility. "We see ourselves as a citizen of the world," says Bakke. This value presumes that AES has a responsibility to be involved in projects that provide social benefits, such as lower costs to customers, a high degree of safety and reliability, increased employment, and a cleaner environment. "We try to do things that you'd like your neighbor to do."

One might question whether a commitment to these shared values might be detrimental to profits or shareholder value. "We have specifically said that maximized profit is not our objective," says Bakke. In fact, the company's prospectus states, "Earning a fair profit is an important result of providing a quality product to [our] customers. However, when a perceived conflict has arisen between these values and profits, the company has tried to adhere to its values—even though doing so might result in diminished profits or foregone opportunities. The company seeks to adhere to these values, not as a means to achieve economic success, but because adherence is a worthwhile goal in and of itself."

How are values at AES connected with teams and strategy? Answering this question deserves careful consideration. Many, if not most, companies define their strategies in terms of profit potential, market share opportunities, or minimization of financial risk. Although these elements are important to AES, the company considers them within a larger framework represented by the question: Does this strategy enhance or diminish our achievements when evaluated within the context of the four shared values? As Roger Naill explains: "We have a business strategy that has certain goals—for example, the corporate goals in our strategic plan—and our values represent the rules that we play the business game by."

As an example, consider the element of risk. Most corporations seek to contain or minimize the financial risk of a potential strategy, and AES is no exception. For each new cogeneration project, the capitalization and legal entity are deliberately made distinct from the main AES corporation. The project must stand or fall on its own merits without directly threatening the financial integrity of AES as a whole.

Nevertheless, financial risk does not seem to generate the greatest debate and most careful consideration within the company. The issue of whether a potential project (strategy) threatens the shared values seems more prominent. For one project, the company was considering an investor partner for a proposed cogeneration venture. This partner owned a tobacco subsidiary. The so-called risk of this project was not considered predominantly in financial terms but in terms of whether the association with this particular financing partner would be consistent with the shared values of the company. Dennis Bakke provided another example: "When considering what to do about mitigating carbon dioxide emissions and their effect on global warming, the company decided on a strategy of planting and/or preserving trees, including the planting of 52 million trees in Guatemala. This strategic decision turned on the company's social responsibility value rather than the fact that the cost of tree planting exceeded the company's net profit in the year the decision was made."

Bakke describes the relationship between strategy and values as follows: "There is both a strong linkage and no linkage at all. All strategy for meeting the electricity needs of the world is developed in the context of the shared values. But whether the strategy we choose and implement is successful in actually meeting the world's need for clean, reliable electricity has almost nothing to do with the shared values." Sant elaborates:

> The thing we made clear was that the values were not likely to change over time. Those were considered fundamental truths. There wasn't ambiguity about them. There might be ambiguity about what's fair or not fair, but there wasn't ambiguity that we really wanted to be fair, and it was not likely to change to wanting to be unfair, whereas strategy is going to change constantly. We may be doing something now that says coal plants are really a great strategy, but we ought to know that those things are going to change. We're not going to get locked into those or, if we do, we're in trouble. So we should be very clear that there are some things that we are tight on. In Bob Waterman's book, *In Search of Excellence*, he called those tight-loose. We're tight, very tight, on values; very loose on almost everything else. What is important, though, is that the strategy chosen not be inconsistent with the values.

AES's shared values contributed to the team spirit that pervades the company. The content of the values encourages AES personnel to think of themselves not as individuals but rather as members of the larger AES team. Integrity stresses the need for individuals to fulfill commitments—their own and those made by their teams and the company. Fairness generates sensitivity to the positions and perspectives of others, both within and outside the company. Fun, as defined at AES, results from using one's abilities to contribute to the effort of the whole. Social responsibility stresses being aware of and serving the needs of others. Together, these values build an outward-looking orientation in the minds of AES personnel and foster a desire to work cooperatively with others.

The processes by which the values are implemented and evaluated contribute to AES's team orientation. For example, each manager is rated annually on "values performance"— that is, how he or she performs in relation to the four shared values. According to Bakke, "We rate each other, fifty-fifty, on the basis of technical performance and values performance." More broadly, all AES employees are encouraged to challenge any and all others on how strategic and operating decisions reflect the core values. This fosters an air of mutual accountability and serves as a constant reminder that all are members of the same team. Thus, the shared values contribute to a companywide culture that is characterized by a teamlike atmosphere. (See the box, Executive Plant Visits.)

The Operating Committee: The Core of the Strategy Team

AES's Operating Committee is the core organizational unit (team) through which strategy is developed. Think of the committee as an onion with three layers (Figure C4.2-1). The inner layer consists of the three founding officers: Sant, Bakke, and Bob Hemphill, the executive vice-president. This is the core vision team—the group that provided the initial guiding vision of the company and is still most actively involved in the extension,

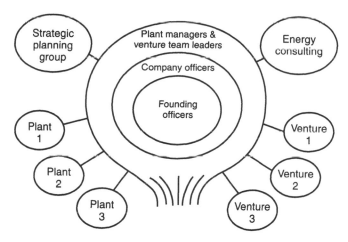

Figure C4.2-1 Operating Committee at AES

enhancement, and communication of that vision. This core vision team is also "first among equals." That is, although all members of the Operating Committee have equal access to and opportunity in the strategy process, in practice, Sant, Bakke, and Hemphill are generally seen as having more influence than the others, and typically they are more engaged in managing the core values of the company.

The middle layer of the "onion" consists of company officers who are not founders: Ken Woodcock and Tom Tribone (senior vice-presidents) and Mark Fitzpatrick, Roger Naill, and Barry Sharp (vice-presidents). They have been with AES for several years and carry out important policy and operating roles. This middle layer also has one important external linkage, Roger Naill, charged with leadership of the planning team, which has responsibility for scanning the environment for ideas for new ventures. The planning team also serves as a technology assessment unit that evaluates the potential of new and alternative technologies.

Executive Plant Visits

We Have Met "They" and "They" Are Us

An important process through which AES has become a whole unified team has been the annual visits of the plants by the corporation's top executives. Dennis Bakke, president, states:

Every officer has to go once a year to one plant for a week. Partly symbolic, partly it's a tremendous time to get to know some of the folks. It lets them give us a bad time. They love it, to see us dirty, or whatever—make fools of ourselves. And partly it's a chance for them to tell us what things are right or wrong. While I was out there, I started to realize, "These people are no different. I don't understand. They have the same motivations, the same concerns, and they like to care about things and about people and about the company. What's different about them? Why are we treating them differently? Why are they being managed in a different way from what we do in Arlington?" I started asking a lot of questions about that. "Why are we doing it differently? Why are the maintenance people all here in their own group and office people in another? And here are operators, and the operators can't do any of this? Maintenance people have to come and do these kinds of things? It's the old union thing, where you hold the plug and I'll plug it in. I said, 'Why do we do that?'"

One guy was complaining, "Well, you know, maintenance guys never do this. They never get it done. I put the work order in, and it never gets done. And they wouldn't let us do that. And they ...," I started saying, "Well, who in the world is 'they'? What do you mean by 'they'"? "Well, uh ... the guys in Arlington," or "the people in the administration building," or "the plant manager." They very seldom could tell you who "they" was, but it was somebody out there. Somebody other than themselves was responsible for their job and making them helpless. We heard all kinds of comments like that. And that bothered us a lot.

Bob Hemphill came up with an idea for a major Anti-They campaign. Everyone had a great time with it. Anti-They. The big international symbol: "They" with a line through it. Everyone gets caught saying "they." Everybody. Even I do. A guy in the control room would say, "Well, they won't. They don't care. They don't want to do this." We'd say, "Who's they?" Now they do it to each other. Trying to get people to say "we." In fact, a reporter came out to do a report one time on one of our plants, and that was his headline on the article. . . . "Everybody Says We."

The campaign against "they" is but one outgrowth of the annual visitations of senior executives to operating plants. Each executive voluntarily spends at least one week at a specific operating plant—not to review or receive briefings but to participate in the everyday activities of the plant by carrying out the work assigned to a specific job. In essence, each executive takes on at least one job per day, and some of these jobs can be fairly rough or dirty. Bob Hemphill recollects: "Since it was my big idea, I got to go first. It actually turned out that Dennis went the same week I did, in August. We both spent a week doing whatever they told us, basically. And since we had no skills, it meant we got to do whatever was hot, or wet, or dirty, or usually hot and wet and dirty. And although these are highly automated plants, there's still a bunch of lugging, toting, hauling, lifting and shoving. And it was very, very interesting."

These visits have two positive results. First, it is an opportunity for executives to listen and learn from direct experience on the firing line. More important, it is an extraordinarily vivid symbolic message to each employee. In keeping with the company's core values, it conveys the notion that each job is important, and no one is too good to work at any job—no matter how rough or dirty it is. More recently, company executives have begun a program of reciprocal visits; groups of employees from each location make periodic visits to the company home office at Arlington.

All of these exchanges evoke a strong sense of loyalty, commitment, and sense of ownership throughout the company. In addition to membership in their immediate work team, each employee feels a part of the larger organizational team.

The outer layer of the onion generally contains two groups: the plant managers and the team leaders of new-venture teams. The plant managers carry out the operations of the current energy generating projects. They work at operating locations geographically distant from the home offices in Arlington.

The team leaders are charged with the responsibility of opening and starting up a new project location. These members of the outer layer also serve as important linkages to the other parts of the organization. The plant managers are the primary links to each operating location, and the team leaders are the primary links to the new-venture teams.

Although distinctions between the three layers can be observed in terms of function, the distinctions do not represent rigid separation; the boundary between layers is very porous. The involvement and influence of individuals in the strategy process are largely dependent on personality and interest rather than organizational structure. On some decisions, according to Naill, "A project development leader might be more influential than some officers, just on the basis of their insights and gifts."

The Operating Committee serves as the core infrastructure through which the strategy process is carried out. In essence, the committee is a network of teams, of which the core vision team is the most central.

The Strategy-Making Process

The strategic management literature distinguishes between the processes of strategy formulation—defining a strategy—and strategy implementation—putting the strategy to work. Although this distinction makes theoretical sense, in practice, the line between the two processes is often unclear. This is certainly the case at AES, where issues of formulation and implementation are addressed in an integrated and continuous fashion. In our description, we combine formulation and implementation and call the process strategy making.

Roger Naill states, "We're always changing our strategy. It's changed at least once a year and maybe twice a year every year that I've been here. We never have the same strategy." Indeed, strategic flexibility has been characteristic of AES from the start. In describing the founding of the company, Roger Sant remembers, "We had a whole bunch of notions that were inaccurate. The data were identifying an opportunity of one kind, and the market was identifying an opportunity of another kind. So, as we went along, we adapted to the opportunities and quickly decided that the cogeneration side of the business was the only one worth pursuing."

An Annual Process

AES engages in an annual strategic planning process that is bottom-up in approach (Figure C4.2-2). The strategic planning group prepares and distributes a book of planning data to all participants in the process. Then one-day strategic planning meetings are held at each plant every September. At these meetings the plant personnel come together to address the strategic direction of their own plant and the company as a whole over the next five years. These one-day meetings are also attended by a senior member of the strategic planning group (Roger Naill or Sheryl Sturges) and, typically, two other officers—one of the core vision team (office of the CEO: Sant, Bakke, Hemphill) and one of the other vice-presidents.

The meeting is led by the plant manager. The agenda is somewhat structured but discussion is fairly loose, designed to get people to talk openly about their ideas and their responses to the discussion materials. The corporate officers serve as resources, share information (sometimes through presentations on issues), and carry the results of the meeting back to the home office. Summaries of each meeting are prepared and distributed to members of the Operating Committee.

For the purpose of strategic planning, the corporate home office is treated as a plant. Participants there include the corporate officers and the team leaders of the new-venture groups. The meeting is structured similarly to the plant meetings, but it provides a forum

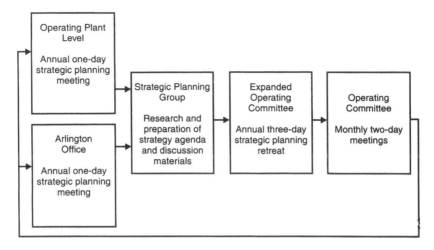

Figure C4.2-2 AES's strategy-making process

for addressing the unique needs and concerns of the new-venture teams rather than those of plant operations.

The one-day meetings are, in effect, mini-strategy meetings for the plants. Although corporate strategy is discussed, most decisions at this level are focused on specific plant—or site—issues.

Later in September, all senior management (officers, plant managers, heads of new-venture teams), as well as a number of additional representatives from across the company (sometimes chosen at random), meet at a Washington-area retreat center. Attendees at the three-day session, the primary corporate strategy vehicle, are provided with a briefing document (about 200 pages) containing the current strategy statement and reviewing the current market situation, competitors, technologies, and potential customers. This briefing document serves as a basis for brainstorming important issues and decisions facing the company—for example, Should we go public? Should supervisors be elected? Can and should we create a partnership with our plant construction supplier? How should we open our plants? Why aren't we signing more contracts? What changes should we make?

All of the attendees will have attended one or more of the one-day plant meetings, and all have responsibility for initiating issues raised and reflecting opinions voiced at these earlier sessions. As in the one-day sessions, a summary document is prepared and distributed.

A Continuous Process

Strategy making does not end with these annual meetings; rather, the process is much more fluid than the previous description implies. Strategic issues are often dealt with outside the annual planning structure, in a process that is virtually continuous. According to Roger Naill, "We start dealing with issues outside of this structure, as well as in it. What we end up talking about in September ends up sort of being whatever's current in September. Something else will come up in December and we'll deal with that one, and something else will come up in January or March, and we'll deal with that one. We're always changing our strategy."

By "always changing our strategy," Naill means in an incremental fashion: "You don't really change 'strategies' every few months. Strategic issues arise naturally outside the formal cycle, that could lead to a major change in strategy. It doesn't happen often, and mostly, because so much effort is spent thinking strategically during the annual cycle, strategy is changed annually."

Issues raised outside the annual planning structure become topics for discussion and action by the Operating Committee and its various subcomponents. In support of the committee's role in the strategy process, the planning group prepares short, focused reports and briefing documents on selected issues that arise throughout the year. For example, one report contained a market analysis that listed all the utilities in the United States and ranked them according to their attractiveness as potential customers.

The Operating Committee meets for two days each month. On the first day, primary attention is given to implementation issues. The manager of each project, from those in the earliest stages of development to plants in operation, gives a short presentation, bringing before the group issues that require brainstorming or decisions. He or she usually identifies several alternatives for action, including the alternative the manager thinks is most appropriate. The discussion following the presentation is likely to address whether the proposed alternative is in accordance with AES's values, as well as the technical and financial aspects of the specific situation. The final decision remains the manager's, but he or she has the resources of the Operating Committee to draw upon.

On the second day, attention turns to more general management issues. Committee members can place any item on the agenda and are encouraged to raise issues that pertain to the values of the company. Topics for discussion may relate to strategy formulation or implementation. One example of a formulation issue related to the core value of social responsibility was, says Bakke, "Should we continue our project in Poland? We face huge problems of poor environment to work in, currency issues, AES people working there, uncertainty about privatization by the government, etc. However, there is great potential for making a positive contribution to air and society." An example of an implementation issue also related to social responsibility was, "Should we build schools for strapped counties around [a U.S.] plant in lieu of taxes that state law exempts us from?" Because the committee addresses both strategy formulation and implementation issues as they arise, the formulation and implementation processes are carried out by the network of teams and are truly integrated and continuous.

Integrating the Whole

Various teams within the company play different, though overlapping, roles in the strategy process. The corporate officers and especially the core vision team have primary responsibility for defining the core values of the company.

Roger Naill and the strategic planning group provide a unique contribution to strategy making. They do not directly make strategy but serve as the primary information and analysis source from which strategy emerges. Thus, the function of the strategic planning group is not to provide the strategic plan, but, rather, to provide the information necessary for the company to act as "informed opportunists." Naill looks at the role for the strategic planning process as providing information: "It's not to provide a plan. My role is to provide information to the planners, which turn out to be as broad-based a group as we can get in the company. We're actually trying to involve everybody."

The planning group focuses its attention on many strategic issues. Should we be in the coal business or the gas business? Should we be building coal plants or gas plants? What is the Clean Air Act going to do to our business? If the Clean Air Act Amendment passes, should we build fluidized-bed coal plants, or should we build standard boilers with scrubbers? What kind of technology should we be involved in? Analyses of these and other issues result in the briefing documents prepared by the planning group for the annual and monthly meetings.

Members of the new-venture teams, especially the team leaders, also have a unique influence on the direction of the company, sometimes through their own interests and personal objectives. AES is committed to the development of its high-caliber personnel and encourages accomplished new-venture developers to seek out and define their own opportunities. AES became involved in international activities primarily as the result of the interests of several experienced new-venture developers seeking more responsibility and broader opportunities.

Finally, plant personnel, especially the plant managers, contribute to the strategy process as it more closely relates to the core business: the cogeneration of electricity and steam. Input from the plants precipitated the strategic concern with operating excellence and continues to define and refine this concept through implementation.

Despite the expected contributions made by each of these groups to strategic management, it is clear that AES expects all participants in the process to be concerned about and take ownership and responsibility for all aspects of the company. Plant managers are encouraged to challenge corporate officers on issues relating to values, new-venture team leaders are expected to provide market information, and the planning group contributes to discussions of operating efficiency.

The Team Structure

The term "team" is not widely used in everyday vocabulary at AES. Nevertheless, a sense of "teamness" pervades the company. Roger Naill articulated it best: "I don't think 'team' is an AES word, in the sense that we don't go around calling ourselves teams. But the concept is clear. For example, Project Honeycomb [see the box, Teams at the Plants] is clearly a team-oriented exercise. Work teams at the plant call themselves 'families.' Our strategic planning group is a 'group.'"

The essence of teams is synergy; that is, what is accomplished by the team is more than could be accomplished by a collection of individuals. By way of analogy, the best basketball teams are those whose members work well together to achieve a common objective. Although individual skills are important, it is their refined combination that maximizes performance. That is why the All-Star games, in which the teams are composed of highly skilled individuals who are not used to playing together, are less elegant than championship games. All-Star teams typically lack the capacity to come together into the well-oiled machines we often see in championship teams.

Teams at the Plants: Operation Honeycomb

AES attempts to evoke employee psychological ownership by individuals through the use of teams at the generating plants. As outsiders, we would call these structures "self-managing teams" or "employee involvement teams," but AES uses the term "Honeycomb." Dennis Bakke describes the evolution of Operation Honeycomb:

Our plants were running wonderfully when we said, "This isn't really consistent with our values and the way we want people to operate and relate to each other. We need to make huge changes in the way we do operations if we're going to be consistent with our values." We did this massive change that came to be known as Operation Honeycomb. We changed how our plants are organized and how people relate to each other. It's based on the premise that people will take responsibility and can be trusted. We didn't want arbitrary rules, detailed procedures manuals and handbooks, punch clocks, etc. We wanted a "learning organization," where people close to the action were constantly creating and re-creating and where these people were making the decisions—strategy, financial, and capital allocations. For example, I went down and asked, "What if you didn't have shift supervisors? What if you didn't have this manual that tells you everything to do?" Two months later, they totally revolutionized the place. We discovered these people are no different from the managers. They have the same motivations, the same concerns, and they like to care about people and about the company. Why were we treating them differently? Why were they being managed in a different way?

We outlined several elementary principles to be used in a Honeycomb structure. Cut the number of supervisor levels to improve communication, and get out of people's way. And then one of the plant people came up with, "Why don't we just divide up into teams?" The next thing I knew, the plant manager called me and said, "We got this all done. We've implemented it." They said, "We're going to call this stuff Honeycomb," and they had worked out all this symbolism regarding beehives and how all the bees were working together.

Of course, the supervisors had to change. Some have adapted extremely well and are real stars. Others moved to special jobs that don't require them to supervise. A few have had to leave completely. So, it's all over the map.

Now, the plants do their own capital allocations. The plant managers decided to change the order of criteria for hiring. First, how well does this person fit with our shared values; then, technical skill. They make almost every decision. They have the responsibility and authority to make every single decision in that plant. There are no exceptions that I know of.

Today, all AES generating plants are organized according to some form of self-managing teams. Since the process of change essentially is implemented bottom-up (although mandated top-down), the specific forms, labels, and language vary considerably from plant to plant. Furthermore, the path leading to self-management has been quite different among the plants. Some were "changeovers" of existing nonunion plants; one was a changeover of a union plant; finally, others have been implemented from the beginning.

This variety of implementation and form has given AES a tremendous diversity of experience while adapting to the specific condition unique to each plant. Nevertheless, the conversion to "honeycomb"-like teams has always been inspired and guided by the organization's core values. It always features a bottom-up process that displays great confidence that the employees have a special capability to work out the details of implementation that will suit them best.

Today, the Honeycomb principle is an important part of AES's strategic philosophy. The company believes that operating excellence is a distinctive competence that provides a special competitive advantage. In turn, critical factors in achieving operating excellence are the responsibility, pride, and sense of ownership that stem from the Honeycomb operating philosophy. "Most important," says Bakke, "is that Honeycomb provides an environment where the 'fun' value can best work itself out for each AES person."

For synergy to be achieved, a combination of specialization, interchangeability, and trust is required. Individual team members can contribute to the team effort if they can develop some level of unique skills, but specialization is complemented by a basic understanding and skill level in all of the team's functions. Thus, to use the basketball analogy again, play makers can take open shots, shooters can rebound, and rebounders can initiate plays. To make the rapid and continuous switching between specialization and generalization within the context of a fast and competitive game, each player needs to be able to trust that teammates can and will make the right play at the right time. Trust provides the confidence to extend oneself to the limit.

Given this definition of a team, AES obviously exhibits team characteristics in numerous ways and at many levels.

The core vision team, each energy-generating plant, the new-venture groups, the strategic planning group, and the Operating Committee all act like teams. They provide a unique stimulus to enhance the motivation, initiative, and self-responsibility of employees throughout the company. Indeed, the word "ownership" best describes how teams influence the psychological perspective of employees. Employees feel ownership in the company and, especially, in their own jobs. Ownership leads to strong motivation and sometimes exceptional effort to perform well (see the box, Individual Ownership). Thus, individual ownership contributes to organizational competitiveness.

Individual Ownership: A Team Member Takes Initiative

One result of AES's team structure has been a high level of psychological ownership of the company on the part of workers at every level. Such ownership has been an objective of the core vision team since the company's inception. From the beginning, says Sant, the core vision team wanted "something that really makes people feel that they own us. Our instincts were that everybody likes to feel important. We did. We'd been in jobs where we were constantly told that we probably weren't important, and we thought that probably wasn't the way to turn young people on."

AES has been extremely successful in attaining the goal of ownership. Dennis Bakke provides this powerful example:

Let me give you one example of what happened, the kind of thing I think we've had example after example of. We had a guy who, after this Honeycomb process, went Saturday shopping with his wife at one of the discount stores. He was waiting around, waiting for her to get done, and he noticed that they had fans on sale. He looked at the fans, and he realized that they were almost the same kind of fans that we were using at the plant in the process of making gypsum at the back end of our plant. We use a lot of them; they end up wearing out because there's a pretty dirty atmosphere, and so they burn out real fast. He looked and saw that they were selling them for something like $24 apiece, and he remembered that we were spending $75 from the original manufacturer who supplied them at first, and we kept going back to the same guy, at $75. Once or twice a month, we were paying to get new fans. So he immediately took his credit card and bought the entire stock in the store, period. Just bought it.

Now that is the kind of action we're talking about. This is a nonsupervisor, just a regular guy in the plant. What had to be the situation for him? First of all, he had to understand what the technology was, that it was the same kind. He was aware that this was the same kind of fan, or very similar to it, and it would do the same thing in the plant. Second, he had to know all the cost numbers. Third, he had to know that he had authority to do it, that it was safe. And if he was wrong, it would be okay. If he really feared for his job in doing this or that he would have to pay for these hundreds of dollars of fans he had just bought, for a normal guy . . . he knew he would be backed up on it.

That is the epitome of Honeycomb. That is responsibility-taking. We've had guys who have done that and been wrong. A guy did a whole bundle on an air heater and got it all done, and it was totally wrong—spent, I don't know, $10,000. But no one went back and said, "That's terrible, and you're getting your salary docked." We want to encourage that kind of thing. But that's the epitome of the Honeycomb story. We're trying to publicize it and be happy to have more people do it, every day. That kind of wraps it up.

In addition, the use of teams leads to a highly adaptive, nonrigid organizational structure. Job assignments and roles are not engraved in granite, and they sometimes change significantly as the situation demands. The phrase "that's not my job" would be highly incompatible with the team system at AES.

Contrary to most other companies, AES deliberately avoids drawing and publishing a formal organization chart. The use of teams provides an adaptive structure that can change quickly to meet the demands of an emerging situation or a shift in strategic implementation.

The team structure strengthens AES's ability to scan its environment and identify strategic opportunities very early. Although the strategic planning group is specifically charged with environmental scanning activities, the new-venture teams—with their external contacts in the market, financial, and regulatory communities—and the plant personnel—with their expertise in operating plants—also provide insight into environmental opportunities and threats.

Teams also contribute to strategic flexibility. Rapid communication among and between teams provides a process for revising strategic implementation without undertaking a whole new formal planning process. The annual strategic planning cycle is seen mainly as a starting place; often, significant strategic changes are undertaken with short notice.

Finally, teams contribute to high productivity and competitiveness. The bottom-line results speak for themselves. AES's energy-generating plants significantly exceed industry standards of availability—that is, the proportion of time that energy generation is on line. AES plants typically operate at less than 50 percent of allowable emissions. Voluntary turnover of people is under 1 percent. Accident rates, especially severe accidents, run far below the industry average, and the real cost per kilowatt-hour of electricity produced has been falling for three years. Finally, the company as a whole has maintained high profitability over the years.

"We think it's too early to draw long-term conclusions concerning our 'experiment' with regard to these traditional measures of excellence," Bakke is quick to point out. "We are fairly bullish, however, regarding adherence to the values, especially the fun environment that has been created by the decentralized teams and other aspects of the corporate approach."

The Network of Teams as the Strategy Team

We found the interlocking dynamics between the de facto teams and strategy making at AES unique and provocative. First, strategy making is consistent with an articulated and differentiated set of core values. The philosophy represented by these core values is pervasive and affects strategy making in a profound way. Second, we discovered that teams were not only useful for the day-to-day issues and operations, as typically found in other companies, but were also an essential element in the total strategy-making process. Both within-team and between-team elements provide the crucial structure and process for essential communication that makes broadly based strategy making at AES possible.

Strategy making essentially begins as a bottom-up process. However, the between-team processes, as represented by the annual strategy meeting and the monthly Operating Committee meetings, are the mechanisms that foster aggregation and integration from the diverse parts of the company. Moreover, the bottom-up approach to strategy making provides the means by which the integration of goals, objectives, and ways to achieve them, across all parts of the company, becomes possible.

AES emphasizes the importance of teams and teamwork throughout the entire organization. Its executives do not see themselves as bosses, and they have attempted to design a total organization that represents the essence of teams. Whatever the label, AES has found a way to make teamwork an essential strategy-making ingredient through a network of teams.

KEY LESSONS FROM THIS CASE

1. Teams can be coordinated with one another through a set of core values that pervade the total organization.

2. Monetary profit is only one measure of team effectiveness. Other measures such as social responsibility and team member satisfaction should be included in evaluations.

3. A core set of values can aid the process of team evaluation. Team activities that enhance the values are desirable and evaluated positively; activities counter to the values should be evaluated negatively.

4. A network of interlocking teams can be used to develop organizational strategies. At AES, teams meet on an annual cycle, but strategy is continuously being revised and adapted across teams.

5. Cooperation across teams is enhanced by intentional contact among members of different teams. One method of doing this is to have members of the top-management team "stand in" as a temporary member of other teams throughout the organization.

6. Organizations need to develop a sense of "we" rather than "they" to facilitate interteam coordination and cooperation.

7. Teams at the top can become a model for other teams throughout an organization.

NOTE TO CASE 4.2

1. Most of the quotations in this case are from on-site interviews conducted from 1990 to 1992. We are especially thankful to Dennis Bakke, who facilitated the project, and to the special cooperation of AES employees. Other material is excerpted from AES's June 1991 prospectus and the 1991 annual report.

CASE

4.3

The Team at W. L. Gore & Associates

This case was written by Frank Shipper and Charles C. Manz.[1]

Not all teams are formally designed. This case tells the story of the highly creative and successful W. L. Gore & Associates, where teams are created as needed. The Gore recipe includes associates, not employees, who interact directly with whomever they need to get the job done rather than through a chain of command. "Unmanagement," "unstructure," empowerment, and individual self-leadership characterize this high-performing organization. Understanding the Gore process provides a glimpse of the possible future for work teams.

W. L. Gore & Associates offers many potential advantages and benefits of formally established work teams without the formality of designated teams. Instead, the whole work operation becomes one large, empowered superteam in which each person is individually self-managing and can interact directly with everyone else in the system. Gore relies on self-developing teams without managers or bosses but with lots of leaders.[2]

In the Beginning: The Wilbert L. Gore Story

W. L. Gore & Associates evolved from the late Wilbert L. Gore's personal, organizational, and technical experiences. While he worked at E. I. Du Pont de Nemours, he was part of a team to develop applications for polytetrafluoroethylene (PTFE), more commonly known as Teflon. After some experimenting, he realized this material had the ideal insulating characteristics for use with computers and transistors.

He tried several ways to make a PTFE-coated ribbon cable without success. A breakthrough came in his home basement laboratory. He was explaining the problem to his son, Bob. Bob saw some PTFE sealant tape made by 3M and asked his father, "Why don't you try this tape?" His father then explained to his son that everyone knows you cannot bond PTFE to itself. Bob went on to bed.

Bill Gore remained in his basement lab and proceeded to try what everyone knew would not work. At about 4 A.M., waving a small piece of cable, he woke up his son, saying to him excitedly, "It works, it works." The following night, father and son returned to the basement lab to make ribbon cable coated with PTFE.

For the next four months, Bill Gore tried to persuade Du Pont to make a new product, PTFE-coated ribbon cable. But his employer was not interested in fabricating a product (Du Pont wanted to remain a supplier of raw materials), and so Gore struck out on his own.

On January 1, 1958, their twenty-third wedding anniversary, Bill and his wife, Genevieve, founded W.L. Gore & Associates in the basement of their home. After finishing their anniversary dinner, Vieve turned to her husband of 23 years and said, "Well, let's clear up the dishes, go downstairs, and get to work." They viewed this as a continuation of their partnership. Bill Gore was 45 years old with five children to support when he left Du Pont. He left behind a career of 17 years, and a good and secure salary. To finance the first two years of the business, they mortgaged their house and took $4,000 from savings. All of their friends told them not to do it.

The first few years were rough. In lieu of salary, some of their employees accepted room and board in the Gore home. At one point 11 employees were living and working under one roof. A few years later, the Gores secured an order for $100,000 that put the company over the hump, and business began to take off.

W. L. Gore & Associates has continued to grow and develop new products primarily derived from PTFE, including its best-known product, Gore-Tex. Today W. L. Gore makes a wide range of products in four categories: electronic, medical, fabrics, and industrial products. Bill Gore died in 1986 while backpacking in Wyoming. Before he died, he had become chairman and his son, Bob, president. Bob continues to occupy this position. Vieve remains the only other officer, secretary-treasurer.

The Organization Without Bosses

W.L. Gore & Associates is a company without titles, hierarchy, or any of the other conventional structures typically associated with enterprises of its size. The titles of president and secretary-treasurer are used only because they are required by the laws of incorporation. The management style at Gore has been referred to as "unmanagement." The organization's development was guided by Bill's experiences on teams at Du Pont and evolved over time to adapt to current needs.

In 1965, W. L. Gore & Associates was a thriving and growing company with a facility in Newark, Delaware, and about 200 employees. One morning, Bill Gore was taking his usual walk through the plant and realized that he did not know everyone there. The team, he decided, had become too big. As a result, the company developed a policy that no facility would have over 150 to 200 employees. Thus was born the expansion policy, "Get big by staying small." The purpose of maintaining small plants is to accentuate a closely knit, interpersonal atmosphere. Today W. L. Gore & Associates consists of 44 plants worldwide (some clustered on the same site) with over 5,300 associates. For example, in Flagstaff, Arizona, Gore has four plants on the same site; 27 plants are in the United States and 17 are overseas. Gore overseas plants are located in Scotland, Germany, France, Japan, and India.

Compensation at W. L. Gore & Associate takes three forms: salary, profit sharing, and an associates' stock option program (ASOP). Entry-level salary is in the middle of externally comparable jobs. According to Sally Gore, daughter-in-law of the founder, "We do not feel we need to be the highest paying. We never try to steal people away from other companies with salary. We want them to come here because of the opportunities for growth and the unique work environment." Associates' salaries are reviewed at least once a year and more commonly twice a year. For most workers, the reviews are conducted by a compensation team from the facility in which they work. All associates have sponsors who act as their advocate during this review process. Prior to meeting with the compensation committee, the sponsor checks with customers or anyone else who uses the results of the person's work to find out what contribution has been made. In addition, the evaluation team considers the associate's leadership ability and willingness to help others to develop to their fullest.

In addition to salaries, W.L. Gore has profit-sharing and ASOP plans (similar to an ESOP plan) for all associates. Profit sharing typically occurs twice a year (depending on profitability), with the amount awarded to each associate based on his or her time in service and annual rate of pay. In addition, the firm buys company stock equivalent to 15 percent of each associate's annual income and places it in a retirement fund. Thus, an associate becomes a stockholder after employment at Gore for one year. Bill wanted each associate to feel as if he or she was an owner.

The principle of commitment works both ways. Gore tries to avoid layoffs and pay cuts, which is considered disastrous to morale. Instead, the company has used a system of temporary transfers within a plant or cluster of plants and voluntary layoffs to cope with downturns in business.

Gore is an unusual company by many standards and has also been a highly successful and profitable one for several years. Sales jumped from $6 million in 1969 to $660 million in 1990. This tremendous growth has been financed almost entirely without debt.

A number of features that set Gore apart from other organizations serve as lessons for other organizations that want to enjoy some of the benefits that Gore has obtained. Those benefits stem largely from its unique employee empowerment approach to managing (or unmanaging) an organization.

Culture and Norms Supporting Employee Empowerment and Success

Bill Gore wanted to avoid smothering the company in thick layers of formal management, which he felt stifled individual creativity. Yet he needed a system to assist new people, to follow their progress, and to provide a way of setting compensation. Thus, the firm developed its sponsor program.

Job applicants are initially screened by personnel specialists, as in most other companies. Candidates who meet the basic criteria are then interviewed by associates. Before a person is hired, an associate must agree to be the new employee's sponsor. The sponsor takes a personal interest in the new associate's contributions, problems, and goals and serves as a coach, an advocate, and a friend. The sponsor tracks the new associate's progress, provides help and encouragement, and deals with weaknesses while building on strengths. Sponsoring is not a short-term commitment. All associates have sponsors, and many have more than one. When individuals are hired, they have a sponsor in their immediate work area. If they move to another area, they have a new sponsor in that area. As associates' responsibilities grow, they may acquire additional sponsors.

Because the sponsoring program looks beyond conventional views of what makes a good associate, some anomalies occur in the hiring practices. Bill Gore told the story of an 84-year-old man who applied for a job and spent five years with the company. He had 30 years of experience in the industry before joining Gore. His other associates had no problems accepting him, but the personnel computer did. It insisted that his age was 48. As in this example, the Gore system of "unmanagement" attracts individuals from diverse backgrounds and creates unique success stories.

Bill Gore described three kinds of sponsorship:

1. The sponsor who helps a new associate get started on the job or helps an associate get started on a new job (starting sponsor).
2. The sponsor who sees to it that the associate being sponsored gets credit and recognition for contributions and accomplishments (advocate sponsor).
3. The sponsor who sees to it that the associate being sponsored is paid fairly for his or her contributions to the success of the enterprise (compensation sponsor).

A single sponsor can perform any one or all three kinds of sponsorship.

In addition to the sponsor program, Gore associates are asked to follow four guiding principles:

1. Try to be fair.
2. Use your freedom to grow.
3. Make your own commitments and keep them.
4. Consult with other associates prior to any action that may adversely affect the company's reputation or financial stability.

The four principles are often referred to as fairness, freedom, commitment, and waterline. (The waterline terminology is drawn from an analogy to ships. A hole in a boat above the waterline poses little danger to the vessel. A hole below the waterline puts the boat in immediate danger of sinking. In other words, associates can, and are encouraged to, make decisions on their own as long as the downside risk does not threaten the survival of the organization.)

The operating principles were put to a test in 1978. By this time, word about the qualities of Gore-Tex was being spread throughout the recreational and outdoor markets, and production and shipment had begun in volume. At first, a few complaints were heard, then, some of the clothing started coming back and finally, a great deal of the clothing was being returned. Gore-Tex was leaking. Having high-quality waterproof products was one of the two major properties responsible for Gore-Tex's success. The company's reputation and credibility were on the line.

Peter W. Gilson, who led Gore's fabric division, said of the situation, "It was an incredible crisis for us at that point. We were really starting to attract attention, we were taking off . . . and then this." Peter and a number of his associates in the next few months made a number of below-the-waterline decisions. First, research determined that certain oils in human sweat were responsible for clogging the pores in Gore-Tex and altering the surface tension of the membrane. Thus, water could pass through. They also discovered that a good washing could restore the waterproof property. At first, this solution, known as the "Ivory Snow solution," was accepted.

A single letter from "Butch," a mountain guide in the Sierras, changed the company's position. Butch wrote how he had been leading a group and, "My parka leaked and my life was in danger." As Gilson said, "That scared the hell out of us. Clearly our solution was no solution at all to someone on a mountaintop." All of the products were recalled. "We bought back, at our own expense, a fortune in pipeline material. Anything that was in store, at the manufacturers, or anywhere else in the pipeline," said Gilson.

Bob Gore and other associates set out to develop a permanent solution. One month later, a second-generation Gore-Tex had been developed. In addition, any customer who returned a leaky parka was given a replacement. The replacement program alone cost Gore roughly $4 million.

The Lattice Organization Structure

Gore has been described not only as unmanaged but also as unstructured. Bill Gore himself referred to the structure as a lattice organization, with the following primary characteristics:

1. Lines of communication are direct from person to person, with no intermediary.
2. There is no fixed or assigned authority.
3. There are no bosses, only sponsors.
4. Natural leadership is defined by followership.
5. Objectives are set by those who must make them happen.
6. Tasks and functions are organized through commitments.

The structure within the lattice is complex and evolves from interpersonal interactions, commitment to responsibility, natural leadership, and group-imposed discipline.

Bill Gore explained this structure: "Every successful organization has an underground lattice. It's where the news spreads like lightning, where people can go around the organization to get things done." Another description is that the lattice structure is characterized by the constant formation of temporary cross-area groups; there are teams similar to quality circles going on all the time, but they are not formally designated. The cross-level and cross-functional interpersonal accessibility created by this structure enables teams to form in response to specific needs. Associates can team up with other associates, regardless of area, to get the job done.

The lattice structure does have some similarities to traditional management structures. For instance, a group of 30 to 40 associates who make up an advisory group meets every six months to review marketing, sales, and production plans. As Bill Gore has conceded, "The abdication of titles and rankings can never be 100 percent."

An outsider observing the meetings and other activities will no doubt notice the informality and humor with these groups, but words such as "responsibilities" and "commitments" are frequently used. This is an organization in which members take what they do seriously, but not themselves.

For a company of its size, W.L. Gore may have the shortest organizational pyramid found anywhere. The pyramid consists of Bob Gore, the late Bill Gore's son, as president and Vieve, Bill Gore's widow, as secretary-treasurer. All the other members of the Gore organization are referred to as associates. Words such as employees, subordinates, and managers are taboo in the Gore culture.

Leaders

Gore has no managers but many leaders. Bill Gore once described in an internal memo the kinds of leaders who are needed and the role they play:

1. The associate who is recognized by a team as having special knowledge, or experience (for example, this could be a chemist, computer expert, machine operator, salesman, engineer, lawyer). This kind of leader gives the team guidance in a special area.
2. The associate the team looks to for coordination of individual activities in order to achieve the team's agreed upon objectives. The role of this leader is to persuade team members to make the commitments necessary for success (commitment seeker).
3. The associate who proposes necessary objectives and activities and seeks agreement and team consensus on objectives. This leader is perceived by the

team members as having a good grasp of how the team's objectives fit in with the broad objective of the enterprise. This kind of leader is often also the "commitment-seeking" leader in 2 above.

4. The leader who evaluates the relative contribution of team members (in consultation with other sponsors) and reports these contribution evaluations to a compensation committee. This leader may also participate in the compensation committee on relative contribution and pay, and reports changes in compensation to individual associates. This leader is then also a compensation sponsor.

5. The leader who coordinates the research, manufacturing, and marketing of one product type within a business, interacting with team leaders and individual associates who have commitments regarding the product type. These leaders are usually called product specialists. They are respected for their knowledge and dedication to their products.

6. Plant leaders who help coordinate the activities of people within a plant.

7. Business leaders who help coordinate the activities of people in a business.

8. Functional leaders who help coordinate the activities of people in a "functional" area.

9. Corporate leaders who help coordinate the activities of people in different businesses and functions and who try to promote communication and cooperation among all associates.

10. Intrapreneuring associates who organize new teams for new businesses, new products, new processes, new devices, new marketing efforts, new or better methods of all kinds. These leaders invite other associates to "sign up" for their project.

Leadership is widespread in our lattice organization, and it is continually changing and evolving. The reality that leaders are frequently also sponsors should not confuse the fact that these are different activities and responsibilities. Leaders are not authoritarians, managers of people, or supervisors who tell us what to do or forbid us from doing things; nor are they "parents" to whom we transfer our own self-responsibility. However, they do often advise us of the consequences of actions we have done or propose to do. Our actions result in contributions, or lack of contribution, to the success of our enterprise. Our pay depends on the magnitude of our contributions. This is the basic discipline of our lattice organization.

Many other aspects are arranged along similar lines. The parking lot contains no reserved parking spaces except for customers and the disabled. There is only one area in each plant in which to eat. The lunchroom in each new plant is designed to be a focal point for employee interaction. Dave McCarter of Phoenix explains, "The design is no accident. The lunchroom in Flagstaff has a fireplace in the middle. We want people to like to be here." The location of the plant is also no accident. Sites are selected based on transportation access, a nearby university, beautiful surroundings, and climate appeal. Land cost is never the primary consideration. McCarter justifies the selection by stating, "Expanding is not costly in the long run. The loss of money is what you make happen by stymieing people into a box."

Gore's leadership approach focuses on empowering and enabling others to perform on their own and to the best of their ability. In a sense, the only real bosses for Gore employees are themselves. Gore promotes the development of creative, innovative self-leaders through SuperLeadership (leading others to lead themselves).

Working Without Structure and Management

Not all people function well under such a system, especially newcomers. Those accustomed to a structured work environment may face adjustment problems. As Bill Gore said, "All our lives most of us have been told what to do, and some people don't know how to respond when asked to do something—and have the very real option of saying no on their job. It's the new associate's responsibility to find out what he or she can do for the good of the operation."

The vast majority of new associates may flounder initially but usually adapt quickly. For those who require more structured working conditions and cannot adapt, Gore's flexible workplace is not for them. According to Bill Gore, for those few, "It's an unhappy situation, both for the associate and the sponsor. If there is no contribution, there is no paycheck."

Ron Hill, an associate in Newark, has pointed out that the company will work with associates who want to advance themselves." Associates are offered many in-house training opportunities. They tend to be technical and focused on engineering because of the type of organization it is, but it also offers in-house programs in leadership development. In addition, the company has cooperative programs with associates to obtain training through universities and other outside providers. Gore covers most of the costs for the associates, but the associate must take the initiative.

Anita McBride, an associate in Phoenix, realizes that Gore is "not for everybody. People ask me, Do we have turnover, and yes, we do have turnover. What you're seeing looks like utopia, but it also looks extreme. If you finally figure out the system, it can be real exciting. If you can't handle it, you gotta go—probably by your own choice, because you're going to be so frustrated."

In rare cases an associate "tries to be unfair," as Bill Gore put it. Such "unfairness" might involve chronic absenteeism or stealing. "When that happens, all hell breaks loose," said Bill Gore. "We can get damned authoritarian when we have to."

Over the years, Gore has faced several unionization drives. It neither tries to dissuade an associate from attending an organizational meeting nor retaliates when flyers are passed out. Each attempt has been unsuccessful. Bill believed that no need exists for third-party representation under the lattice structure. He asked, "Why would associates join a union when they own the company? It seems rather absurd."

Being an associate at Gore can be a unique and challenging experience. Consider Jack Dougherty's experience. Dougherty, a newly minted M.B.A. from the College of William and Mary, bursting with resolve and dressed in a dark blue suit, reported to his first day at W.L. Gore. He presented himself to Bill Gore, shook hands firmly, looked him in the eye, and said he was ready for anything. Gore replied, "That's fine, Jack, fine. Why don't you look around and find something you'd like to do?" Three frustrating weeks later, he found something. He was dressed in jeans, loading fabric into the maw of a machine that laminates Gore-Tex, the company's patented fabric, to other fabrics.

Sixteen years later, Jack had become responsible for all advertising and marketing in the fabrics group.

This story is part of Gore's folklore. Today the process is slightly more structured. New associates take a journey through the business before settling into their own positions, regardless of the specific position for which they are hired. A new sales associate in the fabric division may spend six weeks rotating through different areas before beginning to concentrate on sales and marketing. Among other things he or she may learn is how Gore-Tex is made, what it can and cannot do, how Gore handles customer complaints, and how it makes its investment decisions. Anita McBride related her early experience at W.L. Gore:

> When I first came to Gore I had worked for a structured organization. I came here, and for the first month it was fairly structured because I was going through training. "This is what we do, and this is how Gore is" and all of that, and I went to Flagstaff for that training. After a month I came down to Phoenix, and my sponsor said, "Well, here's your office," it's a wonderful office, and "Here's your desk," and walked away. And I thought, Now what do I do, you know? I was waiting for a memo or something, or a job description. Finally, after another month, I was so frustrated, I felt, What have I gotten myself into? I went to my sponsor and I said, "What the heck do you want from me? I need something from you," and he said, "If you don't know what you're supposed to do, examine your commitments and opportunities."

Anita did find something to do: she heads up the personnel function in Phoenix.

Unstructured Research and Development

Like everything else at Gore, research and development is unstructured. There is no formal research and development department, yet the company holds over 150 patents. Most inventions are held as proprietary or trade secrets. Any associate can ask for a piece of raw PTFE, known as a silly worm, to experiment with. Bill Gore believed that all people have it within themselves to be creative.

The best way to understand how research and development works at Gore is through an example. By 1969, Gore's wire and cable division was facing increased competition, so Bill Gore began to look for a way to straighten out the PTFE molecules, the way, he thought, to "a tremendous new kind of material." If PTFE could be stretched, air could be introduced into its molecular structure. The result would be greater volume per pound of raw material without affecting performance. Thus, fabricating costs would be reduced—and profit margins increased. Going about their search in a scientific manner with their son, Bob, the Gores heated rods of PTFE to various temperatures and then slowly stretched them. Regardless of the temperature or how carefully they stretched them, the rods broke. Working alone late one night in 1969 after countless failures, Bob yanked at one of the rods violently. To his surprise, it did not break. He tried it again and again, with the same results. The next morning Bob demonstrated his breakthrough to his father, but not without some drama. As Bill Gore recalled, "Bob wanted to surprise me, so he took a rod and stretched it slowly. Naturally, it broke. Then he pretended to get mad. He grabbed another rod and said, 'Oh the hell with this,' and gave it a pull. It didn't break . . . he'd done it." The new arrangement of molecules changed not only the wire and cable division but led to the development of Gore-Tex and a host of other products.

Initial field-testing of Gore-Tex was conducted by Bill and his wife, Vieve, in the summer of 1970. Vieve made a hand-sewn tent out of patches of Gore-Tex. They took it on their annual camping trip to the Wind River Mountains in Wyoming. The first night out, hail tore holes in the top of the tent, but the bottom filled up like a bathtub from the rain. As Bill Gore stated, "At least we knew from all the water that the tent was waterproof. We needed to make it stronger, so it could withstand hail."

The second largest division began on the ski slopes: Bill was out with a friend, Ben Eiseman, a surgeon at the Denver General Hospital. As they were about to start a run,

Bill Gore remembered, "I absent-mindedly pulled a small tubular section of Gore-Tex out of my pocket and looked at it. 'What is that stuff?' Ben asked. So I told him about its properties. 'Feels great,' he said. 'What do you use it for?' 'Got no idea,' I said. 'Well, give it to me,' he said, 'and I'll try it in a vascular graft on a pig.' Two weeks later, he called me up. Ben was pretty excited. 'Bill,' he said, 'I put it in a pig, and it works. What do I do now?' I told him to get together with Pete Cooper in our Flagstaff plant and let them figure it out." Now hundreds of thousands of people throughout the world walk around with Gore-Tex vascular grafts.

Every associate is encouraged to think, experiment, and follow a potentially profitable idea to its conclusion. At a plant in Newark, Delaware, a machine that wraps thousands of yards of wire a day was designed over a weekend by Fred L. Eldreth, an associate with a third-grade education. Many other associates have contributed their ideas through both product and process breakthroughs.

Innovation and creativity work very well at Gore, even without a research and development department. The year before he died, Bill Gore claimed that "the creativity, the number of patent applications and innovative products is triple" that of Du Pont. Overall, the associates appear to have responded positively to the Gore system of un-management and unstructure. The year before he died, Bill Gore estimated that "the profit per associate is double" that of Du Pont.

Use with Caution: Unmanagement and Unstructure Have Limitations
Although the lattice structure and the unstructured management approach used at Gore appears to be a remarkable and promising organizational innovation, it should be considered with some caution. Just like any other new system, it should be evaluated in terms of its fit with the organization, its culture, and its objectives.

Bill Gore stated, "I'm told from time to time that a lattice organization can't meet a crisis well because it takes too long to reach a consensus when there are no bosses. But this isn't true. A lattice, by its very nature, works particularly well in a crisis. A lot of useless effort is avoided because there is no rigid management hierarchy to conquer before you can attack a problem."

The lattice has been put to the test on many occasions. For example, in 1975, Dr. Charles Campbell, the University of Pittsburgh's senior resident, reported that a Gore-Tex arterial graft had developed an aneurysm, a bubblelike protrusion that is life threatening; if it continues to expand, it will explode. Obviously, this kind of problem has to be solved quickly and permanently.

Within a few days of Dr. Campbell's first report, he flew to Newark to present his findings to Bill and Bob Gore and a few other associates. Bill Hubis, a former policeman who had joined Gore to develop new production methods, had an idea before the meeting was over. He returned to his work area to try some different production techniques. After only three hours and 12 tries, he had developed a permanent solution. In three hours, a potentially damaging problem to both patients and the company was resolved. Furthermore, Hubis's redesigned graft went on to win widespread acceptance in the medical community.

Other critics have been outsiders who had problems with the idea of no titles. Sarah Clifton, an associate at the Flagstaff facility, was being pressed by some outsiders to reveal her title. She made one up and had it printed on some business cards: "Supreme Commander." When Bill Gore learned what she did, he loved it and recounted the story to others.

One critic, Eric Reynolds, founder of Marmot Mountain Works Ltd. of Grand Junction, Colorado, and a major Gore customer, thinks the lattice has its problems with the day-to-day nitty-gritty of getting things done on time and out the door. "I don't think Bill realizes how the lattice system affects customers. I mean, after you've established a relationship with someone about product quality, you can call up one day and suddenly find that someone new to you is handling your problem. It's frustrating to find a lack of continuity." Nevertheless, "I have to admit that I've personally seen at Gore remarkable examples of people coming out of nowhere and excelling."

Bill Gore thought that "established companies would find it very difficult to use the lattice. Too many hierarchies would be destroyed. When you remove titles and positions and allow people to follow who they want, it may very well be someone other than the person who has been in charge. The lattice works for us, but it's always evolving. You have to expect problems." He maintained that the lattice system works best in start-up companies by dynamic entrepreneurs.

Summary

The approach described in this case features no permanent work teams and no managers. The lattice structure and "unmanagement" at Gore might be regarded as a self-developing team approach without bosses. With the lattice structure, all Gore employees interact directly with all other organizational members. In a sense the entire organization becomes one empowered interacting work team. In addition, a variety of temporary and fluid teams spring up to address specific projects and issues. The Gore approach is a remarkable alternative to a more formalized work team approach and may provide one positive window to the future of work teams.

KEY LESSONS LEARNED FROM THIS CASE

1. A lattice-type structure can be used in small organizations to encourage teamwork. The structure has the effect of creating a large team in which each associate can interact directly with anyone else in the system without concern about going through a formal chain of command.

2. Some of the void that is left by lack of structure and formal management, in a traditional sense, can be filled by culture and norms. At Gore innovation, teamwork, and independent effort are valued.

3. Self-developing temporary teams can increase teamwork and allow an organization to benefit from teams without a formal team structure.

4. In small organizations the lattice metaphor provides a mechanism for developing an organization-wide team.

5. Effective teamwork can be evoked and created without having to rely on formally designated and relatively permanent teams. Indeed, in the future effective team applications may involve people joining together informally whenever teamwork is needed.

NOTES FOR CASE 4.3

1. A number of sources were helpful in providing background material for this case. The most important sources were the W.L. Gore associates who generously shared their time and viewpoints about the company. We especially appreciate the assistance of Anita McBride, who spent hours with us and provided many resources, including internal documents and videotapes.

2. A number of published sources are available for obtaining more information on Gore, including the following: S. W. Angrist, "Classless Capitalists," *Forbes,* May 9, 1983, pp. 123–124; J. Hoerr, "A Company Where Everybody Is the Boss," *Business Week,* April 15, 1985, p. 98; K. Price, "Firm Thrives Without Boss," *AZ Republic,* February 2, 1986; B. G. Posner, "The First Day on the Job," *Inc.* (June 1986): 73–75; L. Rhodes, "The Unmanager," *Inc.* (August 1982): 34; J. Simmons, "People Managing Themselves: Unmanagement at W.L. Gore Inc.," *Journal for Quality and Participation* (December 1987): 14–19; A. Ward, "An All-Weather Idea," *New York Times Magazine,* November 10, 1985; "Wilbert L. Gore," *Industry Week,* October 17, 1983, pp. 48–49.

Index

Abilities/skills, 38-41
Acceptance, 89
Accommodation, 89
Action teams, 31
Additive tasks, 142
Adjourning, 88
Advice teams, 30, 31
AES Corporation, 163-175
Affective conflict, 94
Agreeableness, 41
Alcoa, 11
Antecedent modification, 39
Anticipation, 88
Arousal, 143
Assertiveness, 91, 92
Attraction-selection-attrition hypothesis, 42
Automobile manufacturing, 33
Avoidance, 96

Baby boomers, 9
Baby busters, 9, 10
Bargaining, 91, 92
Book, overview, 13, 15
Brownfield, 157

Cases
    AES Corporation, 163-176
    Charrette Corporation, 108-117
    Fitzgerald Battery Plant, 47-51, 70-79
    IDS Financial Services, Inc., 52-68
    independent insurance company, 118-124
    Lake Superior Paper Company, 126-136
    Texas Instruments Malaysia, 17-28
    W.L. Gore & Associates, 177-185
Categorization, 146
Centralized communication networks, 41
Challenger Space Shuttle, 84
Challenges to team effectiveness, 155-161
Changing, 105
Charette Corporation, 108-117
Charismatic leader, 99
Chicago Bulls, 139
Coalition, 91, 92
Coercive power, 91
Cognitive conflict, 94-95
Cohesiveness, 84

Collaborative problem solving, 40
Common enemy, 148
Common goal, 148
Communication skills, 40-41
Compatibility, 41, 42
Compensation plans, 148, 150
Competition between teams, 146, 147
Compromise, 97
Conflict, 94-97
Conflict resolution, 40, 96, 97
Congressional committee, 92
Conjunctive tasks, 143
Consequent modification, 40
Coordinators, 74-78, 97
Cost-reward equation, 9
Critical events, 83-84
Curriculum, 152

Daily administration, 24, 25
Daily management, 25
Decentralized communication network, 41
Deming, W. Edwards, 19, 22
Disjunctive tasks, 143
Diversity in teams, 43
Divisible tasks, 142

Drucker, Peter, 19
Dunlap, Al, 102

Eberle, Charles, 12
Effectiveness teams, 20, 21
Emotional stability, 41
Employee surveys, 152
Empowered leadership, 104–105
Empowering leader, 102
Environmental scan, 57
Equity, 147–148
Executive plant visits, 166, 167
Expert power, 91
External facilitator, 98, 99
External supervisor, 98
Externally managed teams, 35
Extroversion, 41

Facilitator, 98, 99
Federal Express, 11
Fit, 42, 43
Fitzgerald Battery Plant, 47–51, 70–79
Five S's, 24
Florida Power & Light, 25
Foreperson, 97
Formation for survival, 4
Forming, 82–83
Friendliness, 91, 92
Functional theory of formation, 4, 5
Fundamental requirements for success, 158–159

Gainsharing, 150
General Motors Company, 7, 8
Generation X, 9, 10
Giving feedback, 70
Goals, 36
Greenfield, 158
Group cohesion, 83

Group decision-making survival experience, 152
Group heterogeneity, 43
Groupthink, 84, 85

Hackman, Richard, 4
Harmful stereotyping, 146
High-involvement learning tools, 152, 153
Higher authority, 91, 92
Homogeneity, 43, 44
Honeycomb principle, 171, 172

IDS Financial Services, Inc., 52–69
Imposition, 97
Individual goals, 37
Individual ownership of company, 174–175
Influence strategies, 92–94
Informal rules, 83, 84
Information sharing, 78–79
Input-process-output model of teams, 13
Integrative bargaining, 97
Interdependence, 31–34
Internally elected leader, 98, 99
Interpersonal theory of group formation, 5
Interteam cooperation, 145–150

Japanese organization, 7
Job analysis, 151
Juran, Joseph M., 20, 21, 22

Kaizen, 21

Lake Superior Paper Company, 126–137
Lattice organization, 179–181, 185

Lawler, Edward, 7
Leaderless teams, 97
Leadership, 97–105
Lectures, 152
Legitimate power, 92
Lesson plans, 153
Lorenzo, Frank, 102
Loyalty, 148

Malaysia, 18
Manufacturing sector, 8
Maximizing tasks, 142
Member satisfaction, 141
Milliken & Company, 25
Miner, John, 11

Negative anticipation, 61
Negative feedback, 70
Norming, 84–86
Norms, 84–86

Objective performance indicators, 139
Obstacle and rope courses, 153
Operation Honeycomb, 171, 172
Operator self-control, 20, 22, 22
Optimizing tasks, 142
Outcome assessments, 154
Outdoor obstacle and rope courses, 153
Overall goal (shared by team members), 37
Overpowering leadership, 100, 101
Overview of book, 13, 14

Participant learning, 154
Participant reactions, 154
Peer pressure, 78
Performance appraisals, 152

Performing, 86–88
Personality traits, 41
Pooled interdependence, 32
Power, 90–92
Power-building leadership, 103–104
Powerless leadership, 103
Proactive analysis, 151
Procter & Gamble Company, 7
Production teams, 30
Profit sharing, 150
Project teams, 30
Psychological ownership of company, 173

QC story, 21, 22
Quality circles, 20
Quality garden (shrine), 23
Quality improvement teams, 20

Reactive analysis, 151
Reason, 91, 92
Reciprocal interdependence, 33
Referent power, 91, 92
Refreezing, 105
Relationship conflict, 95, 96
Retrofit, 158
Reward power, 90, 91
Rewards/reprimands, 71
Role-play, 111–114, 153
Roles, 38, 39
Rubbermaid, 11

Sanctions, 91, 92
Scarcity, 146
Self-goal setting, 39
Self-leading teams, 36
Self-learning, 153
Self-managing teams, 35
Self-management, 19
Self-management skills, 40
Self-observation, 39
Sense of direction, 36

Sequential interdependence, 32
Service sector, 8
Shared goal, 149
Simplification, 146
Skills/abilities, 39–42
Social comparison process, 6
Social exchange, 9
Social facilitation, 144
Social identification, 146, 147
Social trap, 95
Socialization, 88–90
Socioemotional inputs, 41–42
Socioemotional roles, 39
Sociotechnical systems (STS) theory, 6, 7, 56, 57
Specific abilities, 39
Sponsorship, 179
Stereotyping, 146
Storming, 83
Strongman leaders, 100
STS theory, 6, 7, 56, 57
Success, requirements for success, 157, 158
SuperLeader, 101
Supervisor anxiety, 63
Supervisor resistance to teams, 105–106

Task applications, 30–33
Task conflict, 94
Task inputs, 39
Task interdependence, 31–34
Task roles, 39
Team building, 154
Team composition, 38–43
Team development process, 82–88
Team effectiveness, 139–140
Team effectiveness potential, 142–143
Team goals, 36, 37

Team meetings, 151
Team member compatibility, 41, 42
Team self-leadership, 34–36
Team staffing, 38
Team viability, 140
Teams
  defined, 3
  effectiveness, 10–12. See also Team effectiveness
  historical development, 6–8
  reasons for formation, 4, 5
  settings where used, 8
  viability, 9, 10. See also Team viability
Teamthink, 85
Technical analysis, 57
Texas Instruments Malaysia, 17–28
Theory X, 158
Theory Y, 159
Total productive maintenance, 24
Toyota, 25, 33
Training and development, 149–154
Transactor leader, 100
Transformational leader, 99
Transition from supervisors to facilitators, 61–63

Unfreezing, 105
Unitary tasks, 142
Unmanagement, 178
Unstructured management, 179–181, 184, 185

Verbal reprimands, 71
Verbal rewards, 71
Viability, 140

Visionary Hero leader, 101

Volvo, 33

W.L. Gore & Associates, 177-187

Wayne, John, 102

"We" vs. "they" phenomenon, 59

Weyerhaeuser, 11

Win-win negotiation strategies, 40, 41

Within-team leaders, 97, 98

Worker preferences, 9, 10

Worker self-management, 19